General Władysław Sikorski, 1881–1943

General Władysław Sikorski, 1881–1943

The Life and Controversial Death of Poland's Leader in Exile

Evan McGilvray

Pen & Sword
MILITARY

First published in Great Britain in 2024 by
Pen & Sword Military
An imprint of Pen & Sword Books Limited
Yorkshire – Philadelphia

ISBN 978 1 52679 514 4

A CIP catalogue record for this book is available from the British Library

Typeset by Mac Style
Printed in the UK by CPI Group (UK) Ltd, Croydon, CR0 4YY.

MIX
Paper | Supporting responsible forestry
FSC® C013604

Pen & Sword Books Limited incorporates the imprints of After the Battle, Atlas, Archaeology, Aviation, Discovery, Family History, Fiction, History, Maritime, Military, Military Classics, Politics, Select, Transport, True Crime, Air World, Frontline Publishing, Leo Cooper, Remember When, Seaforth Publishing, The Praetorian Press, Wharncliffe Local History, Wharncliffe Transport, Wharncliffe True Crime and White Owl.

For a complete list of Pen & Sword titles please contact:

PEN & SWORD BOOKS LIMITED
47 Church Street, Barnsley, South Yorkshire, S70 2AS, England
E-mail: enquiries@pen-and-sword.co.uk
Website: www.pen-and-sword.co.uk
or
PEN AND SWORD BOOKS
1950 Lawrence Road, Havertown, PA 19083, USA
E-mail: uspen-and-sword@casematepublishers.com
Website: www.penandswordbooks.com

Contents

Acknowledgements		vi
Introduction		vii
Chapter 1	The Early Years, 1881–1918	1
Chapter 2	The Fight for Frontiers, 1918–1921	11
Chapter 3	Sikorski, 1921–1939	19
Chapter 4	Poland and France, 1939–1940	34
Chapter 5	Relocation in London, 1940	72
Chapter 6	Settling In: London, 1940–1941	83
Chapter 7	The Polish-Soviet Treaty, June–July 1941	94
Chapter 8	Conflict in the Army, Anders vs Sikorski	113
Chapter 9	Anders	126
Chapter 10	Sikorski and Anders, a Toxic Relationship	135
Chapter 11	Katyń and the End of Sikorski's Soviet Policy	144
Chapter 12	The Final Trip East	170
Chapter 13	Gibraltar, July 1943	176
Chapter 14	Investigation	183
Notes		195
Bibliography		215
Index		221

Acknowledgements

This book is very much my Covid book.

I researched it after returning from hospital, recovering from Covid in April 2020. Therefore, I would like to dedicate this work to the staff at St James' University Hospital ('Jimmy's'), Leeds. Doctors, nurses and auxiliary staff at Jimmy's and elsewhere worked throughout the pandemic at great risk to themselves. They did not party as others who should have known better did. And claps don't pay the bills.

I would also like to thank Jan Jarzembowski who sourced images for this work and then annotated them – all for free.

And many thanks to Matt for his humorous e-mails!

Thank you all.

Evan McGilvray
11 July 2024

Introduction

General Władysław Sikorski was the most well-known Polish general of the Second World War. However, as the now long retired American political scientist Sarah Meiklejohn Terry recalled, as late as 1976, Sikorski was still a 'hot potato' to members of the Institute of History of the Polish Academy of Sciences. Nevertheless, within five years Sikorski was back on the menu as it were and what had been taboo subjects in communist Poland were openly discussed even if Poland was to remain communist until 1989. As Meiklejohn Terry noted the atmosphere had changed.[1]

Even so, in the modern western world Sikorski remains virtually unknown unless one is part of that small circle of westerners who study or have studied what is often dismissed as east-central Europe or the former Soviet bloc. In the light of the Russian invasion of Ukraine in February 2022 and the war that is raging as I write this introduction, I consider that this biography of Sikorski would go some way towards informing those who wish to know more about countries such as Ukraine and others such as Poland who are now threatened by Russia, and how the world has arrived at the appalling war now being fought in Ukraine, and how history and indifference has allowed this to happen.

To introduce Sikorski, it should be recognised that he was best known pre-war in British and French military-political circles owing to his splendid service with the Polish Army during the Polish-Soviet War of 1919–1920. After 1920 and until 1926 Sikorski served in various ministerial roles, including prime minister, in various Polish governments. However, after May 1926 his star began to wane and then he was left in isolation until the defeat of the Polish Second Republic during September 1939 following the twin invasions of Poland by Germany and its major ally, the Soviet Union.

May 1926 was when the so-called liberator of Poland, Józef Piłsudski, after nearly five years of sulking, launched his coup and once more was the undisputed ruler of Poland, a position he enjoyed until his death in May 1935. Piłsudski had been suspicious of Sikorski, even though he had served Poland well since 1914 when Poles had begun more earnestly the struggle for re-independence.

Poland was overrun during autumn 1939 and many Poles began to trudge out of that country towards exile or internment. Sikorski was one such figure heading towards probable internment in Romania when he was intercepted by the French authorities and spirited to Paris where he was to establish a Polish government-in-exile as well as a Polish army. Sikorski was well prepared for this situation owing to his inter-war experience while the French government was happy to work with him as he was not tainted with the excesses and failure of the inter-war Polish military junta which was known as the *Sanacja.* Sikorski, without doubt, was a talented man but he was not prepared for the situation which met him in 1941. He was expected by the British government to work with the Soviet government following the German invasion of their former ally, the Soviet Union, in order to prosecute the war until the eventual defeat of Germany and Nazism. Poland and its people had been brutalised by the Soviet occupation of its lands with millions of Poles deported, enslaved or murdered. In 1941 surviving Poles were released from Soviet captivity including the Polish general, Władysław Anders.

General Anders had endured horrific captivity at the hands of the Soviets and was quite understandably very anti-Soviet, but Sikorski should have learned to work with him. Sikorski knew nothing of Russia while Anders had served in the Imperial Russian Army and spoke fluent Russian. However, the two men clashed when they should have been working together to secure a decent settlement for Poland at war's end rather than allowing the Soviet Union to annex the country and occupy it until 1989. Later elements within the so-called Anders' Army began to plot against Sikorski and eventually Sikorski died in an aircraft accident off Gibraltar on 4 July 1943. It had been proved that Polish officers had tried to kill Sikorski in air trips previously and that the only people who wanted Sikorski dead were those in Anders' Army or, to give its correct form, II Polish Corps. No matter how much the Poles try to pretend that Winston Churchill or Joseph Stalin tried to kill Sikorski, the evidence is lacking while Churchill even remarked to Stalin that Sikorski was the only Pole with whom they could work. Therefore, it made no sense to kill Sikorski from the Allied point of view especially as Stalin was getting what he wanted anyway. Only Anders' people had a reason to kill their Prime Minister and Supreme Commander.

So, simply, the tale of Władysław Sikorski is one of a decent man who tried to do his best for his country and its people in the most extreme of times. True he was guilty of playing at politics when he perhaps should have concentrated on strategy and securing the future of Poland post-war. War is always a difficult time and eventually he was outmanoeuvred by the more capable Anders and paid with his life. It should be recalled that Anders also failed to gain anything for Poland. The country, with others, was quietly forgotten by the British and Americans after 1945, allowing the Soviet Union to establish a European empire. Sikorski's story is of glory, betrayal, hubris and nemesis which will astound the western reader more used to sniping in a debating chamber than those of the politics of exile and internecine strife.

Chapter One

The Early Years, 1881–1918

The future General Sikorski was born on 20 May 1881 in Tuszów Narodowy, a village in Mielec county in south-eastern Poland, then part of the Austro-Hungarian Empire. The young Sikorski, Władysław Eugeniusz Sikorski, son of Tomasz and Emilia, was born into humble circumstances which worsened in 1884 when Tomasz died. Emilia was left with four young children of whom the young Sikorski was the third born. Sikorski had no memory of his father. The young widow Emilia took her family and returned to her family home where her family gave her a small house in which Emilia lived for many years. Things were difficult for the Sikorski family with money always tight; however, with the financial aid of Emilia's family, life was not as bad as it might have been. When Sikorski was seventeen years of age money was made available by his grandparents for training in a profession. The Polish historian Olgierd Terlecki observed that, without the generous help from Emilia's family, it was unlikely that history would have heard anything of Władysław Sikorski had it not been.[1]

Nevertheless, after studying and training, in 1908 Sikorski graduated as an engineer from Lwów University. It was during this period that Sikorski together with others, including Kazimierz Sosnkowski and Marian Kukiel, became involved with the struggle for the re-independence of Poland. All three, Sikorski, Sosnkowski and Kukiel, were destined to become leading lights after 1939 in the politics of Poland in exile. On being forced out of Poland in 1939 none of the trio was to return to their homeland. The Polish historian Andrzej Garlicki claims that Sikorski was involved in the Polish underground movement as early as 1907 and first encountered Piłsudski in the same year. Piłsudski was attending lectures on tactics for the 'militia groups' of the Polish Socialist Party (*Polska Partia Socjalistczna* – PPS) given by Sikorski in Lwów.[2]

This was rather audacious, given that the then twenty-six year old Sikorski had only had one year of army service and field training but held the rank of lieutenant in the Imperial Austrian Army.[3] However, this was never a handicap to the Polish revolutionaries seeking independence and future power. They were an incredible group of blaggers! Sikorski was no exception and, later in life, seemed ashamed of his humble beginnings and claimed, somewhat unjustifiably, kinship to the aristocratic Kopaszyna-Sikorski family.[4]

Roman Wapiński wrote that 1908 was a significant year in Sikorski's life. He had completed his engineering studies as well as becoming involved in the political struggle which was to define him. In 1910 Sikorski was one of the founders of the Riflemen's Union (*Związek Strzlecki*) as well as becoming head of one of its departments. Around this time Sikorski also wrote an instruction manual – *Drill Regulations for the Riflemen's Union and Elementary Infantry Tactics*. However, this is to jump ahead a bit as Sikorski first had to complete his military service after graduation and then, in June 1909, he married Helena, the adopted daughter of the Zubczewska family. On 30 September 1909 Sikorski began work as a trainee in the Department for the Construction of Water Installations in the Emperor-King's vice-regency works in Lwów (today L'viv). Sikorski was a model employee and interested in his work. He wrote and published articles on flood control and the use of waterways. He was also a good family man and always seeking ways to improve the family financial situation – perhaps the difficult childhood years had made a mark on him but, whatever, his domestic happiness could have only been increased with the birth of his daughter Zofia on 2 March 1912.

It should be considered that by the time Sikorski had finished his studies he had already become associated with the liberal-progressive movement in Poland and, after his graduation, he became one of its leading advocates. On 21 November 1910 in Lwów he helped to organise the Polish Progressive Party (*Polski Stronnictwo Postępowe*) and became one of its leaders. It is thought that Sikorski's ideas of how to retrieve Polish independence were largely based on three main factors which were reflected in the party journal. The three ideas were education, wealth and military power. There is much of this reflected in Sikorski's life: his time as a student in a teacher training college in Rzeszów where he pursued educational goals; his work as an engineer helped to increase the nation's wealth and his activities in the Union for Active Struggle (*Związek Walki Czynnej*) and in the Riflemen's Union led to the foundation of the modern Polish Army during November 1918. Sikorski's involvement with the military increased after 1911 as it was increasingly obvious that war would break out soon in Europe.

From the summer of 1911 Sikorski, with Józef Piłsudski, Sosnkowski, Kukiel and Włodzimierz Momentowicz, participated in activities designed to further the goals of a general uprising and the struggle for independence in Galicia and the Congress Kingdom, respectively the Austrian and Russian sectors of Poland. However, despite this closeness between Piłsudski and Sikorski, Sikorski was never to be one of Piłsudski's inner circle. Their backgrounds were quite different. Sikorski was educated, having trained as an engineer and had grown up in the more-or-less politically tolerant and autonomous Galicia. This caused to him to be more pragmatic and cautious compared with Piłsudski when it came to the matter of Poland and the cause for re-independence.

Sikorski was willing to work towards a solution rather than take it head-on with the imperial powers ruling Poland. An example came on 29 July 1914 during an assembly of the Interim Commission of Confederated Independence Parties when Sikorski had tried to persuade those assembled of the need to 'start negotiations with a government'. He meant the Austrian government with which indeed those Poles striving for independence did work, fighting alongside the Austrian Army against the Russians. But this was happening anyway as cousin fought cousin depending on which part of Poland they were living in as the three partitioning powers all conscripted their Polish subjects to fight for Kaiser, Tsar or Emperor-King, just dependent on where one lived.

Piłsudski was more ambitious. He wanted the Russians gone from Poland, hence his support for Austria in 1914 as well as internationalising the Polish question. Sikorski, however, saw the development of a Polish military force as a factor which would help towards building a Polish state and did not encourage anything that might endanger this.

The differences between Sikorski and Piłsudski did not immediately become apparent at the outbreak of the First World War, but its roots can be found there. On 6 August 1914 the Polish Rifles decided to embark on an independent campaign against the Russians. It was a disaster, both politically and militarily. It was feared that the Austrian authorities might disband the rifle companies. This, of course, would have been a major setback for Polish independence. Sikorski, having successfully negotiated his release from the Austrian Army, was from 6 August 1914 heavily involved in trying to rescue the situation which faced the Polish Riflemen owing to their incompetence on the battlefield and Piłsudski's poor political judgement. Piłsudski was a cunning man but not a political genius and Sikorski had to pick up his shortcomings.

After meeting with Piłsudski on 11 August 1914 at Miechowo, Sikorski drafted a memorandum to the headquarters of the Austrian Army, suggesting that a Polish Auxiliary Corps be founded. Sikorski's suggestion was that this formation should consist of two legions based on the existing rifle movement. He wrote, 'In organising such a Corps, appropriate use should be made of the abilities, expertise and popularity of Piłsudski, who is the representative of the independence movement in the Congress Kingdom of Poland.'[5]

Sikorski feared that the Polish rifle companies would be dissolved and so with Sokolnicki and Ignacy Daszyński took part in the proceedings of the Interim Commission of Confederated Political Independence Parties. This led to an agreement with the Polish caucus in the Austrian Parliament which was to see the creation on 16 August 1914 of the Supreme National Council (*Naczelny Komitet Narodowy*). With the establishment of the Committee Sikorski was appointed Head of the Military Department of its western section. From there

Sikorski and others found a base of support for the proponents of an Austro-Polish solution. Sikorski also assisted a group which was trying to enlist Poles living in German and German-occupied territory for the Polish cause. On 21 September 1914, together with Witold Jodko-Narkiewicz, Sikorski went to Berlin to try to obtain arms for the Legions as well as pursue the question of recruitment from Germany and German-held areas. The visit failed and so Sikorski doubled down on his idea of Polish action being based on support from Austria. From October 1914 Sikorski developed the Legions and began to organise their cavalry, sapper and service support units. He also made efforts to recruit officers from the rifle movement to senior posts and establishing a military college.

At this point Sikorski's relationship with Piłsudski was good. Sikorski was doing as Piłsudski wanted by aiding Piłsudski's attempts to continue independent military operations in the Kingdom of Poland as well as expanding the Legions' 1st Regiment. All of this illustrated how useful Sikorski was. However, when Sikorski was appointed commander of the Legions' 4th Regiment and made preparations to leave his command of the Military Department, Piłsudski did his best to prevent him leaving. Piłsudski feared that Sikorski's successor at the Military Department would be a Polish career officer from the Austrian Army. If this was to happen it would seriously damage Piłsudski's ability to maintain an independent policy regarding the Supreme National Committee and the Legions' Command.

The damaged relationship between Sikorski and Piłsudski remained unnoticed until the summer of 1915. The two men agreed in principle with the concept of independent Polish action in the Congress Kingdom of Poland. It may have been that Sikorski had underestimated how swiftly and significantly the ranks of the Legions swelled but he had also realised that the establishment of a proper Polish Army rather than a legion of temporary legionnaires was a long-term project. He needed to overcome public feelings of aversion and indifference to the Legions' work with the Central Powers. Sikorski knew that working with the Russians was a non-starter and would have only retarded the work already done by himself and Piłsudski. However, no matter how much Sikorski tried to iron out the differences between the Military Department and the Legions' First Brigade, he and Piłsudski were destined to become further estranged.

It should be considered that, as much of Sikorski's work was based on the development of the Legions and therefore the beginning of a post-independent Polish army, that Sikorski began to regard himself increasingly as a politician rather than a soldier. His circle of contacts certainly reflected that, including those from conservative and conservative-minded circles. This was important as it was a riposte to Piłsudski's attitude which could be seen as extreme – he did not shy away from advocating the assassination of Russian officials. Piłsudski was a Socialist: just how deep this ran is uncertain but in today's world he would have been regarded a terrorist and he was extremely anti-Russian.

In 1915 Sikorski had not abandoned his idea that the best way to move towards an independent Polish state was a union of Galicia and the Kingdom of Congress Poland both under Austrian rule. He also hoped through the leadership of the Supreme National Committee and of the Austrian Army Headquarters to get the Austrian monarchy involved in the Polish Question. This had a pre-history as in 1867 the Austrian Empire was forced into sharing governance with Budapest; thus, the Austro-Hungarian Empire. The empire was vast and becoming unmanageable. A compromise with the Poles and perhaps other Slav people was logical.

However, Piłsudski was looking at the Polish Question in the round. He was not willing to consider a localised solution as Sikorski appeared to be doing but saw the problem as a whole and was deeply concerned with the fate of those Poles who remained under Russian governance. Piłsudski wanted all Poles liberated and not just those in Austrian-occupied territory. A fault of Sikorski, which ultimately was to cost him his life, was his inability to understand Russia and its rulers whether it was a Tsar or Stalin. Initially Piłsudski tried to win Sikorski over and ensure that he obeyed orders. In a letter of 30 May 1915, Piłsudski certainly tried to reach out to Sikorski but, to be honest, the letter of that date is somewhat vague and couched in metaphors from card games; Sikorski remained unimpressed and Piłsudski's attitude towards Sikorski hardened.

From then on their relationship was always chequered; the struggle between Piłsudski and Sikorski and the Military Department began. From 1916 Piłsudski, supported by the Colonels' Council, established at Piłsudski's suggestion and consisting of commanders of the Legions, set about the dismantlement of the Military Department or, in other words, Sikorski's political base. From here, the Colonels, aided and abetted by Piłsudski, set about demonising Sikorski and his supporters. Fake news is not a new thing. Indeed, Roman Wapiński gives an example of the poisonous and unnecessary rhetoric of Piłsudski regarding Sikorski.

> That parasite came later when the artificially developed command of the Legions started to look for support in the army, producing officers and giving out promotions to its officers, regardless of their military value. To say nothing of the whole political role carried out in the rear by Mr Sikorski.[6]

Interesting use of language predating the use by the Nazis of 'parasite' when referring to the Jews. Of course, it was rank hypocrisy from Piłsudski who did exactly what he claimed Sikorski was doing. Many of Piłsudski's followers had not attended a military academy; Piłsudski certainly had not, while officers who tended to side with Sikorski more often than not were trained military officers from the Austrian Army. This taking of sides was to store up further trouble which came to a head in May 1926 when Piłsudski launched a successful military coup against the democratically-elected Polish government. Sikorski was not entirely blameless, far from it, but this feud between the two men set the tone of the politics of the inter-war Polish state, the Second Republic.

Later, in the face of an extremely aggressive Germany and Stalin's Soviet Union, Poland's fate was sealed. During the autumn of 1939, both countries invaded Poland and conquered. Post-war the Polish Second Republic was only to exist in name only in the UK as the Polish government-in-exile and eventually recognised by nobody. But in 1990 it was able to prove its legitimacy when the Polish Presidential seals of office were returned to Poland following the election of Lech Wałęsa to the office of the President of Poland. The seals of that office had been kept safely in London since 1940 for the day when a genuinely democratically Polish president was elected. It took over fifty years before this happened and, at a stroke, the illegitimacy of communist rule in Poland was exposed.

Piłsudski should take the larger share of the blame for the destruction of the Second Republic as it was his backward-looking military policies that left Poland with an inadequate army commanded by incompetents which had been loyal to him up to his death in 1935. But, as Piłsudski had overturned the 1921 Polish Constitution during the time of his coup in May 1926, he was left with no room to criticise Sikorski who, as we shall see, tried to keep Poland on a democratic course between 1921 and 1926. Simply, Piłsudski was a wrecker and his political failings allowed for enablement of fascism and a pro-German foreign policy from 1933 until spring 1939.

The main difference between Sikorski and Piłsudski was the manner in which they conducted their campaigns. Piłsudski, acting very much like a Bolshevik, relied on a tight group of dedicated supporters who were ready to carry out every order given by him. Sikorski, however, worked within an elite group of followers, one which failed to connect with the masses. By early 1916 it was seen in the Congress Kingdom that Piłsudski was the symbol of the Polish independence movement while Sikorski was seen 'merely as a proponent of the Austro-Polish solution'.[7] This sent a signal to Piłsudski's followers to begin hostilities against the Military Department. This was well received in anti-occupation circles. It reached a crisis on 4 July 1916 when the Piłsudski-ites serving in the Department carried out Piłsudski's instructions and delivered an ultimatum demanding the halting of further recruiting and greater co-operation between the leaders of the

Department and Piłsudski and the Colonels' Council. Sikorski rejected these demands which caused the Piłsudski-ites to walk out of the Department and the offices that controlled it. The Military Department, led by Sikorski, was derided by Piłsudski and his followers as being an institution serving Austria and Sikorski's ambitions. The Piłsudski-ite campaign caused Sikorski to move from the Department to take one of the senior posts of the Legions and he was finally appointed commander of 3rd Regiment on 9 September 1916. The Austrian Army High Command considered this to be a temporary post. But Piłsudski had not really won the argument. He was also to learn that he had not conquered Sikorski.

Undaunted by the loss of Piłsudski-ites at the Military Department, Sikorski continued to make the Polish Question relevant to German policy. What Sikorski wanted to do was to transform the Polish Legions into a Polish Auxiliary Corps. This resulted in the Act of 5 November 1916 where the German and Austrian emperors agreed to re-establish a Congress Kingdom on the territory of the Russian partition zone. During negotiations to reach this point Sikorski put forward his ideas in an article, 'The Legions – A Polish Corps'.

Sikorski considered this to be the nucleus of a future Polish army. An army which he saw not only as an instrument with which to bargain with the Austrians and Germans but also as a basic element towards the establishment of a new state. In his article, Sikorski had written:

> Although the Polish Legions from the very start represented ideas and aspirations which are contained in the heart of every Pole, and they were a new and wonderful embodiment of the sacrificial struggle for independence waged with iron resolve by four generations against the fundamental Polish enemy – Russia – still the will of the nation did not declare its emphatic support for them. This was the result not only of the initial, complicated situation on the battlefields, but above all because the Polish Question had not been the subject of an official declaration. Indeed, the Central Powers (Austria and Germany), preoccupied with day-to-day events, did not, in the early part of the war, devise a programme for a Polish state.[8]

Sikorski admitted that, by writing that 'the nation did not declare its emphatic support for them', he was observing the failure of every revolt against imperial rule in Poland since 1830. The failure lay with the fact that more-or-less the only people who stood to gain by a successful revolt against any of the occupying imperial powers were the Polish ruling classes. Ordinary people, especially the peasantry, would have only exchanged one ruler for another. However, the Austrians, Germans and later the Russians learned that the way to destroy the Polish aristocracy was to remove serfdom from their lands. This meant land reform with the illusion that the peasants were now free to till their own land while before they had had to work so many days a year free for the local landowners. This was abolished which ended popular support for aristocratic uprisings against the imperial powers. Land reform always appealed to the Polish peasants, and it was often quite deceitful, especially in the Russian occupation zone.

Sikorski and, indeed, Piłsudski both realised that this state of affairs had to be got around and that any revolt or move to independence should be a popular move reinforced by a proper Polish army and not one full of enthusiastic amateurs as Piłsudski's men largely were. The 5 November 1916 Act for Sikorski was evidence that progress had been made on the National Question. As Sikorski regarded the Polish Auxiliary Corps to be the foundation of a future Polish army which, as we have seen, he considered to be a basic building block for an independent Poland, he opposed the plan of the German Governor General of Warsaw, General von Beseler, who wanted Polish military forces to be commanded by German officers. Sikorski was also opposed to Piłsudski's attempts to employ officers from the Polish Military Organisation (*Polska Organizacja Wojskowa* – POW), another of Piłsudski's paramilitary groups, while it was still being formed. In a memorandum of January 1917 Sikorski declared that the Military Department should be considered to be the basis of a future Ministry of War and should be entrusted with the main role in creating the army. Sikorski also declared that he was in favour of conscription as volunteer recruitment was only a temporary measure.

Sikorski continued to develop his view on the importance of Poles developing their own national military force, not a paramilitary force as Piłsudski led, and its role in the struggle towards a solution to the National Question. Sikorski was astute enough to realise that it only partially answered this question. Piłsudski, as his actions were to later prove, sought power rather than genuine independence. He wanted to be dictator as he actually was after 1926. This explains why when, after March 1917 when the Russian ruler, Tsar Nicholas II, was overthrown, Piłsudski's attitude towards a national Polish military force became more negative. This led to the 'oath crisis' of July 1917 which saw Piłsudski and most Legionnaires interned by the Germans for refusing to swear an oath of allegiance to the Central Powers.

The 'oath crisis' also created a setback for Sikorski, but he remained true to his view of the necessity of creating a Polish Army. On 24 August 1917 he resigned his post as head of the State Recruitment Inspectorate and also refused to take part in the organisation of the Polish Armed Force. With the Polish Auxiliary Corps, which after the 'oath crisis' consisted only of Austrian citizens, Sikorski left the Congress Kingdom of Poland. On 1 September 1917 he became head of the Corps' Recruiting Board. Nevertheless, his hopes of a resolution to the question of the re-independence of Poland remained linked to the policies of the Central Powers.

The signing of the Brześć Treaty between the Central Powers and the Bolshevik government on 3 March 1918 gave large swathes of former Russian territory, especially western Ukraine, to the Central Powers. This led to widespread protests amongst the Polish population living in Ukraine. Sikorski identified with that part of the Polish Auxiliary Corps which had forced its way to the Austro-Russian front. With other soldiers from the Corps, Sikorski was interned in Hungary and court-martialed.

Sikorski was acquitted at his court martial. Indeed, it gave him a platform to criticise Austrian and German politicians whom he considered were trying to wreck the Legions, especially as they became divided after the oath crisis. This was probably the beginning of the splits in the inter-war Polish military-political elite circles. At the time it is certain that the Austrians and Germans were not interested in Polish independence while it was unlikely that anybody could have predicted the travails of inter-war Poland which largely had its roots in the weak establishment of Piłsudski and the Legions. Sikorski stated at his trial, 'Having been left in Warsaw on the orders of General Beseler, along with three other Polish colonels, I went to the Polish Auxiliary Corps of my own free will, thinking those orders to be a German attempt to wreck my Polish and military programme.'[9]

The Central Powers' attitude towards Polish aspirations in 1918 merely caused Sikorski to double down on his efforts to establish a national Polish army as part of the foundations of a modern resurrected Polish state. On 22 April 1918 he issued an order to officers leaving the Dulfalva internment camp in which he stated:

> The Polish Legions survived all the reserves of fortune. Even the hardest one, which was the result of misunderstanding and lack of appreciation, on the part of our own nation, of the idea represented by them. This resulted in quarrels and internal wrangling which tore apart the body of the Legions. It was a simple result of an inability to carry out those programmes, which were the reason for the Legions' creation. Today, more than ever, it is true that because of their military value, as well as their inherent ideological value, the Polish Legions organised in 1914 on the territory of the Polish Piedmont – Galicia – were, and remain, eminently suitable to perform the role of the cadre for the Polish Army.[10]

This was possibly the first time that Sikorski had publicly stated the concept that the Legions were the nucleus of a future Polish army.

Since the outbreak of war in 1914 many things had changed regarding the question of Polish re-independence, especially the various Polish militias which had sprung up during this period. Sikorski had not really benefited from his exertions in trying to champion the Polish cause within the Central Powers; he had become an accomplished politician, an esteemed members of the Galician elite and was popular in Vienna. However, Piłsudski had trumped Sikorski's position and had become the symbol of the Legions and Polish liberation. Furthermore, the Legions were slowly being taken over by younger people who had no political background and were fiercely loyal to Piłsudski, the Commander. They were not partners, as Garlicki writes, but 'executors' of Piłsudski's will and ready to undertake his wishes.[11] This was despite Piłsudski having been in prison since 1917. Sikorski was outside this circle of what can only be called revolutionaries. However, in November 1918, with the defeat of the Central Powers, Poland regained its independence for the first time since 1795 but its troubles were just about to begin.

Chapter Two

The Fight for Frontiers, 1918–1921

On 11 November 1918, the First World War finished at 11:00 hours. The giants had fought; the aggressive Central Powers had been defeated. Russia had defeated itself the year before with revolution. In 1918 Russia was undergoing the convulsions of civil war as the Bolsheviks who had, under Lenin, launched a coup in November 1917 against the Kerensky government which had ousted the imperial order in March 1917, tried to obtain complete control of Russia. Poland achieved independence on 11 November 1918 but it had nothing to do with Piłsudski or Sikorski; it was down to events and at times pure dumb luck. Poland was about to undergo a gruelling three years which were to mark it down as a democracy and lay the foundations for its failure as a state which was to disappear for fifty years and only re-emerge as an independent state in 1989.

In contrast to Piłsudski, the so-called 'liberator' of Poland, Sikorski was a colonel, but he was a trained officer even if only to a modest extent and his rank had been inflated by the consequences of war. Nevertheless, he was about to prove himself to be worth more than this rank and Piłsudski's superior. Garlicki claims that the difference between Sikorski and Piłsudski is that in both of their internments Piłsudski won great political gains while that of Sikorski was proof of the failure of his political ideas and his personal standing.[1] However, this cannot be true as both men had either failed or succeeded if they were both interned. Piłsudski was the more ruthless and could only succeed in disorder such as a time of war or eventually in a coup. This is not success while Sikorski worked better within the confines of stability and lawfulness.

Whatever, on 10 November 1918 on returning to Poland from prison in Magdeburg, Piłsudski had no real rivals in his bid for power. Sikorski was starting from scratch. Poland was in chaos and about to fight wars on several fronts. The wars which were beginning in east-central Europe Churchill dubbed the wars of pygmies, a statement he prefaced with the concept that the fighting between 1914 and 1918 had been the war of giants. This gives a subtle hint at just how the western powers, including the defeated former imperial powers of Russia, Austria and Germany, perceived states such as Poland after 1918. There was a sense of sneer about the new states as they tried to proceed forward. In

November 1918, Poland moved straight to war as it began to try to establish the new state's frontiers. It was not alone as east-central Europe had become a wild west (or east) as the new states moved hither and yon establishing borders at the expense of one another. The west had no real interest in what was going on in the east, save for the case of Poland. American President Woodrow Wilson had championed the case for Polish re-independence; it seemed the right thing to do but the reality was that Poland was to be the bulwark of the eastern fringes of Europe.

West European elites had always been suspicious of Russian intentions towards the more civilised end of Europe. With the November 1917 Bolshevik coup the situation between the two understandings of Europe was exasperated. The Bolsheviks were cast in the role of being the return of Attila the Hun and his perceived barbaric horde. The Bolsheviks were the antithesis of everything that the ruling classes believed in. Of course, the Bolsheviks were savage but so were their enemies, the Whites and, at times, the Poles. There were other concerns such as a pandemic while there was little appetite for war in the west, but the so-called pygmies had war and conflict thrust on them. As the skirmishes in the west were toughed out between principally Polish, German and Czech paramilitaries, two serious conflicts were to erupt in the east.

The first war was between Poland and the Western Ukrainian Republic and was principally over who was to rule over that section of Ukraine. Poland, despite often playing the historical victim, was also a very nasty overlord, indeed a bully of weaker nations such as the Ukrainians. Western Ukraine was, and is, overwhelmingly Ukrainian but since at least the seventeenth century Polish landlords had ruled the area and had imposed their will over the native Ukrainian peasantry. In the middle of this was the city of Lwów, a seat of Polish culture and it was over this city that the Poles and Ukrainians clashed during the winter of 1918–1919. Nearby oilfields naturally added an extra element to this conflict.

The Poles, against the odds, fought well during the winter and by spring 1919 defeated the Ukrainians and secured Lwów and its surrounding areas for a generation. Today Lwów is L'viv and in modern Ukraine. The fighting in the east attracted attention from the Bolsheviks and, as the Poles moved eastward, the Bolshevik army, the Red Army, moved westwards towards Poland. Bolshevik ideology, stemming from the thoughts of Karl Marx and brutally reinforced by the writings of V.I. Lenin had a mission statement: World Revolution.

The aim of the World Revolution was the successful spread of communism around the world. The first communist revolution had just happened in Russia. A country which Marx would have found strange as he had considered it to have been too backward for such an event. He had always considered Germany to be the most suitable country to see a communist or Marxist revolution. According to Marxist theory only the industrial worker was capable of successfully understanding, wanting and carrying out such a radical act. To Marx, Russia was a largely agricultural state with an uneducated peasant population. The Bolsheviks wanted to move their revolution westwards towards Germany through Poland as if to fulfil Marxist theory. As Germany immediately after 1918 was in a state of turmoil and revolution itself, western leaders feared that the Bolsheviks would indeed move via Poland into Germany and might actually be able to export the World Revolution.

In Poland there was also fear of the Bolsheviks who were touted as being godless heathens. As the Bolshevik revolution came out of Russia, Poles were also easily persuaded that the Bolsheviks needed stopping as they were another example of Russian imperialism. Which was true. The west saw that Poland needed aiding once Polish armies and the Red Army clashed on the still wild eastern border lands. However, events were not as simple as two enemies clashing on the battlefield.

Even though the Poles and Ukrainians had fought during the winter of 1918–1919 by 1920 they were allies. Ukraine also wanted independence and looked to the Poles to aid them in this. The Ukrainian leader, Petliura, had arranged with Piłsudski to send a Polish Army into Ukraine in an attempt to stem the advance of the Red Army. The Polish advance was so successful that by May 1920 the Polish Army arrived at the Ukrainian capital, Kiev (today Kyiv). At this point the Red Army counter-attacked and began to drive the Polish Army back westwards.

The westward advance of the Red Army concerned the west. There had been western intervention in Russia as the British, Americans, French and Japanese had each landed forces to try to prevent the success and expansion of the Bolshevik Revolution. Indeed, Churchill, the arch anti-Bolshevik, wanted Bolshevism strangled at birth. This was to prove to be ironic as we shall see as he and Sikorski tried to work with Stalin and the Soviet government after 1941. Often, for pragmatic reasons, Churchill had to bully Sikorski to fall in line with Stalin's bidding. However, in 1920 the British government was doing its best to pull the Polish irons out of the fire as it seemed that the Bolshevik advance could not be stemmed. The Polish Army was wholly lacking in defensive skills while the Red Army was in many ways nothing but a peasant rabble.

However, in both armies there were a few good commanders. In the Polish Army these appeared to be from the ex-imperial Austrian Army and not from Piłsudski's paramilitary Legions while the Red Army had a more perplexing situation. With Allied intervention in Russia the Bolsheviks were forced to return to those professional officers from the former imperial Russian Army. But, as the Bolshevik leadership did not trust these men, their work was overseen by Bolshevik activists, simply political officers who were checking that the Red Army and the revolution was not being betrayed. Stalin was one such man. Nevertheless, the Red Army was led both brilliantly and ruthlessly by Leon Trotsky, seen by many as Lenin's right-hand man and probable successor. It was not to be.

It should be remembered that even though Polish independence was a main point of Wilson's points for an armistice in 1918, many western politicians were not enthusiastic about the plan, including British Prime Minister David Lloyd George. However, the revolutionary Bolshevik advance into Europe frightened enough senior politicians, but not the workers in the west who considered that the new regime might just have a point if it meant the end of the capitalist system and an equal society. That was just wishful thinking, but it did prevent the initial supply of arms to Poland as British dockers refused to load the ship, the SS *Jolly George*, with arms destined for Poland or, as the dockers under a future British Foreign Secretary, Ernest Bevin, saw it, supply arms to Poland to invade Russia. When Bevin became Foreign Secretary in 1945, he had learned a lot about the Bolshevik revolution and the horror of Stalinism. Using diplomacy, as British Foreign Secretary after 1945, Bevin fought the Soviet government tooth and nail and was instrumental in establishing NATO in order to prevent further Soviet expansion.

The only useful tools which the two western powers, the UK and France, could supply was diplomacy, with the hope of trying to obtain a ceasefire with good terms for Poland which seemed doomed by the summer of 1920. The other tool was the military missions supplied by the two powers. However, the Poles proved to be less than co-operative and, quite frankly, militarily useless. Polish troops were often led by quite craven officers. There appeared to be no idea in the Polish Army of how to lead a war. Staff work was even worse with no one seemingly in command with few, if any orders, actually being issued by senior staff. Allied commanders trying to retrieve the Polish army from the mire in which it had got itself stuck discovered that Polish commanders simply lied whenever they had made a hash of things. In many ways it might have been easier to have let the Bolsheviks have the country as it seemed at times that the Poles did not really want to defend their homeland, or they would have co-operated and fought the better. However, unlike the short termism of Polish elites, the west understood what would happen if Poland was taken: the World Revolution would have been at hand.

The events of the Polish-Soviet War have significance but few of any importance to be fair. A breakthrough was the use of a Captain Benedykt, a brilliant mathematician and codebreaker, who was Chief of Intelligence of the Second Polish Army. Benedykt had been able to intercept and decipher despatches from the Budyonny Army which was steadily advancing into

Poland. The weaknesses of the Red Army were learnt by this skilful piece of intelligence work; it was discovered that Budyonny was nearly out of ammunition, especially artillery shells. Furthermore, the exact position of the Soviet Brigade Headquarters was revealed as being in the Korca area. This information allowed Second Army to go on the offensive against the Budyonny.[2] This incident proved the possibility of having a correct modern Polish army, but it was not to be.

As late as 1937, General Władysław Anders, who was to be become one of the great exiled Polish leaders, also criticised the failings of the Polish Army and how it had failed to modernise. He considered officers of the Nowogródska Cavalry Brigade, of which he had just taken command, to be 'hidebound' in their attitudes. Anders reported that his brigade could not fight armoured units while in war games his officers were always too quick to charge forward without any reconnaissance.[3] This was also an observation made by the commander of the British Military Mission to Poland in 1920.[4] Quite simply, most Polish officers never bothered to check what might be around the corner or further ahead while out in the field or when taking up a position for the night. As Suchcitz, in his conference paper, noted, Anders was not a lazy or negligent officer and took his duties seriously.[5] Without doubt, the state of the Polish Army by 1937 depressed Anders.

It is worth considering just what the state of the Polish Army in 1920 was and how the British certainly viewed its progress. The Polish Army, as we have seen, had only come into being in November 1918. It was born out of various sources. Major General Radcliffe, the senior British officer in the British Military Mission during the summer of 1920, left Paris for Poland on 22 July after a meeting with Ignacy Paderewski. Paderewski, in addition to being a well-known concert pianist and advocate of Polish independence before 1918, was also the Polish prime minister and foreign minister, appointed by Piłsudski. Paderewski was Radcliffe's starting point for his work in Poland.

Radcliffe noted that, in spite the fact that on 19 October 1919, the unity of the Polish Army had been declared, the evidence was that this was not true and that officers trained and led their men in the manner in which they had been trained. This, of course, led to quite different methods of leadership and outcome. After his meeting with Paderewski, Radcliffe noted three major failings of the Polish Army at this point.

1. The incapacity of the Polish Command and its Staff.
2. The inferiority of Polish armaments and equipment compared with that of the Russians which had greatly improved with the capture of weapons and by an increased output of their own munition works.
3. Political intrigue and the 'deplorable organisation' under which the Head of State (Piłsudski) was also the executive Commander-in-Chief.

Paderewski suggested that it was essential that the office of C-in-C of the Polish Army be separated from that of Head of State and suggested two names: General Dowbór-Musnicki and General Józef Haller. The French Military Mission considered that Piłsudski's roles made him the 'evil genius' of Poland. The French noted that Piłsudski was more interested in political intrigue rather than military operations and preferred leaving such matters to younger favourites.

On reaching Poland the Mission found that the situation was worse than Paderewski had hinted at in conversation with Radcliffe. Radcliffe observed that First and Fourth Polish Armies, which were fighting on the Polish left wing, were of little fighting value. Those on the right flank were little better. It was reported that the worst feature of the entire Polish campaign was that many Polish officers had fled in panic in the face of the Soviet advance; their morale undermined by Bolshevik atrocities they had left the ordinary Polish rank and file without leadership. This meant that the British and French had to provide officers to 'stiffen' Polish troops and to remind Polish officers of 'an officer's duty'.

Piłsudski initially made a poor impression on the French general, Maxime Weygand. General Weygand also considered that Piłsudski was only interested in political intrigue and not urgent military matters. Piłsudski displayed a complete lack of frankness and seemed to have no interest in taking Weygand into his confidence or learning from Weygand's military experience. It was also noted that Piłsudski lacked 'military common sense' but was very astute when he summed up the Bolshevik mentality; they pretended to negotiate but were planning to exploit their military advantage with force of arms.

The situation faced by the Military Missions in Poland in 1920 was serious. The Polish Army could not fight, and the Polish Staff did not function. Indeed, the Polish staff work was a disgrace. It kept no regular hours; written orders were rarely given. Instead, vague instructions by telephone were issued. A further problem was the lack of honesty on the part of the Poles. The loss of the town of Briansk was concealed from Weygand for nearly forty-eight hours. Military appointments were vague while visits to the front revealed poor deployment of Polish troops. This meant it was difficult to control or co-ordinate any movements owing to an extended front and also explained the Polish inability to defend. There was also no concept of correct military procedure: outposts were unknown; the Polish method was to occupy a village and then sleep totally unaware of what was just down the road. Constant retreats badly affected the morale of Polish troops while there was no attempt to deter stragglers and deserters. The Polish government was hopeless and was described as being a government of 'all vices' and had taken no serious attempts to rally the Polish for the defence of their country and 'seemed blind to both the gravity of the situation and to the incapacity of the High Command to deal with it'.[6]

Therefore, it became very obvious that most of the Polish officer corps had little professionalism about them and even less honour and merely sought to save themselves while their newly-born country could go hang! This meant that if Poland was not to be lost the British and French would have to try to intervene and convince the Poles they actually needed to fight or lose their newly-born country. The British placed themselves at the disposal of Weygand while steps were taken to re-supply Poland with British troops unloading arms destined for Poland at the Free City of Danzig.

The French observed in a meeting held during the first week of August 1920 a distinct cleavage between Polish ministers and the Polish military staff – the Polish ministers had more faith in Weygand than they did in their own Chief of General Staff, General Rozwadowski, who offered to resign in favour of Weygand. The French general refused to take over but wanted it made quite clear that he would not be held responsible for any further failings of the Polish Army. Even if they were being heard, the French felt that they did not exercise any real influence on events. The French concluded that the eventual Polish success at Warsaw was the inefficiency of the Red Army which largely relied on untrained peasants who were prodded onwards towards Polish lines with the use of political officers which prevented any attempts to retreat. Only two Polish officers made any impression on the French Military Mission: General 'Sigorski' (this was actually Sikorski), Commander of Fifth Army, and so confirming that the French meant Sikorski and the Allied inability to understand Slavic names, a trend that was to continue into the Second World War. The other officer was Colonel Zagorski, Chief of Staff to General Józef Haller. It was decided by the French that there was a need for a properly trained Polish Officer Corps and Poland was to look to France for assistance in this matter.[7] Sikorski had already distinguished himself in March 1920 when the Polish 9th Infantry Division under his command seized Mozyr on the river Pripet in the centre.[8] This was significant as it was one of the few Polish gains that year until victory at Warsaw and then that was under French tutelage.

The summer of 1920 was to set the politics for the entire history of the inter-war Poland, the so-called Second Republic. The main problem, according to the British, was the Polish over-reliance on Piłsudski. Sir Maurice Hankey, Secretary to the British Cabinet, told Lloyd George that the Polish Nationalist leader, Roman Dmowski, despite being the most bitter of opponents of Piłsudski, admitted that it was only Piłsudski could maintain unity of the Polish Army.[9] Hankey had already commented on the failings of the command of the Polish Army in a letter to Lloyd George. Hankey reported that Weygand wanted Piłsudski to give up the command of the Polish Army which was not compatible with effective exercise of supreme command.

The French General Paul Henrys had already made a poor defence of Piłsudski, his military policy and strategy. Nevertheless, Henrys was supported by Sir Horace Rumbold, the British Ambassador to Poland, the French Ambassador and the pro-Polish British general, Sir Adrian Carton de Wiart. They all considered that it would be 'absolutely impossible' to remove Piłsudski. The French Ambassador thought that such a move would be impossible without a civil war. However, the entire group considered that Polish officers were 'appallingly bad' and that Piłsudski was surrounded by ex-officers of the Austrian Army who they considered to be the 'worst type'.[10] This was not a reference to the professional officers of the former Imperial Austrian Army but the legionnaires, those military amateurs who had fought alongside the Austrians until it became impractical politically to continue to do so.

Hankey, a veteran of the First World War, drew on his military experience and rated Polish officers from the ex-Imperial Russian Army as being better than the legionnaires while he considered that the best Polish officers came from the Poznań area which also provided the best troops. It was further observed that these officers had little military experience owing to German prejudice against Poles who served in the ex-Imperial German Army.[11] Hankey further observed to Lloyd George that the French Military Mission during July 1920 had been paralysed until the removal of Henrys. This was due to Henrys' subservience to Piłsudski as well as the fact that some Polish officers refused to take any notice of the French mission. Paderewski had already been critical of Piłsudski's poor performance as a military commander and feared that Henrys was already under his spell.[12]

The attitudes of Polish officers, and especially the flaws of Piłsudski as observed by the British and French Military Missions, goes some way towards explaining events in Poland after 1921. It also explains how and why elements within the Polish military were able to seize control in Poland during the May coup of 1926. Those same attitudes allowed the Polish military to establish a junta and demolish democracy in Poland as well as retain power until the invasions of Poland by Germany and the Soviet Union in September 1939. Despite having fought the largest European war between 1918 and 1939, Poland stagnated in all ways including militarily until 1936.[13] The problem was the domination by Piłsudski and his cohorts of Poland until his death in May 1935. Piłsudski was succeeded by a so-called Marshal of the Polish Army, Edward Śmigły-Rydz, a sycophant of Piłsudski and of no obvious talent in any direction. It was no wonder that Poland fell to its enemies in 1939 and remained as a vassal state in one shape or another until the summer of 1989. Now we should return to the examination of the life of our subject, Władysław Sikorski, and consider his role in Poland between the wars.

Chapter Three

Sikorski, 1921–1939

Sikorski may have come to the notice of the British Military Mission in August 1920, but it was to be of no consequence in his career in the inter-war Polish Army. During the first years of the Second Republic, Sikorski tried to obtain democracy for Poland. He was doomed to fail. Piłsudski still held all of the trump cards – he was popular with many Poles, and he had the corporate support of the army or, more to the point, of the First Brigade, those men who had rallied to him in 1914, performed badly on the battlefield but had blagged their ways as liberators.

Sikorski was destined to be a legislator and to try to make democracy work in Poland. It was an unfashionable position to be in and despite his best attempts Sikorski failed in the short term. Nevertheless, the borders of Poland were established in 1921 in the terms of the Treaty of Riga. Some consider that this treaty was a brilliant piece of Bolshevik diplomacy since the Poles were duped into accepting more Ukrainian territory than the western powers wished, and more than the Poles could handle. McCauley considers that the Bolsheviks gave more territory than it was willing to accept in the belief that the more non-Poles there were in Poland, the more unstable Poland would become.[1]

The Soviet government was not wrong as the 1931 Polish census revealed that only 69 per cent of Polish citizens were of Polish nationality. Fifteen per cent of Polish citizens were of Ukrainian nationality, predominantly living in eastern Poland, exactly as the Soviets had planned. By the 1930s, a Ukrainian resistance force (OUN) in Polish-occupied Ukraine began a guerrilla war proper against the Polish government and Polish landlords.[2] This led to a so-called 'pacification' operation by the Polish Army which was badly handled and saw it rampaging across eastern Galicia or the '*Kresy*' as Poles tenderly called their borderlands.

This action cannot be ignored as it was to be part of the problem for Sikorski as he tried to re-organise the Polish Army in exile after September 1939. Later, after 1941, Sikorski was forced to negotiate with Stalin the question of eastern Poland which had been annexed by the Soviets in 1939, lost to Germany in 1941 and, once the Soviets returned to the offensive after 1943 and the Red Army began its westward march towards Germany, it annexed all territory before it. Stalin made it very clear to Sikorski that eastern Poland was not up for debate but was part of an enlarged Soviet Union or quite simply an enlarged Soviet empire.

The inter-war Polish military junta made further mistakes during the 1930s which were to haunt Sikorski even though he had nothing to do with them. It should be realised that the Polish military was very successful in encouraging young Poles to make careers in the armed forces. Indeed, it was a great way to advance socially and was a route for a bright young man to escape the rural drudgery which was the lot of many Poles. However, the same cannot be said about encouraging recruits from the minorities such as Ukrainians and Byelorussians. A major problem was that such recruits were often posted far from home in western Poland, possibly in an attempt to 'polonize' them.

Furthermore, aggression in eastern Poland, notably in Volhynia, by the Polish Army, lack of promotion in the army for minorities, military doctrine and propaganda laced with anti-Semitism caused many from the minorities to conclude that they had little, if any reason, to identify themselves with Polish nationhood. This should be contrasted with perception of ethnic Poles which figured just under 70 per cent of the total population of inter-war Poland, of the army being a guarantor of Poland's national sovereignty.[3] These were problems that confronted Sikorski during his period of office between 1921 and 1926 and later as Polish Prime Minister and Supreme Commander in exile between 1939 and 1943.

To further the narrative of Sikorski's actions between 1921 and 1926 an examination of the Polish Army during this period is required. The most prominent grouping within the army was that from the wartime Legions of which the veterans of the First Brigade, fiercely loyal to Piłsudski, seemed dominant but were overshadowed by those who had served their war in the Imperial Austrian Army, had been properly trained and had genuine combat experience. Garlicki remarked that the First Brigade was often associated with a particular brand of radicalism which combined Piłsudski's socialist past with a colourful and aristocratic tradition.[4] The Legionnaires were deeply distrustful of the ex-Austrian Army Polish officers owing to their former allegiance to the former Austrian Army. The ex-Austrian officers in turned expressed their contempt for the Legionnaires, scoffing at their lack of formal military training and overall military incompetence.[5]

In 1919 it was estimated that 95 per cent of all generals in the Polish Army were veterans from the former imperial services, of whom the majority were from the Imperial Austrian Army. In 1918 it was considered that there were over 100 generals who had formerly served in the Imperial Russian Army but, as they were scattered across the former Russian Empire, they could only return to Poland slowly and with great difficulty. There were few 'German' Polish generals in the new Polish Army owing to the discriminatory promotional practices in the German Army.[6] Therefore, by sheer force of numbers, members of the former Imperial Austrian Army officers initially dominated the early profile of the inter-war Polish Officer Corps. By 1922 with the return of the 'Russian' Polish generals to Poland, there was near parity in numbers with those ex-Austrian Army generals.[7]

Between November 1918 and November 1922 Piłsudski held the offices of Head of State and Supreme Commander. However, Piłsudski's personal power was stymied by democracy with the introduction of the 1921 Polish Constitution and the election of a president. Many had thought that Piłsudski would stand for the presidency but he refused to stand for office as he considered that the new constitution weakened the president's (and his power), and this altered the relationship between the *Sejm* (Polish parliament) and the Polish Army. The reason for this change was the nature of next period of Polish history, 1921–1926, which was largely an attempt to subject the Polish Army to civilian oversight.[8]

Civilian oversight of the Polish Army was partly conducted through the office of the President as laid out in the 1921 Constitution. The President was not responsible to the *Sejm*, but his power was exercised through his ministers who were. The President was the highest ranking military officer but in time of war, according to Article 46 of the 1921 Constitution, could not be Supreme Commander. Instead, the President, in collaboration with the Cabinet and the Minister of Defence, would appoint a Commander-in-Chief. These checks to the political power of the Polish Army and a check on Piłsudski's possible personal powers. This infuriated him. Piłsudski rejected the principle of direct civilian control over the military by the government and parliament, arguing that the highest authority over the army should be the Commander-in-Chief.[9]

Furthermore, Piłsudski opposed this degree of civilian control as he feared that the army would become a political tool. He also believed that he had moral responsibility for the army and was entitled to speak on its behalf.[10] However, the Polish civilian political elite, which was normally disunited, was determined to curtail the popular appeal of the Polish military, especially that of Piłsudski, and bring it under civilian control and so presented a united front to do so.[11] However, the various civilian administrations were weak. This allowed Piłsudski to make forceful arguments for an experienced soldier to hold the post of defence minister and so a pattern was set in Poland which saw high-ranking generals hold that post between the wars.[12]

Piłsudski did not have it all his own way as the various Polish governments between 1921 and 1926 removed 'Piłsudski-ites' from positions of power and replaced them with their political opponents, both military and non-military.[13] It was during this period of democracy that Sikorski began his political career at a higher level than before when he was nominated as Chief of the General Staff in April 1921.

In this role Sikorski faithfully served Poland but he was heading for future clashes with Piłsudski who, since 1921, had withdrawn from politics and was sulking in his villa just outside Warsaw. Polish politics were turbulent as the new country, after establishing its frontiers, had to function as a normal country which was not easy since it inherited three imperial traditions, legal systems, several currencies and there had at one point even been two different ways of calculating the calendar. However, there was worst to come when, on 16 December 1922, Polish President Gabriel Narutowicz was assassinated after only five days in office. Sikorski was appointed prime minister on the same day. The murder of Narutowicz infuriated Piłsudski who became embittered with the political process in Poland. The Polish historian Wacław Jędrzejewicz asserts that, following the assassination of Narutowicz, Piłsudski became particularly incensed with people in the government whom he considered to be responsible for the murder and that this was one of the reasons for his seizure of power in 1926.[14] Garlicki observes that, after the death of Narutowicz, there were persuasive arguments that those (not named) who were morally responsible for his assassination may have also been working towards murdering Piłsudski. During May 1926, Piłsudski said that the assassination of Narutowicz had been brutal and that he blamed himself for being unable to prevent it; an alleged attack on Piłsudski's children had provoked this statement.[15]

In 1923 Sikorski was nominated as Inspector General of the Infantry and later accepted the post of Minister of Military Affairs. It was during this period that the Polish government began to reform the Polish military as already mentioned in this narrative. As related, Piłsudski was furious and began a campaign against Sikorski in order to gain public sympathy and to remove a public enemy as he by then viewed Sikorski.[16] The senior British officer, Lieutenant General Sir Adrian Carton de Wiart VC, a keen observer of inter-war Poland, remarked in his autobiography that Piłsudski was a very jealous man and when anybody achieved higher office than he, he sought to get rid of him. This included Sikorski and Paderewski, both of whom Carton de Wiart observed 'stood high in the eyes of the world'.[17]

By 1923 Piłsudski had withdrawn from public life. He was angered by the political situation in Poland where he considered that those responsible for Polish re-independence had not been given enough credit for their efforts. Polish governments however, between 1921 and 1926, made a major mistake in ignoring the concerns of Piłsudski's veteran legionnaires and so allowed them to nurse grudges against successive democratically-elected Polish governments. It should be remembered that Piłsudski did not look to the Polish Army for support but to his veterans from the Legions, notable the First Brigade and he was willing to represent them.[18]

It was not surprising that Piłsudski was able to successfully launch his coup in May 1926. He was popular throughout Poland. The country was governed by democratic governments but were seen as ineffective civilian administrations. Meanwhile many officers remained loyal to Piłsudski and to the nation and not to the government elected to administer the country. It was a disaster waiting to happen but when Piłsudski seized power many were relieved that he had done so.[19]

Piłsudski justified his coup as forestalling chaos in Poland. As the majority of Polish civilians trusted the Polish Army rather than an elected democratic government, the Polish Army became the main political force in Poland.[20] This was something that Piłsudski had spoken out against earlier as he did not want his political opponents using the army, but he had no qualms in using it if it bought him personal political power. Piłsudski claimed that he knew what was best for Poland and was 'an educator rather than a dictator'.[21] Indeed, he was a dictator but a rather junior one in the age of dictators headed by Hitler and Stalin. And the majority of Poles readily accepted the rising influence of the Polish Army in Polish politics and governance. This was partly due to the belief that soldiers were guided by patriotism and dedicated to the nation as it was perceived that this had been demonstrated by the defence of Poland from Soviet Russia and the spread of communism in 1920.[22]

But this was not to look closely at the actions of the Polish officer corps in that year when the French had to virtually take command of the Polish Army owing to the craven behaviour of Polish officers. As already noted, Sikorski was one of only two Polish senior officers who, according to the French, came out with any credit in the Polish-Soviet War. Piłsudski was considered to have been a bit of a joke regarding his homespun theories of war.

Nevertheless, Piłsudski ploughed on with his own political-military agenda. After seizing power, military professionalism took a backseat. The large numbers of ex-imperial Austrian Army officers serving in the Polish Army and political enemies of Piłsudski were subject to a 'Piłsudski-ite' purge. After the coup many junior officers complained that they had been passed over for promotion for having been on the wrong side of the coup through supporting the elected government. Their predicament coined a new adjective '*Zmajowany*' or 'May-ed'. More seriously, senior officers including Sikorski were placed into a professional 'limbo' being neither purged nor involved in Polish military life.[23]

Piłsudski's desire to cleanse Poland and its political system, rather like Donald Trump wanting to drain the 'Washington swamp', led to the Polish military junta ruling Poland being dubbed *Sanacja*, derived from the Polish for 'sanitation'. Part of the sanitation programme was the reduction of the French Military Mission which had been involved in trying to re-organise and modernise the Polish Army.[24] This, according to Piłsudski, was to keep the Polish Army immune from politics.[25] This, of course, is laughable as the Polish Officer Corps was already highly politicised with the situation becoming worse between 1926 and 1939. But this fallow period gave Sikorski time and space to think and to pronounce.

Sikorski used his time wisely, writing a history of the Polish-Soviet War in which he had served with distinction, at least in the eyes of the professional officers from the Anglo-French Military Missions. In addition, he wrote a treatise on modern warfare which in many ways was a critique of military rule in Poland and how Piłsudski and his sycophants had held back any progress in modernising the Polish from 1926. *Nad Wisłą i Wkrą*, Sikorski's study of the Polish-Soviet War was published in 1928, the year in which Piłsudski relieved him of his command (Commander of the Lwów Military District). It is quite a wide-ranging book and discusses just how the Polish-Soviet War was won and it was not by due dint of the First Brigade but by a number of factors including the input of General Weygand who, it could be said, at least guided the Polish Army to victory. It should be noted that Charles de Gaulle, who served in the Polish-Soviet War as part of the French contingent, states in his autobiography that Weygand in 1920 'had made Piłsudski adopt a plan which saved Poland'.[26]

One can only speculate why Piłsudski had to be forced to adopt Weygand's plan. Was Piłsudski merely militarily incompetent of which there is no doubt or was there something more sinister afoot? Was Poland expected to lose in 1920 and allow the Red Army to sweep into a dysfunctional Germany? Whatever, Sikorski's work is an accurate account of the summer of 1920 and the eventual Polish victory over the Red Army at Warsaw. Sikorski refrains from attacking the Piłsudski legend of 1920. He does not add to it but, rather as he did during fighting of the May Coup, did nothing to aid Piłsudski or to detract from him. Even Piłsudski dismissed the Battle of Warsaw as a minor incident despite the fact that it prevented the spread of Communism across Europe for a generation.

However, one who is not a Pole but understands Polish history can only wonder if the failure of the Red Army in 1920 was not a disaster for Piłsudski; he had been part of a terrorist movement prior to 1910 and, as the Polish historian and veteran, Marian Romeyko, observes, had been a personal friend of the Bolshevik leader and dictator, Lenin.[27] One can only wonder just on which side Piłsudski was actually working between 1919 and 1920. It would seem that it was only a matter of ideological tactics which separated the two men.[28] But Sikorski had become an enemy of Piłsudski as Piłsudski illegally seized power in Poland. The next book published by Sikorski *Przyszła wojna*, in English *War in the Future*, was published in Polish in 1934 and translated into French in the same year. The work only appeared in English in 1943. This was a product of great thought and critical analysis by Sikorski – the fact that it was swiftly translated into French in the year of the original publication is evidence of the importance and relevance of Sikorski's work. Given that the work was only translated into English in 1943 illustrated the irrelevance of eastern Europe to British military planners. Indeed, the continent of Europe remained largely outside much of British planning. British strength lay with its navy. Nevertheless, Sikorski's book remained insightful and should have prepared Poland for war in the modern world.

The First World War had changed some perceptions of warfare. In the west it was clear that horsed cavalry no longer had a role to play on a western-style front that depended largely on defensive positions which could only be taken with great effort and bloodshed with often a massive artillery bombardment opening any major offensive. Tanks were to later assume their role as an alternative to horsed cavalry while military aviation rapidly expanded its role between 1914 and 1918. In eastern Europe, horsed cavalry still had a role to play and the fact that the efforts of Polish cavalry contributed heavily to the victory against the Red Army in 1920 convinced many Poles, especially Piłsudski and his cronies, that there was little or no point to replace horses for motorised infantry.

And so, the status quo remained until Piłsudski's death in 1935. However, Polish military minds were not as antediluvian as it might appear since many Polish officers such as Anders and Maczek, both doomed to serve Poland from exile after 1939, advocated modernity for the Polish Army while even the British Army delayed mechanising the regular cavalry until the mid-1930s, owing to the lack of suitable vehicles to replace horses.[29] It should also be remembered that the almighty German Army throughout the Second World War was largely reliant on horses; it was only in North Africa that German forces were wholly mechanised.

At the time of the appearance of *Modern Warfare* the reality of Nazi Germany was not totally apparent. It was clear that Hitler's regime was aggressive towards all, but anti-Bolshevik in nature, which was something that many Poles could understand whilst the virulent anti-Semitism was probably not taken too seriously by the world. Anti-Semites in politics were not uncommon. What concerned Sikorski in his treatise on warfare was how advances made in military technology and thought should be embraced by the Polish Army. By 1934 there was not even any thought of how Poland should be defended – there was no defensive planning at all. There had been between 1921 and 1926 but curiously, after Piłsudski's coup, there was little thought at Staff level regarding defending Poland: so much for Piłsudski being a great military thinker. The reality was that he was an incompetent amateur as witnessed by his performance between

1914 and 1920. It was charisma and the efforts of others which always carried Piłsudski and little else.

Sikorski, as with anyone with imagination could see the greater role that aircraft would have in another major war. This proved to be true in the Spanish Civil War of 1936–1939, which was almost a dry run for the 1939–1945 war for the Germans and Italians who supported the Spanish fascist leader, General Franco. Franco led a coup against the legitimate Spanish government in 1936, defeating it in 1939. The fighting in Spain allowed the German and Italian air forces to hone their skills as military aviators, as well as spreading death and destruction with the bombing of civilian targets which became a feature of the Second World War by all sides. Obviously, Sikorski also saw an enhanced reconnaissance role for aircraft and, incredibly, he refers to the use of helicopters being able to carry, land and deploy troops, basically close land-air co-ordination or air cavalry. He also called for an independent air force.[30]

The call for an independent (Polish) air force is important as in Poland the air force was part of the Polish Army. (The US Air Force was not formed until 1947 prior to which it had been part of the US Army.) Moreover, the use of helicopters showed imagination from Sikorski. He had been schooled in an army of cavalry and here was a man discussing something that was very much on the drawing board. It is true that in Alfred Hitchcock's 1935 film, *The 39 Steps*, a helicopter is seen searching for the hero Richard Hannay across the Scots glens but this would have been fantastic to the 1935 cinema audience, many of whom would not have understood what they were seeing. The question is just how did Sikorski know of such an innovation and just what did the Polish military junta think of such an outlandish contraption as no doubt they would have viewed it at the time.

In 1928, following an unsatisfactory election which returned Piłsudski and his government, Piłsudski decided to rid himself of Sikorski. Between 1926 and 1928 in his writings and thoughts Sikorski had displayed too much independence and criticism of Piłsudski but it seemed that he was still unsure of just how he should deal with him. The 1928 election result decided Piłsudski that he should rid himself of Sikorski. Just a week after his so-called victory in the March 1928 election, Piłsudski removed Sikorski from his command and had him placed on the reserve list.[31]

Sikorski made the most of his enforced premature retirement and it might have served Piłsudski and his junta better if they had kept Sikorski close. Sikorski, after his dismissal, went to France from where he applied for four months' sick leave, but he actually wanted to study recent innovations in French military thinking. He still considered that the junta would re-appoint him to some post or, as he suggested to his wife, as 'an active position abroad'.[32]

He could not have been more mistaken as, after a delay, he was granted indefinite leave and was not to hold any office either military or civilian until after the Polish defeat of September 1939. For the next four years Sikorski spent most of the time in France and Switzerland and only returned to Poland for family and festive occasions. This meant that Sikorski was out of Poland for much of a time of increased political tension as the junta continued to dismantle the fragile democracy which Sikorski had tried to build between 1921 and 1926. This was a source of dismay for Sikorski as he was outside Polish politics and had no input to the situation. Simply, he was frustrated both in political and military affairs within his homeland.

What is interesting is that Sikorski retained respect for Piłsudski right up until the latter's death as so many victims of a dictator often don't blame the man himself but the regime. Some people wondered if Sikorski was actually railing against the regime or waiting to be asked to join it. Amazingly, Sikorski considered that Marshal Edward Śmigły-Rydz, a most incompetent officer and even worse statesman, might modernise the Piłsudski regime. Sikorski seriously believed that Śmigły-Rydz would at least restore an element of democracy to Poland and remove the military junta.[33] Sikorski could not have been more wrong.

Śmigły-Rydz, who did succeed Piłsudski, was an unexpected choice. It had widely been expected that Piłsudski's favourite, Walery Sławek, would replace him. However, many of Sławek's colleagues considered that he lacked the gravitas to fill Piłsudski's shoes. Śmigły-Rydz was a general in 1920 when he took the Polish Army to Kiev but, outside the army, even in 1935, he remained an unknown figure. He was considered to have been 'a stiff and unimaginative' officer when he assumed Piłsudski's 'mantle' which he never quite filled.[34] Nor the role. Śmigły-Rydz was just another incompetent Polish leader.

As Piłsudski's health worsened he began to spend increasing periods abroad. This coincided with Sikorski's return home in 1932. As Polonsky notes, this was the height of the depression years which hit Poland badly economically. It was also the period when Colonel Józef Beck, another incompetent officer and unqualified diplomat, began to spread his black wizardry over Polish foreign policy. Between 1932 and 1935 it would seem that, even though Sikorski explored various avenues to try to return Poland to democracy, his plans never really attracted enough support and even he was willing to leave things be until Piłsudski's death.

This was also a period not only of economic stagnation for Poland but also one of increasing danger from Germany. Sikorski was aware of this the increasing threat but was not in a position to do much about it except write and warn. Indeed, the revisionist foreign policy of Nazi Germany so alarmed Sikorski that he wrote in *Kurier Warszawski* on 8 July 1934:

> the differences which divide Poland from Soviet Russia result solely from the Bolshevik system and have a general character … Against this, the revisionist aspirations of Germany are directly aimed at the territory integrity and independence of the Republic.[35]

Quite simply, even as early as July 1934, Sikorski was clear that Nazi foreign policy included the absorption of Poland in the guise of re-uniting Germans. A major disaster of the Versailles peace treaty, which was to have concluded peace in Europe, was the division of Germany with East Prussia being cut off from Germany fully with the re-establishment of Poland. To exasperate the situation, the port of Danzig, today Gdańsk, was designated a 'Free City', basically independent, but should have shared port facilities with Poland. Once the Nazis came to power in Germany the situation altered as the German majority in Danzig, egged on and supplied by Germany, began to behave with hostility towards Poles and Poland in general.

Eventually, one of the German attacks on Poland came from German warships in Danzig on 1 September 1939. The fact that Sikorski saw the German danger and considered allying with the Soviet Union is incredible as few Poles would have considered this possible. Indeed, Polish foreign policy between 1935 until March 1939 should be seen as pro-German as traditional Polish sentiment was antipathy towards all things Russian, whether under the Soviets or the Tsars. Despite the ideological hatred between the Bolsheviks or Soviets under the iron rule of Stalin since 1929, there was nobody who could fill Piłsudski's vacant position and so hoped that there might some return towards democracy.

Sikorski still held back as he continued to believe that he could work with members of the Polish junta and reach an understanding with some of its leading actors. By the end of 1935 it was quite clear that Sikorski was not going to be offered any political or military office and that any hopes of restoring democracy in Poland were an illusion. Furthermore, Beck felt able to strengthen his own position from the Polish Foreign Ministry. The new regime, largely headed by Śmigły-Rydz, strengthened Beck's foreign policy as he began quite openly to follow a pro-German stance. Simply, the new Polish junta, far from restoring Polish democracy, set about totally dismantling it.

To be fair, the post-1935 regime attempted to modernise Polish defensive plans as well as to establish an industrial weapons manufacturing system. However, it was a while before anything happened. Piłsudski had been Inspector General of the Polish Army, his only genuine rank but he ruled Poland from behind the scenes. He had taken this role as he insisted that by doing so, he kept the army out of politics while there was no constitutional basis for involvement in government affairs, but it did allow the holder to interpret the role as he wished.[36] Śmigły-Rydz certainly took full advantage of the position.

Trying simply to replace Piłsudski with Śmigły-Rydz was always going to be awkward since the latter lacked Piłsudski's charisma and the corporate support from the legionnaires. Furthermore, personal conflicts within the regime began to take on ideological tones. After the death of Piłsudski the former ruling group of ex-legionnaires began to disintegrate while Śmigły-Rydz's group, the Non-Party Bloc (*Bezpartyjny Blok Współpracy z Rządem* – BBWR) and in 1937 the Camp of National Unity (OZON) was created. During the same year Śmigły-Rydz began to lose support from ex-legionnaire associations and from the army, owing to the growing fascism within his regime. Furthermore, the rhetoric of the regime suggested that OZON was preparing a coup in order to establish a totalitarian regime.[37] On 12 October 1937 legionnaires presented a resolution to Śmigły-Rydz which condemned the Polish Youth Movement, the *Falanga*, as fascist and accused OZON of dismantling Piłsudski's legacy.[38] The reaction against OZON by the legionnaires and the army caused Śmigły-Rydz to back down. He dismissed the OZON leaders and broke all connection with the *Falanga*.[39]

However, what should be taken from this episode is that until the army and the legionnaires more-or-less mutinied the Polish leadership was quite happy to embrace fascism and only baulked when it was realised that it lacked the corporate support of the military which was also the only body that could prevent such a measure. When Poles yesterday and today talk about inter-war democracy in Poland and how it was lost, they are peddling a myth. Poland was near fascist, extremely anti-Semitic and a close ally of Nazi Germany. It was only once Colonel Beck realised that Hitler wanted nothing out of Poland other than being a stepping-stone towards the Soviet Union that Polish foreign policy finally moved away from its pro-German stance.

Śmigły-Rydz's lack of popularity with the military also translated as such with the civil population as it should be remembered that the army was the most trusted institution in Poland. If the army did not trust the regime the people did not trust it either. Śmigły-Rydz should be seen as a failure. His character was best summed up by Frank Savery as recorded by Hugh Dalton. Savery, had been, prior to the German invasion of Poland, the British Consul General in Warsaw, who noted that Śmigły-Rydz was vain, secretive and traditional. However, what is most damning was his military thinking which spoke only of a 'strategy of mobility' which required no fortifications but relied merely on large-scale cavalry raids into Germany. This was his primary offensive weapon.[40] Clearly, the Polish regime had little notice of what had been happening in

Germany since 1933 or the number of works detailing modern military thought, including that of Sikorski.

Incredibly, it was not until October 1938 that the Polish High Command ordered exercises based on reality rather than what was hoped to be. The main exercise was based on war with the Soviet Union – Poland was yet to fall out with Germany. The exercise, Plan 'W' (*Wschód* – East), revealed a shortage of ammunition available to Polish forces.[41] Plan 'W' was finally completed on 20 March 1939. A plan for war with Germany, Plan 'Z' (*Zachód* – West), did not begin until 4 March 1939. Plan 'Z' was defensive in nature with the time, place and method of attack being chosen by the enemy. By this time Poland was already surrounded by Germany on three sides.[42] Sikorski was critical of the defensive nature of Polish defence plans, remarking that a professional army should always be 'ready to strike'. The inference was quite clear but even Sikorski was too optimistic about the abilities of the Polish Army after 1935.[43] September 1939 laid clear the failings of the Polish Army to complete its most basic task, the defence of Poland.

It is ironic to note that by 1939 Poland had fewer military plans than it had in 1925. This was despite the fact that 50 per cent of the Polish national budget was spent on defence between 1935 and 1939. It was a huge expense for an undeveloped country but was nowhere near enough to match that of Germany. German data for the same period illustrated that Germany spent thirty times more on the Heer alone.[44] Ironically, between 1921 and 1926, the period of Polish democracy and prior to military rule, two plans had been provided for in readiness for war with Russia or Germany.[45] Polonsky remarked that it was all rather late.[46]

The reason that it was 'rather too late' was that, despite Poland belatedly beginning to build an arms industry complex after 1936, it seemed that the regime wanted to compound its military folly by building factories too close to Germany. Basically, the Polish ruling elites could only imagine war with the Soviet Union and never with Germany, even though it was quite clear that Germany was definitely the greater threat. Piłsudski had always advocated 'Eyes East!' Russia was the enemy and this policy had always served him well and his successors saw no reason to change it.[47] Poland's final act of co-operation with Germany was the annexation of the disputed area of Teschen in Czechoslovakia, during October 1938. This was the nadir of the OZON regime, and was to have repercussions later during the war whenever the Poles cried betrayal; their allies would retort by resurrecting this misdeed. It has been claimed that the annexation of Teschen was an attempt to boost Śmigły-Rydz's flagging reputation in Poland.[48]

All Sikorski could do realistically was to criticise, but from the side-lines; he remained an outsider. He travelled to France and to Czechoslovakia making political allies who were to prove of use later after 1939 but in the mid-to-late 1930s Sikorski seemed to be a voice in the wilderness. Sikorski was dismayed as he saw his country become increasing more fascist in political outlook; he opposed both the extreme right and the extreme left as he considered that both were anti-religion, and that fascism was a result of the middle-class fear of communism.[49] Sikorski also considered what many in the 1930s was perceived to be 'the Jewish problem'.

Hitler's enemy number one was the Jews. In Germany there were few Jews, and most were integrated. In Poland, there were millions, and many remained outside traditional Polish society, marked by religious observance and by outward appearance with a majority especially in rural areas wearing traditional clothing, sporting beards and ear locks. They were clearly different and not really accepted by the majority of Poles, especially in the former Tsarist zones of Poland. Sikorski sent mixed messages when he noted that capitalism could only be strengthened if the middle classes are strong. This he claimed would require the gradual lowering of the percentage of Jews living in Poland.[50]

This is not to suggest that Sikorski advocated the slaughter of Jews as was to be the case after 1941 in east-central Europe as the Germans with their allies murdered most European Jews on an industrial scale in death camps, ravines and elsewhere. Any Jews they could lay their hands on, as well as others including ethnic Poles, were slaughtered. Indeed, the Slavic people were also marked for extermination by the Nazis. Sikorski, as with most people, could not have imagined the mass slaughters which were to come. However, prior to 1945 and the realisation of the extent of German near extermination of European Jews, countries which should have known better had tinkered with the idea of removing their Jewish populations to elsewhere in the world. Madagascar was a popular choice for some governments for no apparent reason while there was little consideration of perhaps encouraging Jewish emigration to Palestine. Sikorski was basically repeating a line, a political line which was popular with many throughout the world before 1945: the Jews were a problem and it needed resolving.

Sikorski was certainly alive to the threat which Germany held after 1935 and could see that war was coming before many others did. Clearly, Beck did not, or would not as he continued to direct a pro-German foreign policy which alarmed Sikorski. It was obvious to Sikorski that the Polish Army needed modernising and that would require a loan from France. Sikorski also saw that a French loan might be a way to remove Beck but any attempts to dislodge him came to nothing. Indeed, Beck began to maintain an anti-Czechoslovak attitude which timed in nicely with Hitler's plan to annex Czechoslovakia. In the autumn of 1938, at the height of the Munich crisis, as the British and French prime ministers attempted to salvage peace in Europe, Poland invaded and annexed part of Czechoslovakia.

No doubt, Sikorski was dismayed as he had advocated a bloc of collective security involving the Slavic states and including the Soviet Union as the only way to face down Nazi Germany. The Polish position during 1939 grew worse as, in early spring, Beck finally stood up to Hitler following the complete annexation of the Czech lands during March while Slovakia became a German vassal state. During the same month Beck had finally realised that Hitler merely wanted Poland to become a client state rather than a genuine ally.

Poland may have been following a fascist methodology of rule since the death of Piłsudski, had imposed strict restrictions on their Jewish population and taken a strict anti-Soviet line which had been attractive to Hitler, but Beck finally realised that if Poland became any further involved with Germany, Poland would lose everything. Following the annexation of the Czech lands, after Hitler had sworn that after taking the largely German-populated Sudetenland from Czechoslovakia, he had no further territorial demands to make, Beck could see that the word of Hitler meant nothing. During March, after Hitler began to threaten Poland, Poland made treaties with the UK and France who pledged to declare war on Germany if that country was to attack Poland.

The Franco-British guarantees were quite worthless, and the Polish government were foolish to put too much faith in them. The British had no real army or commitment for a war in Europe – the British Army protected the homeland and policed the Empire; the Indian Army did the same for India with various commitments to British overseas possessions. The strength of the British lay with the Royal Navy. The French had a large and strong army which was touted as the strongest in the world but there was a fatal flaw – to help Poland in the event of a German attack the French Army somehow would have to reach Poland by sea onto the Baltic coast or fight across Germany. It wasn't going to happen. Simply, the Polish government was too foolish to realise that the reality was that Poland was alone. Beck had made an important speech during May 1939 in which he spoke of honour being higher than peace. Morally he was correct, but how was Poland to hold on to its honour if it was to be overrun by Germany?

By the end of summer 1939 the misery for Poland was complete. During August 1939, incredibly Nazi Germany and the Soviet Union made a show of reconciliation, which was a sham, at least on the part of Hitler, and signed a treaty – the Molotov-Ribbentrop agreement. The two countries were allied even if some considered that the Soviet government had signed such a treaty in order to obtain some form of security guarantee from Germany. However, this cannot be accepted owing to the provision under the terms of the pact allowing the Soviet Union to expand its borders and absorb territory from its western neighbours, namely the Baltic Republics of Lithuania, Latvia and Estonia, as well as seizing Polish territory. After the capture of German archives in 1945 it was discovered that within the Nazi-Soviet pact there was a 'Secret Additional Protocol' which read:

> In the event of territorial or political changes taking place on the lands belonging to the Polish state, the boundary between the German and Soviet sphere of interest will run approximately along the line of the rivers Narew, Vistula and San. The question of whether or not it is in the interest of both sides to maintain an independent Polish state, and within what boundaries can only be finally resolved in the light of further political events.[51]

Germany's path into Poland was wide open. It was clear that if and when Germany invaded Poland; the Soviet Union would not attempt to stop the invasion. Poland was alone. The long expected invasion came on the morning of 1 September 1939. The Allies, after a few days, declared war against Germany and did nothing. On 17 September the Soviet Union invaded eastern Poland and in October 1939 Germany and the Soviet Union divided Poland between them. Poland has never received back any of the territory annexed by the Soviet Union in September 1939. Regarding Sikorski, on 30 August 1939 he wrote to Śmigły-Rydz offering to serve in any capacity. He received no reply. This left Sikorski free to follow any path he chose and the following, near on four years, as we shall see, Sikorski chose to serve Poland with honour and distinction until his death in July 1943.

Chapter Four

Poland and France, 1939–1940

The poor and shortsighted treatment of Sikorski by the Polish regime after 1926 probably was his saving. If he had not been excluded, he possibly might have become a member of the military clique ruling Poland in those years. However, as we have seen, Sikorski spent much time after 1926 abroad. Most time was spent in France from where he was able to make contacts which were to serve him well between 1939 and 1940 and later in London.

The British government had already taken a dim view of the inter-war Polish leadership with Field Marshal Ironside condemning the Polish system of governance during a friendly official visit as late as July 1939. Ironside stated of the Polish leadership, 'The President was a figurehead and knows it. The Prime Minister never appeared. The two men who have all the power in their hands are the Foreign Minister, Colonel Beck, and the Marshal Śmigly-Ridz' [*sic*].[1] The naked power of the Polish military was clearly evident, and it did not win many allies.

Poland, invaded by Germany on 1 September 1939 and the Soviet Union on the 17th, was overrun and, despite nationalist rhetoric ever since, was comprehensively defeated. During September 1939, the Polish government fled to Romania where it was interned. In Poland, this created a political vacuum which needed filling to prevent either or both the German and Soviet governments creating a puppet Polish government to rule in their stead in occupied Poland. However, neither Stalin nor Hitler saw any real reason to introduce Polish puppet governments: both wanted to see Poland destroyed but Poles heading westward to exile and the chance to fight another day needed something to rally around and to look to for authority and legitimacy.

The necessity of establishing a Polish government-in-exile was clear to many Poles who wished to oppose the German and Soviet occupations of Poland. It was a symbol of an undefeated Poland. This was perhaps demonstrated best by a man known simply as 'Borecki', who was one of the first Poles to resist the occupations of Poland. Like Sikorski he had been an oppositionist figure against Piłsudski and his regime. In 1939 he joined the Polish underground movement. His story came to light in the report of Jan Karski, the heroic Polish resistor, who in 1943 escaped occupied Europe to the UK. He brought with him a report that alerted the world to the genocide of European Jews being carried out by the Nazis. However, in 1940 Borecki was prepping Karski to see Sikorski in France. Borecki pressed the point that Sikorski's government in France and the underground movement in Poland were all evidence that the Polish state still existed and would return while the 'presence of the German regime is artificial' while 'we cannot tolerate the existence of any Polish government co-operating with the occupants. If any traitors appear, we will kill them'.[2] No doubt if the Home Army (*Armia Krajowa* – AK) had not been destroyed in 1944, Poles working with the Soviets would also have been executed.

In early 1940 Karski had an interview with Sikorski, and was clearly impressed by him, leaving a thumbnail sketch of his leader at that time. He considered that Sikorski was about sixty (he was sixty in 1941) and in good health. His manners were polished, and he stood tall and upright. He had some slight French mannerisms which Karski speculated were acquired owing to his acquaintance with France and the French from the 1920s. Karski noted the absolute faith Sikorski had in the French. Also, interestingly Sikorski told Karski that it would not be enough to merely return Poland to independence once the war was finished but to progress and put Poland on a democratic footing and sweep the former regime away. He called for free political parties and elections. However, the most interesting statement made by Sikorski to Karski was:

> the army shall never be allowed to interfere in political life. We have had enough of that. It must be the armed force of the people, animated by the ideal to serve the people, and not to rule them, not to lead them.[3]

Poland and Poles were fighting for their very existence and needed to ensure that the world knew this. Therefore, the need for a genuine government, albeit in exile, was necessary and recognised in order to head off any puppet government that an enemy regime might try to foist on Poland. It should be noted that, until early October 1939 when Hitler was still trying to format some form of peace negotiation with the British and French, some form of rump Polish state under the thumb of Germany was mooted by the Germans. However, by 10 October 1939 this appeared to have been withdrawn by the Nazi authorities.[4]

Nevertheless, the fear of a puppet Polish government was always real as revealed in a Polish document dated 1 March 1940 known as the 'Whitehall Letter'. This 'letter' was seen by Sikorski and highlighted the fears of the possibility of a Polish puppet government being formed from malcontents from the Polish right wing who had 'swallowed their differences with Colonel Beck's partisanism'. The letter, also discussed as Letter No. 101, was referred to with further detail in which it was revealed that Polish nationalists were 'pursuing a policy for reconciliation with the Germans under the aegis of Hungary'. Basically, certain Polish traitors were willing to form a rival Polish government in Budapest. A potential leader was also discussed. A certain 'Madam Wenda' was mentioned as acting head of this movement in the absence of her husband who was interned in Bucharest.[5]

This clearly was a potential challenge to Sikorski's government and would have been under German control. For reasons which are not discussed, nothing came of this plan. But it does raise the problem of governments rival to that of Sikorski. It also clearly displayed the continued popularity of the pre-war military regime within the Polish Army. The popularity of Beck and Śmigły-Rydz remained undiminished within the military, especially those interned in Romania. It was a perennial problem and one that would eventually defeat Sikorski during 1943. Sikorski never really had an answer to the old regime, and it would finally destroy him.

Legitimacy was all-important and a tall order as the inter-war Polish regime had been anything but legal. Therefore, any exiled Polish government or movement had to convince a host nation that it was acting for the Polish nation and doing so legally. The illegitimacy of the inter-war Polish junta climaxed when the legitimate 1921 Polish Constitution was overturned for a bespoke 1935 Polish Constitution which paved the way for personal rule by Piłsudski but he died within a month of signing the new constitution into law, such as it was. However, it was the 1935 Polish Constitution which served as the basis of the legitimacy claimed by the Polish government-in-exile based in France between 1939 and 1940 and later in the UK between 1940 and 1945. Therefore, the legitimacy of the Polish government-in-exile was compromised as it derived from a document which had illegally usurped the legal constitution of the Republic of Poland. This only became an issue after 1943 when the Soviet government began to question the legality of the London-based Polish government as the Soviets by 1943 had produced their own Polish government, a puppet communist model favourable to Stalin.

The need for continuity in the face of national destruction and defeat meant that the exiled Polish authorities had to refer to the 1935 Polish Constitution as it had been adopted by the Polish Republic and was the document to refer to in order to make sense of how the Polish state should function during wartime and in exile. Any hesitation to have done so might well have spelt disaster as both Germany and the Soviet Union would have taken full advantage of any further discord within Polish elite circles or rather what remained of them. Therefore, the initial stages of the establishment of the Polish government-in-exile in the west were, firstly, the relinquishing of office by the former Polish government, by then interned in Romania. The second objective was the installation of Sikorski from his relative obscurity to becoming the figurehead of Polish resistance and continuity of the Polish state.

The first stage of this plan was to ensure that legal procedure was followed in order to install Sikorski as Polish prime minister in exile. The twin invasions of Poland forced Polish President Ignacy Mościcki out of Poland and into exile in Romania. Before leaving Polish territory, he resigned his office and, using a presidential decree, nominated Władysław Raczkiewicz as his successor.[6] The Polish government in Romania had pressed for this action in order that a Polish government could function in exile from France.[7] The Polish government had fled to Romania and had hoped to get a sympathetic reception from the Romanian government once there, but the German government had already ensured that this would not happen. The Poles considered that all that they required from the Romanians was a single *droit de passage*,[8] the right to traverse Romania en route to France.

Since the outbreak of war German representatives had been in the Romanian capital, Bucharest, to discuss the future of any Poles who might arrive in the country with Gregor Gafencu, the Romanian Foreign Minister. On 14 September 1939 the Romanian government made it clear that if the Polish government and its military commanders crossed into Romania, they would be interned.[9] The British and French governments were already aware of this position as they knew that the Romanian government, under German pressure, would intern Polish officials on their arrival in Romania. On being asked by French officials what would be the Romanian policy towards Poles who retreated into Romania, the Romanian military attaché to Paris admitted that it would most likely be internment.[10] Terlecki observed that orders for the internment of Polish government members and senior Polish figures had been published by the Romanian authorities as early as 6 September 1939. This of course was under German pressure.[11]

Owing to his internment, Mościcki was forced to nominate his successor in order to preserve the continuity of the legal Polish government. His first choice, General Bolesław Wieniawa-Długoszowski, the Polish ambassador to Italy, was instantly rejected by the French, who claimed that his character and private life compromised his ability to hold the Polish presidential office.[12] The British Foreign Office (FO) was very surprised at the attitude of the French government and so conducted its own investigation to establish whether the French allegations could be substantiated and why the UK government had not been consulted before the French government refused to accept Wieniawa-Długoszowski's nomination.[13]

Sir Eric Phipps, the British Ambassador to France, carried out the instructions of Lord Halifax, the Foreign Secretary, and investigated the French allegations against Wieniawa-Długoszowski. Phipps quickly learned that that they were true and that, as Polish ambassador to Italy, Wieniawa-Długoszowski was considered a drunk, a gambler and a drug addict.[14] Despite the apparent truth behind the French allegations, the British government remained irritated by the French government's unilateral decision to veto who was suitable to be Polish president.[15] However, there appeared to have been no follow-up to the British vexation.

The French attitude also annoyed Edward Raczyński, the Polish ambassador to the UK, who considered that, after the military defeat of Poland, all that was left to Poland, was state sovereignty, the Constitution and foreign alliances. The French, by failing to accept the nomination of Wieniawa-Długoszowski, had ignored the Polish presidential prerogative to nominate his own successor. Raczyński also considered that, even after Wieniawa-Długoszowski, Raczkiewicz's nomination was still less than second choice, coming after that of the pre-1918 champion of Polish independence and international concert pianist, Ignacy Paderewski, followed by that of General Kazimierz Sosnkowski, one of the few Polish generals to emerge from the September 1939 campaign with any credit. At the time of his nomination Sosnkowski was still missing. Mościcki decreed that, should Sosnkowski arrive in Paris, Raczkiewicz should resign at once. When Sosnkowski did finally turn up in the French capital, Raczkiewicz did indeed offer his resignation but a compromise was reached as Sosnkowski was appointed as Raczkiewicz's successor if and when this might become necessary.[16] The action of the French government was based on the assumption that the war would last no longer than six months and was fuelled by the desire to see the former Polish government replaced which would allow for French interference while the whole question of Polish independence was left to hang.[17]

The September defeat was the end of the inter-war Polish administration and led to their domestic political opposition forming an exiled Polish government in Paris.[18] The former Polish regime was damned politically and militarily as most politicians and senior officers, more interested in their careers, had fled to Romania while the Polish Army was still fighting.[19] No doubt they also fled for their lives as their compatriots were left in the lurch in Poland to face both the Germans and the Soviets.

Nevertheless, the craven actions of the former Polish government was the opportunity for the Polish opposition to step into the breach and this, according to Beauvois, led to the French government being able to place Sikorski into power within the Polish government being set up in Paris during the autumn of 1939. Indeed, Beauvois claims that the French government had actively sought out Sikorski to install as Polish prime minister.[20] This is an assertion and cannot be verified but, as we have seen, Sikorski spent a lot of time in France during the inter-war period and had met the right people while his book on the future of modern warfare had been quickly translated into French. Therefore, owing to these circumstances, the French had seen Sikorski as a viable and untainted leader of a Polish government-in-exile and so did seek him. This is the line that Sarah Meiklejohn Terry takes as she wrote:

> Although from a constitutional standpoint General Sikorski's emergence as prime minister, as well as supreme commander of the Polish Army in exile, had all the trappings of a legal transfer of power, politically speaking it was tantamount to a *coup d'état*.[21]

She follows this up by agreeing with others that Sikorski profited from having been in the good books of the French and had been able to display that he had no links with the inter-war Polish junta.[22]

What is known is that Sikorski, beyond doubt, denied a military role, was heading from Poland towards Romania and no doubt internment when he was advised on 18 September by Leon Noël, the French ambassador to Poland, to go directly to Paris.[23] The Polish historian Olgierd Terlecki notes that Sikorski travelled on the *Simplon Express* with Leon Noël and the American ambassador to Poland, Anthony Joseph Drexel Biddle Jr, leaving Romania on the morning of 22 September and arriving in Paris on the 24th.[24]

Terlecki's narrative concerning Sikorski's movements after the Soviet invasion of Poland shows how unimportant Sikorski actually was in September 1939. Sikorski had actually reached Romania as we have already seen. On 18 September he was shored up incognito in a small hotel in the Romanian town of Vijnita, known is Polish as Wyźnica. Terlecki observed that Sikorski had no idea that from this modest retreat he was about to embark on the life of being one of the greatest Polish legends.[25] Hyperbole maybe, but relevant for this story at least. The fact that Sikorski was not arrested by the Romanian authorities is significant. He was not that well known to many outside French elite political circles. By going to a small hotel in a provincial town rather than heading towards Bucharest was probably clever, if not shrewd. Sikorski was probably not on a watch list and a small town's authorities were possibly not sufficiently linked up to more central powers but, without doubt, had Sikorski lingered he would have been interned.

Sikorski was penniless and in a predicament. The Romanian state was refusing to accept Polish zloty and even French francs were not convertible in Romania once war broke out. However, this small modest Romanian hotel not only received Sikorski but also Ambassador Noël arrived and very quickly the French General Faury fetched up there as well. Faury had helped establish the Polish Military Academy and was currently Head of the French Military Mission to the Polish High Command.[26]

It seemed that the French had no real plans for Sikorski beyond being a figurehead around whom Poles could rally, as well as being a Polish leader with whom the French government could work.[27] It should also be recalled that the French government considered that the war would last no more than six months. A pre-war British newspaper report spoke of Sikorski being part of a Polish delegation in Paris at the time, February 1939. He was described as a 'leading military expert' and 'an intimate friend of the late Marshal Foch, is outspoken and devotedly pro-French'. It was also reported that, for a long while, Sikorski was denied a passport by the Polish junta and had only recently been granted one.[28] This does not tally with the evidence that Sikorski was widely travelled during the inter-war period and should not detain us in this narrative. *The Manchester Guardian* was just inaccurate in that assertion but does provide a thumbnail sketch of how Sikorski was seen shortly before the outbreak of war in 1939.

The French government found Sikorski attractive as in Poland he was a well-known opposition figure and represented a break with the past. By his absence overseas, Sikorski had not become mired in the dirt that had been the Polish military junta. Other 'clean' Poles arrived in Paris between 1939 and 1940. Lieutenant Colonel Jan Kornaus, fresh from Romania, reported to Sikorski that he considered the former Polish Foreign Minister, Colonel Beck, to be a danger to Polish interests and considered that Beck should remain interned in Romania.[29] There was real anger with the Polish regime in Poland, as was reported by Sir Howard Kennard, the British ambassador to Poland, who stated to Lord Halifax:

> the Polish collapse and hasty retreat into Romania have caused great resentment amongst representative Poles. The Marshal (Śmigły-Rydz) and Colonel Beck are especially criticized, and it is freely stated that Polish people will not trust their future destiny to their former leaders.[30]

This meant that a new Polish administration had to be formed as the former junta and its leaders were no longer credible in Poland or elsewhere. The French wanted Sikorski to head it. The French certainly wanted a clear break from the inter-war Polish regime, especially as they considered that the regime leaders were responsible for the defeat of Poland and held Beck and Śmigły-Rydz particularly culpable.[31] Furthermore, the French government insisted that any new Polish prime minister establishing a new government in France should be well known in France as well as possess the full confidence of the French government.[32] Sikorski certainly fitted the description and so his overseas wanderings began to pay off. With Sikorski enjoying unrivalled support from the French government; the Polish ambassador, Juliusz Łukasiewicz, acting based on the Franco-Polish Military Alliance and under pressure from the Polish Army, conferred the command of Polish Armed Forces on Sikorski.[33]

Whether Łukasiewicz had the constitutional authority to do so is questionable, but the circumstances in which Poles found themselves in by September 1939 were exceptional. There was a danger of a split within the Polish military being created in France at a time owing to the tensions arising from the outrage and frustration at being forced to leave Poland. It might have also been the case that Łukasiewicz was anxious to prevent the French government from imposing Sikorski as commander of Polish Armed Forces onto the Polish government. Therefore, to forestall this, in agreement with his Consul General Aleksander Kawałkowski, who acted as Łukasiewicz's delegate to Polish troops arriving in France, Łukasiewicz claimed that only Sikorski could be trusted with the command of the Polish Army in France and only his appointment could solve the tensions in the army there. On a formal level, as the most senior Polish officer in France, in accordance with Polish military regulations, he could demand that Polish officers obey his orders and that they could be compelled to do so.[34] Terlecki is quite clear in his assessment of Sikorski: Sikorski was definitely the single Polish general and politician in whom the French had any faith.[35] It was, of course, convenient that Sikorski happened to be a soldier and a politician. One would have been unlikely to have found such a combination in a British general, for example. But in 1939 the question was likely to have been which role was Sikorski to see as dominant – that of a soldier or that of a politician? The French just saw him as a figurehead around which a Polish army could be rebuilt.

The French government, using its diplomatic services, put its good offices at the disposal of those Poles whom they wanted to save from Romanian internment. It was quite clear that both the British and French governments wanted the former Polish junta apprehended and to allow for a Polish fresh start. Given the Polish government's previous pro-German stance until March 1939, there was little reason for the Allies to trust the former Polish government. However, in France there was already a Polish commander, Brigadier General Jerzy Ferek-Błeszyński, who had been the Polish Military Attaché to France between 1928 and 1936. During the September campaign, he had been sent to France by Marshal Śmigły-Rydz as commander of a Polish Division to be established there. Ferek-Błeszyński was commandant at the Polish camp at

Coëtquidan until November 1939 when he was removed by Sikorski. From then the two men were sworn enemies which saw Ferek-Błeszyński, following the evacuation of Polish troops from France during the summer of 1940, being detained in the Polish Officers' Camp at Rothesay on the Isle of Bute, Scotland. This was where Sikorski kept certain difficult officers under his command in isolation from the main of the Polish Army once it was evacuated from Europe to the UK. The camp at Rothesay was a source of discontent against Sikorski by fellow Poles with his enemies claiming that it was a concentration camp to detain Sikorski's political enemies.

Noël realised that, in the face of catastrophe, Poland needed a leader with such authority that he would have international influence rather than be a mere leader of exiled Poles. Ferek-Błeszyński certainly was not that man. What the French government was seeking was a Polish national committee in the face of the destruction of the Polish state and the complete loss of its territory to its enemies. The French sought the continuation of the Polish state, albeit in exile, but one which continued to represent Poland and remained the legal Polish state which was recognised worldwide. To this end Sikorski and Noël entered into negotiations.

After discussions with Noël, Sikorski sought Śmigły-Rydz and went directly to Bucharest. In Bucharest Sikorski encountered Stanisław Stroński, one of the most influential junta journalists. This was furthered as Sikorski, without any reference to Noël, went to see Ignacy Paderewski. On 20 September at 14:00 hours Sikorski, presumably under French protection, arrived in Bucharest and communicated all that had gone before with the Polish Military Attaché to Bucharest, Lieutenant Colonel Tadeusz Zakrzewski. The Polish ambassador to Romania, Roger Raczyński, was not a committed follower of the Polish Foreign Minister, Colonel Józef Beck, but was devotedly striving to save Składkowski's team (Felicjan Sławoj Składkowski, Polish Prime Minister, at the time of the outbreak of war in September 1939). At the time of Sikorski's arrival in the Romanian capital, Zakrzewski considered that the Polish situation was hopeless and so put himself at the disposition of Sikorski as he considered that Sikorski presented the last chance for Poland.

On the same day Colonel Jan Kowalewski, who had until recently been the Chief of Staff of the political arm of the Polish military junta and so an official opponent of Sikorski, arrived at Sikorski's hotel to begin negotiations. Despite being an enemy of Sikorski, Kowalewski remained an officer in the east and in Romania and to this end Sikorski commissioned him to prepare notes on the failure of the September campaign as well as discussing with him possibilities for Poland's future. Sikorski was fascinated with a plan to continue the war against Germany from the Balkans and so a repetition of how the First World

War ended. Despite the very poor situation of Poland as found in September 1939, Sikorski was already planning a future Polish victory.

The next day after travelling nearly 500 kilometres from seeing President Mościcki, Raczyński returned to Bucharest. It had been decided by the Polish authorities by now in exile and internment that a new Polish administration had to be established to succeed the former regime which had been presided over by Śmigły-Rydz and his cronies. This naturally had to have a legal basis to protect the legitimacy of the Polish Republic and its future, even in exile. Having fulfilled his thorny mission, Raczyński returned to the Romanian capital with a sealed envelope addressed to the Polish ambassador to France, Juliusz Łukasiewicz in Paris containing the name of the new successor.

Sikorski spent his last few hours in Bucharest with Roger Raczyński. He called for Mościcki's resignation.[36] This was part of the legal process to ensure that any exiled Polish government established was done so legitimately. This process allowed for Sikorski's government to be established in France and then once more in the UK. That situation went unchallenged until, after 1943, the Soviet government decided to undermine the authority of the Polish government-in-exile by establishing its own puppet committee which was pro-Stalin and therefore Soviet friendly and was to eventually become the author of communist rule in Poland after 1948.

As so as already related, on 22 September Sikorski set off by train for Paris in the company of the French and American ambassadors to Poland. What should be noted is that it would seem, contrary to popular belief, that some senior Polish figures were still at liberty in Romania during September 1939. It is quite clear that in the case of Sikorski he was protected by both the French government and at least by the presence of Ambassador Drexell-Biddle whilst he was in Romania and was able to leave unhindered to travel to France whence, he was able to establish a Polish government-in-exile.

Sikorski arrived in Paris on 24 September and was established in the Danube Hotel. He also found Stroński already established there. Once in Paris it was realised that the future of Poland lay with two possible camps. On one hand Ambassador Łukasiewicz, already appreciating the hopelessness of Składkowski's group, still strove to hand over the reins of power to this group. On the other hand, Polish representatives took to care for the restoration of the Polish government while the Polish opposition naturally saw this in a different light. Opposition activists included mainly Stroński, Lieberman, and Pragier. August Zaleski, reputed to be the laziest man in Europe, was joined by Colonel Adam Koc, a senior member of the junta but one who realised that it was not feasible for the junta to carry on in exile. One man who was inclined to give up Polish sovereignty and reduce Polish affairs to that of a national committee was

Lieberman. This should be headed by Sikorski and with the Polish military as nothing else was needed. However, this naïve approach did not find much support amongst Poles.[37]

Of course, Lieberman's approach was wrong. Poland was a sovereign nation which had been invaded by its enemies and overrun losing all of its geographic territory, but it did not cease being a nation. It had not been replaced and there were enough viable Poles outside Poland who could continue to represent Poland and strive for its liberty, but from conditions of exile. However, the exiled Poles were to discover that, even if they received a friendly reception in Paris and later after the fall of France, in London, they were not to have things all their own way.

On 25 September Mościcki's envoy arrived in Paris with a document naming Mościcki's successor as the president of Poland. General Wieniawa-Długoszowski, the Polish ambassador to Rome was nominated.[38] As we have seen, the French refused to accept this decision and were swiftly supported by the British in their refusal to accept Wieniawa-Długoszowski, citing his unfitness to serve in any public office. Therefore, within a month of being invaded and overrun by their enemies, Poles were also to learn that, to maintain support from their Allies, they needed to accept conditions as laid down by the French and British governments. Even in exile Poland was not free to follow its destiny as perhaps it might have expected to have been. The French government made it very clear that it was not going to tolerate any supporters of either Piłsudski or Beck in any exiled Polish government.[39]

On 28 September the Polish capital, Warsaw, fell to the Germans. Its fall caused Raczyński to comment that the most urgent position to be filled was the Polish presidency so that other states, especially neutrals, would be able to see that 'an independent Polish state possessing a President as a symbol of national unity, a government and diplomatic representatives' had not been vanquished by the territorial loss of the Polish state'.[40] The Sikorski camp was, as Tendyra notes, full of pre-war Polish opposition politicians who were presented with a *fait accompli* and so accepted Raczkiewicz as president on 30 September, owing to his earlier nomination. In his turn Raczkiewicz did his best to avoid appointing Sikorski as prime minister but after two abortive attempts to form alternative governments he bowed to the inevitable and appointed Sikorski. This gave Sikorski a dual office, Prime Minister and Commander-in-Chief of Polish Armed Forces, and marked a clear break from the previous regime.[41]

Terlecki observes that Mościcki had four candidates in mind for the Polish presidency after the Allied rejection of Wieniawa-Długoszowski. The four were Cardinal Hlond, Paderewski, the concert pianist, Zaleski and Raczkiewicz.[42] It is quite clear that Raczkiewicz was the best option out of a bad hand as a senior cleric was never going to work well with western democracies. Paderewski was extremely old, Zaleski had a poor reputation. Raczkiewicz was probably the only acceptable face to the Allies if only because he was the blandest of the candidates available.

The Polish government being formed in Paris was not a happy ship and was 'poisonous' owing to the feuding within it.[43] The feuding was due to the question of where the war was going. Many in the west considered or hoped that the war would be of limited duration, perhaps about six months. This caused many in the Polish camp to think that Poland would soon be swiftly liberated and that the exiled Polish government would be the new rulers of a new Poland. However, reality was not a real strength in Polish circles. Many of those who were holding office in the Polish government-in-exile had not held office for twenty years, including Sikorski. It is typical of a long-term opposition party finally coming to office after years in the wilderness to find that political reality and responsibility is more difficult than was remembered or imagined.

The biggest shock though, to most Poles, was defeat and they could not understand how it had happened. Successive Polish governments, despite the evidence contrary, had always declared Poland to be a great power.[44] Sikorski was able to accept that at best Poland was a medium-sized power and that sandwiched between Germany and the Soviet Union a small power. A small power which needed to work with other small powers in order to find strength. There were those such as Łukasiewicz, the Polish ambassador to France, who had considered Poland to be a 'great power', especially after the Polish annexation of Teschen during autumn 1938 while the Polish ambassador to the UK, Edward Raczyński, suggested that the Polish fetish of being a 'great power' had much to do with Piłsudski and his successors who considered that Poles should be more assertive in their dealings with foreigners and not submit to them.[45]

The problem was that the military regime in Poland had always ignored anything which did not suit it until reality interrupted in the form of the September 1939 invasions of their homeland. It fell to Sikorski to try to bring a sense of reality to those who continued to hanker after a restored Piłsudski-ite Poland. As Sikorski was deemed to be allowing foreign powers, especially the Soviet Union, to dictate terms to him and to Poland, he was to feel the wrath of Polish officers who continued to idealise and identify with the inter-war Polish military regime. It was a circle that Sikorski was doomed never to square. Sikorski and his camp were never to find any genuine common ground with either Stalin or Anders, even though Stalin and Anders had nothing in common and hated one another.

However, it might be wrong to suggest that Sikorski was not alive to the situation in Poland regarding the situation there under occupation, as is witnessed by a conversation between Sikorski and British Foreign Secretary Lord Halifax, during November 1939. As the first shocks of invasion and occupation were beginning to recede, Halifax sought information on what the situation was in Poland at that time. Halifax asked Sikorski whether he had any information regarding the development of Soviet policy. Sikorski did but admitted that it was difficult to give a satisfactory answer because, as Halifax noted, Sikorski's reply was 'Soviet policy was many-sided, but he (Sikorski) was convinced that the aim of the Soviet government "was the bolshevisation of Europe"'.[46] That was indeed the true aim of the Soviet or Bolshevik revolution – the spread of its ideology across Europe and, in time, the world. Trotsky may have espoused it and Stalin may have denied it but he never stopped believing in the eventual aim of the revolution. Stalin just waited for an opportune time to return to the offensive and begin to spread the word once more, even if it was at bayonet point.

Sikorski also made an interesting assertion. He considered that the Germans were subservient to the Soviets or Russians. He noted that the Soviets were already in the Baltic republics of Lithuania, Latvia and Estonia. The Soviets had also occupied eastern Poland which, Sikorski informed Halifax, contained a population of five million Poles and millions more Ukrainians. He also said that it was rumoured that the Soviets were planning to occupy the Romanian provinces of Bukovina and Bessarabia in spring 1940. Sikorski asked Halifax if the British and French governments might be able to persuade the Romanian government to reverse their internment policy regarding Poles in Romania. Sikorski thought that it might be possible for the Romanians to use interned Poles to assist Romania if the rumours concerning Soviet aggression against Romania proved to become true.

Halifax also mentioned that large numbers of Poles were interned in Hungary. Sikorski agreed that this was so. He told Halifax that, under German pressure, the Hungarians had closed their frontiers to prevent Poles leaving Hungary and had interned both Polish civilians and military personnel. Sikorski revealed once more his intuition as he said that, eighteen months previously, he had warned in an article of the dangers of German-Russian co-operation and thought that it was a mistake to take the association of the two countries lightly.

Sikorski gave Halifax a briefing of the situation in occupied Poland. Halifax was told that Soviet troops in Poland were talking of conquering Red Berlin. Sikorski had also noted that the Soviets treated the Poles better than the Ukrainians. Nevertheless, Sikorski considered that the German-Soviet co-operation was dangerous, owing to the similarities in their two political systems. Halifax commented that any extension of Soviet influence in Germany would either have to have the approval of Hitler or not. In the first event Hitler would have to state that Nazi policies approximated to those of the Bolshevik movement or, if he tried to deny Soviet influence in Germany, this might led to real problems (with the Soviet government).

Sikorski considered that the second scenario was more likely. At the time any real opposition in Germany to Hitler and his Soviet policy was unlikely to be spoken of publicly at least. Sikorski also noted that Hitler's popularity and prestige had fallen and so a 'new outburst was to be expected'. Halifax considered that this was significant as Hitler was dithering. It was known that Hitler had had many conferences with advisers, but no decision has been reached thus far. Halifax considered that Hitler was possibly in a dilemma. Halifax considered that Hitler must either attack or do nothing in the face of the increasing strength of his opponents.

Sikorski agreed with Halifax's assertion and claimed that an attack on the Netherlands was very possible. He went further, saying that Germany must be militarily defeated in order to re-organise Europe on the basis which assured general security both from military and political points of view. He also informed Halifax of German brutality in occupied Poland. Halifax said that he would see what he could do.[47]

The above talk between Sikorski and Halifax illustrated that Sikorski was aware of what was happening in Poland even when he was in exile. He knew how to articulate his problems to an influential figure such as Halifax who, it should be noted, had sought Sikorski's advice. Sikorski also revealed in this exchange that he had accurately predicted what was to happen in Europe regarding Germany and the Soviet Union and had anticipated Hitler's next moves, which was indeed an attack in the west which rather went against his stated aims prior to the outbreak of war of moving eastwards in order to establish an eastern empire out of the Slav lands of east-central Europe and the Soviet Union. Sikorski was more astute than many credit him.

A few days later, Sikorski had a similar conversation with British Prime Minister Neville Chamberlain. Sikorski told Chamberlain that Hitler's policy was merely the continuation of the German peoples' idea, a situation which had been going on for a long time. Chamberlain replied that the Germans must learn not to do this. Sikorski told Chamberlain that the Germans had to be completely defeated. However, he warned that a German vanquishment could lead to communism in Germany but thought that this might be prevented by the poor state of the Red Army in Poland.[48]

Once more it is quite clear just how astute Sikorski was at this time. He understood both Germany and the Soviet Union and their policies for this period. It is quite clear that he was calling for unconditional surrender and that Germany must be broken rather than subject to the conditions of an armistice as had been the case in 1918, one which Hitler easily broke during the 1930s.

Obviously Sikorski could not have predicted the rapid prominence of the Soviet Union as an ally after 1941 but was correct that Germany could have turned communist in the event of its defeat. It was only the influence and military might of the USA which prevented all Germany becoming communist at war's end. He certainly failed to see the establishment of a Soviet empire in east-central Europe, but who did so in 1939?

Nevertheless, in September 1939, the British government and FO on seeing the composition of the Polish government-in-exile were disappointed. They were yet to assess the skills or otherwise of Sikorski. The appointment of Raczkiewicz prompted Kirkpatrick at the FO to note that Raczkiewicz had been associated with the junta as Interior Minister between 1935 and 1936 remarking that Raczkiewicz had 'not a particularly distinguished career'.[49] Further character assassinations of the Polish government were made by the British when Sir Eric Phipps, UK ambassador to France, filed his report on the Poles. Marginalia dated 2 October 1939 recorded that Raczkiewicz was 'not a strong personality'; Sikorski as 'being once strong' and 'a French creature' who had 'deteriorated during his time in France'; Colonel Koc (former Finance Minister who had been in London during 1939 trying to obtain credit for re-arming) was described as 'well known – friendly but not a "flier"' and, finally, August Zaleski, sometime Polish foreign minister during the 1920s and destined to be so once more, was described as 'notoriously lazy'.[50] Overall, the FO considered that the Polish government-in-exile was second rate. Indeed, it was remarked that 'the Polish Government, is, I fear, stronger in charm than ability'.[51] This was hardly a ringing endorsement from an ally, but it was also very true. Sikorski was the best that the Poles were to get, as was witnessed after his death in July 1943. The second-rate government became third- and fourth-rate governments until the exiled Polish governments became irrelevant during the summer of 1945.

The Scottish historian Peter Stachura asserts that Sikorski accepted the post of Prime Minister and Defence Minister 'out of a sense of patriotic duty and belief in his ability to provide good leadership …'[52] However, what should not be forgotten was that Sikorski had political ambitions as can be seen by his career between 1921 and 1926, as well as his work prior to 1914 when he tried to raise the question of Polish independence. Furthermore, he was also recognised post-1926 as a senior opposition Polish political figure. Polonsky observed that Sikorski was a 'political general'.[53] Wincenty Witos, another senior opposition Polish politician and three times prime minister before Piłsudski's coup, wrote of Sikorski, 'when he needed to be a general, he was a politician and when he had to be a politician, of necessity he then became a general'.[54] This reflected the case that in inter-war Poland the political situation there allowed a military officer to a serving military officer as well as a career politician. Of course, no man can serve two masters and often the military career became neglected as was frequently the case in Poland.

Therefore, it should be seen that Sikorski before 1939 was interested in returning to power in Poland. It can be argued that the Fall of Poland and his adoption by the French presented Sikorski with a chance to return to power in Poland. This would have seen as being realistic as, before Germany's attack in the west during 1940, there was an illusion that the war was to be short and that indeed the Sikorski government would return to Poland and establish a new government there. However, no matter what, the FO certainly had already determined that the Sikorski was second rate, and it is certain that other governments thought the same.

The overall reaction of Poles to the formation of the Sikorski government was mixed. In Romania Polish exiles took it well. Many Poles there considered that the junta had handled the September campaign poorly. Beck and Śmigły-Rydz were criticised, especially their military policies. But there was also discontent as the French government was accused of interfering in Polish affairs. The abortive attempt to have Wieniawa-Długoszowski appointed as president was cited. There were also unconfirmed reports that the French authorities were issuing visas in accordance to the political leanings of Polish refugees. In protest against this alleged practice, Polish pilots made it quite clear that they only wished to serve in the (British) Royal Air Force (RAF) and not the French Air Force.[55]

A report from Poland itself dated 23 December 1939 gave cautious support for Sikorski and his government. It had been accepted in Poland that once the enemy was defeated in the short-term, Sikorski and his government should be installed as a provisional government in lieu of anything better. It was even noted and accepted that aspects of Sikorski's attitude were somewhat dictatorial, but it would seem that Poles on liberation were to take that risk.[56]

However, when Jan Karski meet Sikorski for the second time to deliver his report of occupied Poland as it stood in 1943 in contrast with his meeting in 1940, Sikorski was visibly older. Karski stated that he and all Poles wanted Sikorski to continue to lead them through the difficult times and beyond. Sikorski replied:

> The people must not forget that old General Sikorski is more than sixty-two. He is a very tired man. His only hope and ambition is to be able to contribute to the resurrection of a free and independent Poland.

Karski noted that Sikorski didn't want to be either leader of Poland or its dictator. He only wanted to serve his nation to the best of its ability.[57] That was certainly the case by 1943 but one cannot be too sure of the situation in 1940 when many considered that the war would be of a short duration and perhaps Sikorski, at that time not burdened by the long years of the war, might have considered taking charge of Poland. In what manner we can never know.

One assumes that Poles were willing to accept Sikorski based on his previous political stance between 1921 and 1926 when he did his best to maintain democracy in Poland. In wartime one is more likely to give orders rather than debate as prompt action often had to be taken. Therefore, Sikorski's dictatorial attitudes had everything to do with the conditions of war rather than his political outlook, that is in the eyes of many Poles who were probably thinking in the terms of a proper election at war's end, yet knew that a provisional government was necessary until correct elections for political offices could be held in Poland. This was probably what the Allies sought as well while the model that seemed to emanate from Sikorski was similar to that associated with de Gaulle once France was liberated after June 1944 and democracy and sovereignty were restored to that country. Sikorski and Poland were not to be so lucky.

The alleged French attitude towards the former regime as it tried to engineer a France-friendly exiled Polish government dismayed Sir Howard Kennard, now UK ambassador to the Polish government-in-exile, who noted that the French, in pursuing a pro-French Polish government-in-exile, allowed Sikorski to continue disputes which related to inter-war Polish politics and continue vendettas which had everything to do with Polish inter-war politics and nothing to do with the pursuit of the war against Germany. And so, Sikorski was able to pursue his political enemies even into exile.[58]

Sikorski's problem was that, while he was in Paris, he was never too certain why he was there. He never really understood that he was there on sufferance and because there was little alternative to him. He was certainly not there because of his undoubted skills as a general with a fantastic understanding of modern warfare but while in France he had become tainted with politics. This was the appeal to the French; Sikorski was politically acceptable to the French government and so allowed to act as the symbol of a Free Poland to which like-minded Poles could flock. But it was not Polish troops who were important. Polish troops arriving in France were few and poorly trained. Quite often they were officers while few were non-commissioned officers (NCOs), those experienced corporals and sergeants who are the backbone of any army. The Polish Army in 1939–40 was in disarray but refused to acknowledge the fact.

Nevertheless, on coming to power during September 1939 Sikorski tried to salvage something from the wreckage of the September campaign. Two agreements concluded between the former Polish regime and the French government served as a basis for the establishment of a new Polish army in France. The first, the Franco-Polish Military Accord of 9 September 1939 permitted the creation of a Polish infantry division and the organisation of conscription and enlistment of Poles from within Polish communities living in France to serve in a new Polish force. The second, an executive protocol dated 21 September 1939, made the Polish division operationally subordinate to the French High Command.

The expansion of the Polish division, which seemed to ignore the previous two divisions who had been building up in France, was contentious. In January 1940, the Polish Army bemoaned the lack of uniforms; in April, the French informed the Polish government-in-exile that a certain percentage of Poles conscripted from the coalfields of northern France could not be conscripted at all as they were needed for mining coal.[59] This was quite a shock for the Polish Army as, in inter-war Poland, it was basically a case that if the army wanted something it got it.

The British government was also not enthusiastic about Polish service personnel joining its ranks. An example was the Polish Air Force (PAF). PAF units serving on UK territory were initially assigned to the Royal Air Force Volunteer Reserve (RAFVR). The British also refused to recognise the training, experience and privileges of Polish airmen. The Polish Navy was regulated under the Anglo-Polish Agreement of 18 November 1939. Its status was defined as that of a naval detachment attached to the Royal Navy (RN) and under the operational command of the Admiralty.[60] However, it should be seen that, owing to the conditions of exile, Sikorski and his army could hardly have expected to have been treated with equity and it must be accepted that the bulk of the armed forces, especially the PAF, were not up to speed with modernity. At best they needed a lot of retraining; at worst they could have been used as cannon fodder.

A major problem for Sikorski was the type of military officer reporting in Paris and, as already mentioned, there were too many officers arriving compared with other ranks (ORs). Before September 1939, 65 per cent of commanders of large Polish units had belonged to Piłsudski's Legions Śmigły-Rydz, including the Inspector General, the Chief of the General Staff and his deputies and the Minister for War and his deputy.[61] The disproportionate numbers of officers arriving in the west caused resentment amongst Polish ORs as it was obvious that many officers had abandoned their men and had fled Poland to save their own skins. The craven action of senior Polish officers began at the top with the Polish military junta fleeing as soon as possible.

This should be contrasted to the actions of General Maczek who, as a colonel, had remained with his men of 10th Motorised Cavalry Brigade and had led them into Hungary and, eventually, he and many of his men reached France. After the Fall of France, once more Maczek remained with his men as they left Europe and headed to the UK. The resentment of Polish ORs against their officers was to be the harbinger of the dissent which was to characterise

Sikorski's premiership. Maczek's actions on the other hand bore fruit as his men loved and respected him. This continued post-war when Maczek, unable to find suitable work, took employment in an Edinburgh bar. Whenever his veterans went to the bar, before ordering a drink, they would stand to attention and salute Maczek before ordering a drink. That is how an officer knows he had genuine respect and not mere rank. Sikorski only ever had rank.

At his first officers' briefing on 28 September Sikorski reminded his officers that there was 'no place, nor could there be any place for party politics or the politics of a clique in the Polish Army'.[62] Sikorski needed to reinforce these words and therefore sought the removal of Śmigły-Rydz who, even though he had been interned in Romania, remained a focus for dissent in the Polish Army. Furthermore, he remained Supreme Commander of Polish Armed Forces. By the end of October 1939 Śmigły-Rydz resigned and was formally relieved of his duties on 7 November. Sikorski officially became C-in-C on the same day.[63]

Even though Sikorski could legally demand obedience from Polish Armed Forces, he always struggled to obtain this from Polish military forces which were outside his immediate realm or, in other words, those overseas. By this I mean the Polish secret army operating clandestinely in Poland and, after 1941, II Polish Corps, popularly known as 'Anders' Army' in honour of its charismatic leader, General Władysław Anders. Anders was credited with leading Poles out of Soviet captivity and to the west, establishing a Polish army along the way and taking part in the Italian campaign. Sikorski lacked charisma and was stuck in London under British supervision.

From the very beginning, Sikorski had to maintain a firm grip of the nascent resistance movement established in occupied Poland. Sikorski considered that a Polish underground army would play an important role in the closing days of the war when Sikorski hoped that the Allies, including Polish exiled forces, would liberate Poland. Sikorski lacked any faith in the forerunner of the Polish underground army, the 'Victory for Poland Service' (*Słuzba Zwyciestwo Polski* – SZP) as it was led by two 'Piłsudski-ites', Major General Michał Karasiewicz-Tokarzewski and Colonel Stefan Rowecki, who was Chief-of-Staff. Karasiewicz-Tokarzewski claimed that he and his comrades sought to restore Poland to democracy but very quickly began to challenge the exiled Polish authorities in France.[64] This highlighted another problem for Sikorski and all Poles living in the west; they lost all sense of what was happening in occupied Poland which meant that they became irrelevant to Poles enduring the rigours of Nazi and Soviet occupation. The German government taunted Sikorski and his men as being the 'Sikorski tourists' as they retreated further westward before eventually arriving in the UK.

Part of the task of the Polish underground was the establishment of an 'underground state'. The main criteria of the underground state were the maintenance of the Polish state authorities, departments and institutions in order to prevent a *de facto* break in the continuity of Polish state authority. This was to prevent Poland being left in a state of 'chaos and internal lawlessness' in the face of the relentless violence against the Polish population, especially Jews, perpetrated by the German forces occupying Poland. Instead, a parallel but secret national and local authority was established to combat the anarchy promoted by the Nazis ruling western Poland.[65] This was where Sikorski had no idea of what was really happening in Poland no matter how many reports he received – he could not imagine the fear and horror of living under the twin occupations of the Nazis and Soviets in Poland.

The murder of Maciej Rataj, who twice had been acting President of Poland, shot by the Germans during December 1939, and Henryk Brun, another senior Polish politician, murdered by the Germans on 21 June 1940, as reported by the Polish Foreign Ministry on 30 September 1940 was evidence of the systematic destruction of Polish intellectuals by the enemy.[66] This was horrific proof that the Germans were determined to destroy Poland, its people and its culture. Sikorski's blood must have run cold at this as it became obvious that the Germans had no respect for anybody and could as easily murder a former head of state as they might a Jewish baby. It meant nothing to them. It was clear that Poles had to be aware that there was an alternative to their plight in their occupied homeland and that legitimacy lay with Sikorski and his exiled government. Nevertheless, Poles and others living in occupied Europe still had to endure the horrors of being occupied by those who did not care whether the occupied lived or died. It was an irrelevance to them.

The reports coming out from Poland were important as it at least briefed Sikorski and exiled Poles on the situation in Poland. These reports would also be valuable to informing the Allies of enemy actions in Poland. Even if the Soviet Union was not officially an enemy of the British or French, information on Soviet activities in occupied Poland gave Sikorski a basis to protest to the British government about Soviet outrages against Poland and its people. However, in 1939 much of the Polish ire was concentrated against the occupying Germans. In a report sent from Warsaw during December 1939 the situation in Poland was clearly horrendous. A major concern was that of the *Volksdeutsch*.[67]

This was a reference to ethnic Germans who were Polish citizens but frequently resented Poles and Poland itself. The presence of *Volksdeutsch* was dangerous as they were of ambiguous loyalty, but all too frequently supported the Nazi line, especially in the early days of the war. The other obvious danger was that they could easily pass themselves off as ethnic Poles and infiltrate Polish underground conspiracy groups and ultimately betray them to the occupying Germans.

The December 1939 report from Warsaw noted that all eighteen to forty-five-year-old Polish males were liable to conscription into the German Army. At the same time there was a steady removal of all potential Polish leaders. In the main part of Poland not incorporated into the Reich but occupied nevertheless, known as the GG from its German appellation *Generalgouvernment*, which included the Polish capital, Warsaw, and its second city, Kraków, it was reported that all Polish intellectuals were being imprisoned or executed. The list of intellectuals was more diverse than an English reader might suspect and included not only what one might perceive to be an intellectual but also priests, teachers, politicians and civil servants. Anybody with a secondary education. It was further noted that every aspect of Polish character was being destroyed as Polish monuments, street names and the like were replaced by Nazi symbolism. It was made quite clear that in the GG all leading Poles had been imprisoned. The report asserted that the situation in Soviet-occupied Poland was similar. The Soviets were imprisoning or deporting Poles to the Soviet Union in what the Soviet government referred to as a 'pacific action'.[68]

Regarding the question of intellectuals it should be recognised that inter-war Poland was a largely uneducated society with the army reporting that 50 per cent of conscripts of that time were illiterate.[69] It would also seem from Berling's experience of captivity that the NKVD were more intrusive into Polish society in the areas of Poland in which the Soviets controlled than the Gestapo were in German-occupied Poland between 1939 and 1940 which closed much of the Polish ability to work as an underground movement in Soviet-occupied Poland.[70]

The SZP recognised the importance of establishing a political base made up of the three political parties still tolerated by Poles remaining in Poland after September 1939. This meant securing the support of the leaders of the underground Socialist, National and Peasant parties. This led to the establishment of the Main Political Council (*Głowna Rada Polityczna* – GRP) to work as an advisory body alongside the SZP. Sikorski was deeply suspicious of the predominance of the Piłsudski-ite officers in SZP as he was of the politicians in the GRP who had been hostile to his own inter-war political party *Front Morges*. This meant that he was reluctant to allow a resistance movement to act independently or rival his own government in France.[71]

As a response to SZP, Sikorski began to organise his own underground movement in collaboration with a friend and *Front Morges* ally, Ryszard Świętochowski. In October 1939, as instructed by Sikorski, Świętochowski returned to Poland to unify those Polish military and political groups opposed to SZP and its allies. Świętochowski hoped that this grouping would become the main body in German-occupied Poland to support the Polish government-in-exile.[72] Sikorski refused to recognise both SZP and GRP and in November

1939 established an official military underground movement – the Union of Armed Struggle or *Związek Walki Zbrojnej* (ZWZ) – which took responsibility for resistance activities in Poland.

This was a political act as well as a military one as Sikorski appointed General Sosnkowski, a dangerous opponent and senior in rank to Sikorski, as commander. This placed Sosnkowski under Sikorski's command but was seen as a very good choice as he was seen as having been close to Piłsudski and prestigious.[73] The appointment of Sosnkowski was cleverer than Sikorski had anticipated as later, in 1941, he was able to dismiss Sosnkowski easier than would have been the case if Sosnkowski had held any other post.

In 1939, Sikorski considered that resistance in Poland was to be part of a swift return to Poland and part of his remit. He was wrong as the military and political leadership remaining in Poland refused to accept that a distant exiled government should be making policy for Poland and instead considered that the underground leadership in Warsaw should be responsible for this work. The longer the war dragged on the more apparent this became. However, as Tendyra observes, the exiled authorities with direct diplomatic ties with the Allies and their government seats outside occupied Poland were best placed to represent Polish affairs rather than a shadowy underground leadership operating in secret in occupied Poland.[74]

Therefore, it could be considered that the establishment of ZWZ was a political mistake. This error stemmed from a military miscalculation which was to have serious long-term consequences as in time the Polish underground began to speak in the name of the Polish people. This was what the Polish government-in-exile claimed to do. This would suggest a schism between the official Polish government-in-exile and the Polish underground state. However, as we will see, overall, the military and political wings of the underground state remained loyal and obedient to the government-in-exile.[75]

Not only was Sikorski experiencing difficulties in trying to establish his authority in Poland, he also struggled to obtain equity within the Allies. The French and British looked down on the Poles as inferior and defeated. Throughout the winter of 1939 and spring 1940 Sikorski attempted to impart to the French the lessons he had learned from the September campaign. Sikorski soon discovered that the French were disinterested as they considered the campaign to be unworthy of serious study.[76] However, there is evidence that General Maurice Gamelin, C-in-C French Armed Forces, studied the reports concerning the combined air-armoured assaults, the so-called *Blitzkrieg*, used to destroy the Polish Army.[77] But it is unclear if the French High Command understood the 'shock effect' of *Blitzkrieg*, especially on reservists who had never been under fire before.[78] Therefore it is wrong to suggest that the French refused to learn from the Polish experience of September 1939. They failed to understand what had happened.

The French thought of war as one of defence rather than attack and certainly did not comprehend the rapidity and mobility of the invading German armoured units especially in conjunction with aerial support, namely the Junkers Ju-87 dive bomber, commonly known as the 'Stuka' which was used as flying artillery. Ironically, the French Army had, in equipment, terms undergone modernity replacing horse with vehicles but had not really updated its tactics and preferred to think in the terms of defence rather than attack. French society was also not ready for war and overall was defeatist in nature. The short sharp attacks by the Germans were a genuine shock to the French.

There was criticism of the French from other quarters as the US ambassador to France told the US State Department that Gamelin and his 'aristocratic' High Command had drawn no lessons from the German invasion of Poland and that the French treated the Poles with contempt. The French High Command had decided that *Blitzkrieg* would not have the same effect on the French Army as it had on the Polish Army. As a result, the French Army received no training regarding the German methods of attack. The American ambassador concluded that the same methods were used against the French and had the same effect as had been experienced in Poland. The British historian Martin S. Alexander dismisses this.[79] The September campaign had been studied by the French, but its lessons went misunderstood. The American ambassador's attitude probably stemmed from American anti-French prejudice which started with American President Franklin D. Roosevelt.

However, what seems to have gone unnoticed was the experience that the Germans had gained their service during the Spanish Civil War of 1936–1939. Hugh Thomas, in his seminal work of that war, quoted the words of General von Thoma, commander of the German tank detachment in Spain who later spoke of Spain as the 'European Aldershot'. The Germans had learnt the value of combined aerial and armoured attacks. The French ignored the lessons of mechanised warfare while the Soviets learned them and began to build up a large, armoured force owing to their own experience of the Spanish Civil War.[80] To the Poles' cost, the French continued to deploy armour in small packets but that was probably the least of their problems. It was clearly a huge operational mistake. The major problem was that Sikorski trusted the French too much and placed too much faith in the French Army which he still insisted would easily defeat the German Army.

Sikorski continued to persevere with his faith in the abilities of the French Army, despite the evidence that the French Army and the British Expeditionary Force (BEF) was failing to prevent the rapid German advance into France during

May 1940. Sikorski continued to tell his government that all was going well at the front even though Gamelin had warned him on 21 May of the possibility of the destruction of the French Army.[81] On one occasion, Sikorski assured his minsters that 'France led by Messieurs Reynaud, Mandel and Weygand, will never let us down ... Mandel and Weygand are my personal friends ...'[82] In Polish society, to hail someone as a 'friend' is a serious business and nothing as shallow as the Anglo-Saxon use of referring to just about anyone of one's acquaintance as a friend; therefore it must follow that Sikorski would have been mortified when he discovered that the French High Command had arranged for the Polish Armed Forces to surrender to the Germans. Sikorski refused and in a vicious row with the French commanders decried the 'paralysed defeatism at the top of France's military and political commands'.[83] The Fall of France marked the end of Sikorski's military career and the remaining three years of his life were those of a politician.[84]

After the Fall of France, the priority of the Polish government-in-exile was its own evacuation and that of its armed forces.[85] Any problems which Sikorski had faced in France were exasperated when he arrived in the UK. Sikorski had had an almost blind faith in the abilities of the French. He had considered that the French Army would defeat the German Army. This caused many Poles to accuse him of allowing the French High Command to squander Poland's most valuable asset in the west – the Polish Army. Out of 80,000 troops under Sikorski's command in France, only 19,451 were evacuated to the UK.[86] A further criticism of Sikorski was that he was in effect missing during the crucial period of 11–17 June 1940 as he was at the front where he hoped to lead a Polish division in fighting near the Maginot Line. Gamelin and later General Weygand had promised him that he could lead Polish troops in battle. A close friend of Sikorski, General Marian Kukiel, commented that this was a 'bad habit' amongst Polish military leaders as other military figures, including Piłsudski, had taken charge of the frontline instead of providing 'political wisdom' at government headquarters.[87]

However, Sikorski may have feared that he might have been charged with deserting his troops in the face of the enemy if he did not lead Polish troops in battle. This was what he had accused members of the Polish junta of doing when they fled to Romania while the Polish Army was still defending Poland. During October 1939 Sikorski had considered purging the Polish Army of those officers whose activities during the September campaign gave cause for concern. After condemning those who had endangered the Polish state, Sikorski had urged an atmosphere of 'mutual trust' in Polish exiled circles as he tried to rebuild the Polish Army. To this end Sikorski promised to suspend judgement on the September campaign until after the war. At this point it was commonly thought that the war would be of short duration resulting in an Allied victory. Sikorski also stated that officers who had contributed to Poland's defeat had forfeited the right to fight for Poland and rebuffed members of the junta who had tried to re-join the armed forces and were willing to serve at any rank.[88] Sikorski feared that he might be treated in the same manner and therefore sought to lead his troops on the front rather than scuttling off to safety as Beck and Śmigły-Rydz had done in September 1939.

Sikorski's departure to the front caused major problems for politicians who were located in the temporary French capital at Angers; quite simply communications between Angers and Sikorski had broken down. A letter from the British Air Ministry to the British Air Attaché in Bordeaux relating to arranging the evacuation of Sikorski gave some idea of the difficulties in trying to locate him. The British conceded that they had no idea where Sikorski was. He had last been heard of being with the Polish Division at Nancy and hoped that the Polish Mission in Bordeaux knew where he was.[89] The lack of communications between Sikorski and his government meant that Sikorski's deputy, General Sosnkowski, was reluctant to withdraw any Polish units, even reserve ones, let alone evacuate the entire Polish Armed Forces in case the blame for any aspect to the Fall of France fell on Poland and himself.[90] It is quite clear that if an early decision to evacuate the Polish government and armed forces had been made, the bulk of its army might have been saved and the government's transfer to the UK, less chaotic.

The Fall of France was a disaster for Sikorski. General Bohusz-Szyszko claimed that Sikorski was so absorbed with events at the front that the French government had been able to deceive him on the situation in France.[91] By being at the front Sikorski disregarded his wider responsibilities, those of being Polish prime minister. This revealed him to be irresponsible because that post meant that he should have been overseeing the functioning of the Polish government and its conduct of relations with the Allies. He also had to consider the welfare of his army which should have included its rapid evacuation in order to avoid complete annihilation.

This disastrous confusion of priorities was to lead to the first concerted attempt by President Raczkiewicz, once in London, to force a separation in Sikorski's powers.[92] Equally, Sikorski was not slow to demonstrate his disdain for Raczkiewicz as, when the Polish President arrived with his entourage at Paddington Station in London on 21 June 1940, he was met by King George VI, but not Sikorski. It was several days before Sikorski received his President and several other ministers whom he considered had fled France with indecent haste.[93]

However, it should be realised that the departure of Sikorski and the Polish government-in-exile, once more on the run, was not easy. As might be anticipated, there was a state of chaos in France. It was quite clear that they and the Polish Army would have to be evacuated from France to the UK: the British had already lifted their army and thousands of French troops from the beaches at Dunkirk at the end of May and beginning of June, but most Poles were still in France. Sikorski had been slow to understand that most French people sought a swift departure from the war; indeed, this was something Sikorski preferred to ignore.

On 4 June 1940 the Polish government-in-exile met at their new base at Angers in north-west France as the Germans were within ten days of capturing the French capital, Paris, and therefore the various seats of governance had removed themselves to perceived places of safety. The exiled Polish government, according to Polish writer Stanisław 'Cat' Mackiewicz, took an unrealistic and foolish attitude towards the French and remained optimistic despite the evidence around them that France was being destroyed by the invading Germans and the French seemed almost compliant in their doom. Nevertheless, there were sufficient French commanders who still considered that France might be able to survive the crisis and operations were planned to try to thwart the German invasion even as Paris itself was imperilled.[94] After all, this had happened before in 1914 whilst in 1871 the Prussians had captured the city after besieging in for over four months. In 1814 Paris had fallen to the Russians. It was nothing new and each time the city and France had survived with its people.

Sikorski, being a natural optimist, and, even if he was not, had to maintain aura of calm in order to govern his exiled government. There was no room to consider defeat and so he had to press on the best that he could and try to rescue his compatriots both civilian and military. On 7 June Sikorski received a 'dramatic telephone call' from the French general, Weygand. This exchange was witnessed by an anonymous major. Weygand made the case for defeating the German offensive claiming that every tank and soldier was in place ready to defeat the Germans and that Polish support was necessary for this French initiative.[95] This must have been music to Sikorski's ears. Here was General Weygand who in 1920 had saved Warsaw; was he about to save Paris and France?

Earlier on the same day, Sikorski, as Chairman of the Polish exiled cabinet, had sat considering the trivial problems of the time such as creating a commission to investigate the September campaign of 1939.[96] This may sound fantastic, but it is also typical of the lack of reality within the Polish camp and in many ways the irrelevance of the Polish Army – it was symbolic and without doubt cannon fodder – but nothing else. Sikorski was deluded enough to consider that he and his men were really relevant to the fighting in France. He had already been insulted by the British who insisted that Polish pilots were to be trained with modern aircraft and bought up to modern and disciplined standards – both were lacking in the Polish Air Force. But the phone call from Weygand made

Sikorski feel relevant to the situation in France. However, events in France were beginning to spin out of control.

For a couple of days there had been a series of German offensives which culminated in the collapse of the French front on the river Somme. On 10 June, Italy entered the war on the side of Germany. The Polish 2nd Division during this time moved forward as far as Belfort which saw the last stand of Polish forces in France in 1940. The French government had already evacuated from Paris to Briare near Orleans where a 'war government' was established. At the same time Weygand and Pétain in the presence of Reynaud and Churchill sought a way to try to end the fighting.

Sikorski was not party to these talks as the war spread. Instead, he chose to travel from Angers via Paris to his field headquarters in Lorraine. Sikorski wanted to acquaint himself with the position of every unit of the Polish Army in France. On 13 June the Germans had reached Paris. The Germans had rendered all of the French defences, including the fabled Maginot Line, useless. France was undone. Reynaud requested Roosevelt in a radio interview for immediate assistance stating that only a miracle could save France and that he believed in miracles.[97] This may have had something to do with the so-called miracle on the river Vistula; many Poles believed that the Virgin Mary intervened and prevented the Red Army from capturing Warsaw in 1920 and thus saving Poland, and indeed Europe, from the Bolsheviks, for a generation. The reality was that General Weygand dictated a sound plan for the defence of Warsaw in lieu of rank amateurish nature of the Polish command structure which lacked any real military schooling or discipline.

In the French city of Tours, the heads of the French armed forces proposed to Churchill, an immediate ceasefire. But the reality was that the fighting in France was over. Sikorski was not aware of the overall situation in France and was on his way to Weygand with plans for a grand counter-attack. Sikorski considered that Weygand was just the man to consider any idea of saving France. This was how for a couple of days Sikorski pursued Weygand. This was very much like Sikorski's peregrination on the way to Podola during September 1939. However, events were overtaking Sikorski and any plans that he might have had for a counter-offensive as, by 14 June, he learned that the Polish president, the government and the diplomatic corps had left Angers and were heading towards Libourne, not far from Bordeaux. The French government was also there. On 15 June a German division was between the rivers Seine and Loire.

Kukiel, in a letter to Sikorski on 15 June 1940 sent by courier, wrote that he had sent a telegram to Sikorski previously. The letter was urgent as Kukiel made it quite clear that Sikorski needed to get to Libourne immediately. Sikorski's close confidant Professor Stanisław Kot also dramatically wrote to Sikorski surveying the situation in France as lost and that he should immediately head to Libourne. These messages did not reach Sikorski owing to the state of chaos which reigned in France during the time. Sikorski continued on his quest to find Weygand and on 15 June arrived in Dijon and from there during the evening of the same day moved to Vichy. Sikorski had no idea that a few hours earlier Zaleski had been in talks with Reynaud in Bordeaux and learned from him that France was to capitulate and that Poles who did not want to surrender had three to four days to evacuate from France.

It is without doubt that Sikorski forgot during this tragic time that he was not only head of Polish Armed Forces but above all he was the Prime Minister of Poland, albeit in exile. Sikorski became so engrossed in the unfolding military campaign and how he might be able to reverse the impeding military catastrophe. But, as Terlicki notes, to discuss this is from the perspective of dozens of years but at the time he was probably correct to try to retrieve the military situation. Even from Sikorski's side nothing is said about those critics who later claimed that he lost the Polish army in France. But as already seen circumstances reduced Sikorski's ability to act in the manner in which he wished to proceed. Sikorski was well aware that if the Polish division left the battlefield it would leave the way open for the Germans to advance. What was really necessary to save the Poles was a clear Polish victory in France. Perhaps this was the very reason why Sikorski had undertaken his road trip to Vichy in pursuit of the French military leadership.[98]

However, how realistic was this? The Poles had a very limited army while the greatest land army on paper, at least in 1940, was the French Army and it had just been totally filleted by the Germans. The British had been obliged to leave continental Europe to regroup and face the prospect of invasion themselves. Nevertheless, on 15 June the French were still fighting but there was already talk of Pétain negotiating an armistice with the Germans. It was not the French Army that had been defeated by the Germans, but that French society had defeated its own army by its pessimism and lack of will to defend their own country as reservists had no interest in the war and so deserters and others flocked with refugees along the roads and highways trying to get to God knows where. France was thoroughly defeated by its own people in June 1940.

Throughout 16 June Sikorski waited in Vichy for Weygand. During this period, Zaleski, in agreement with the Polish government-in-exile, had approached the British ambassador to the exiled Polish government and asked him to inform the British government about Polish decisions regarding the situation in France. It boiled down to a few words – no capitulation with the French.[99] Zaleski also informed the Polish Ambassador in London, Edward Raczyński of this declaration as well as telling Colonel Mitkiewicz, Head of the Polish Military Mission in London. Meanwhile, Sosnkowski and Kukiel were exploring the possibilities of a Polish evacuation from France. However, there were two considerations to be taken into account – the first was that France, a Polish ally, was still fighting. The second was that such an eventuality as evacuation could only be made by the Polish Commander-in-Chief.[100] This of course was Sikorski and the Polish government-in-exile had lost touch with him – so what could they do?

As a result of conversations conducted through Raczyński, Churchill on the same day, 16 June, through the British ambassador to the French government told French Prime Minister Paul Reynaud that, even though he knew that the French government would do anything to aid Polish and Belgian military units in France and would even send them to French territory in North Africa, that the exiled Polish and Belgian governments should be evacuated to the UK.[101]

During the evening there was an unexpected reunion with Sikorski and the Podhalian commander General Szyszko-Bohusz. The Podhalians had just returned from Norway after being evacuated from there after the Narvik expedition and had landed at Brest. Sikorski began to issue orders that were more reflective of the Polish position in France. He ordered the Podhalians to get to the west side of the river Loire and destroy their heavy weapons and equipment. They were to be armed only with light weapons. This was in contrast with the French commander in Brittany who was determined to defend the Brittany peninsula.

On 16 June Churchill sought the unprecedented proposal of a union between the UK and France, thus joining the two countries at the hip. However, this proposal could no longer help France. During the evening of the 16th, France was undermined from the interior by its own Cabinet as it was taken over by Pétain – the arch-capitulator. Only at midnight did President Raczkiewicz manage to reach Sikorski by telephone. Sikorski was still waiting for Weygand. Understanding the danger that he was in, judging from the information passed onto him by Raczkiewicz, Sikorski immediately left Vichy. Travelling through the night for over 300 kilometres Sikorski reached Libourne by morning on 17 June. Once he was there, Sikorski was able to discover everything which had happened in his absence.

At the same time Zaleski arrived back from Bordeaux where he had learned from the newly-appointed French Foreign Minister Paul Baudouin that little in France remained free. Sir Howard Kennard, the British ambassador to the Polish government-in-exile, had arranged passage to the UK for President Raczkiewicz and the Polish Foreign Minister. Already waiting out in the estuary off Bordeaux was the cruiser *Arethusa*. Further arrangements had been made for those Poles most endangered by the impending German occupation of

France with 320 places being offered immediately by the British on two ships. While these arrangements were being made Sikorski immediately set out to Bordeaux and to Pétain.

As announcements were broadcast on French radio regarding the capitulation of France, Raczkiewicz and Zaleski were already aboard *Arethusa*. At 20:00 hours of the 17th, after returning from Bordeaux, Sikorski met with the exiled Polish Cabinet in Libourne. His trip had been completely fruitless. Pétain, in Sikorski's opinion, had nailed down the situation, made some vague promises but above all was shocked that the Poles had decided not to capitulate. Such an idea was beyond Pétain's ken.

Things were going wrong amongst the Polish Cabinet. Already Minister Stańczyk was missing as was Vice Minister Jan Graliński, which meant that officials of the Polish Foreign Ministry and Diplomatic Corps were left to their fates while Stańczyk and Graliński should have remained in place until further orders according to the Polish Presidential Protocol. During the night 17–18 June Poles arrived in Libourne as well as at Lourdes, Toulouse and other southern French towns. It was chaos, people were moving along the roads but without any idea of what to do or to where they are going. Regarding the Polish military situation in France – units of 10th Cavalry Brigade not involved in fighting were withdrawing from the Paris area, airmen without aircraft were withdrawing from Lyon while an officers' Legion left the Vichy area.

At dawn, on 18 June, the Germans arrived at Rennes and captured General Altmayer and his entire staff. This put paid to any question of defending the Breton peninsula. As a consequence, the Podhalian Brigade was no more. Several hundred Podhalians left France on British ships. During this period about 9,000 Polish troops were able to leave France for the UK. Pétain, now deprived of any martial spirit or right of determination having lost his most brilliant and best French divisions, seemed angry with the Polish troops such as the Grenadier Division who right up to the French capitulation had faithfully served France and Poland in the fighting in and around Lagarde when suddenly the French threw in their hand. The Polish 2nd Infantry Division were also hard-pressed, fighting for the French at Maiche where they had only the Swiss frontier behind them.[102] It is a matter of record that this gallant division deprived of French support withdrew into Switzerland and internment until war's end.

It was not the result that the Poles wanted but by being interned by the Swiss the Polish infantrymen were beyond the reach of the Germans. Furthermore, it could be considered that if Switzerland had been attacked by Germany, already there was a whole host of experienced soldiers ready to return to the fray in defence of Switzerland and Polish honour. Switzerland was spared any

German invasion and so 2nd Division remained interned until the end of the war in Europe in 1945.

On 18 June in Libourne the exiled Polish Cabinet met for the last time in France. It was a beautiful June morning, but perhaps not so wonderful as the French authorities had seized all Polish ships in port. Pétain's government was already licking German boots. The Poles knew that they had to get away from France and the chances of doing so were getting slimmer by the hour. Sikorski sent a telegram to London which, luckily, coincided with an initiative of Winston Churchill. Before noon a British flying-boat landed in Bordeaux. It contained a very important Polish political actor and highly influential character – Józef Retinger had been sent as a personal messenger by Churchill to Sikorski. Retinger was to take Sikorski from Libourne to London. Retinger was one of probably two Polish figures, the other being Stanisław Kot, in whom Sikorski had any real trust and faith. It is quite clear that Sikorski trusted virtually nobody from the Polish Armed Forces, and he was right not to trust them.

Sikorski's run to London was not as smooth is it might have been owing to the wild scenes and chaos at the airfield in Bordeaux, but with the aid of Polish Air Force officers, including Colonel Iżycki having to requisition a French vehicle at pistol point, Retinger arrived in Libourne. In the French sub-prefecture building occupied by the exiled Polish authorities, the French finally found out about events that morning relating to General Sikorski's departure when they broke into his office finding a note 'gone to have lunch with the General'.[103] The general being of course Sikorski. The cheeky note was the result of Sikorski asking Retinger what he was doing in France and, as it was more or less lunchtime, Retinger replied something to the effect of having dropped in for lunch.[104] Hence the cheeky note left for the French to find.

The coolness of Retinger's note is quite remarkable as in his memoir it is clear that his trip out to France was anything but easy. Retinger had been uneasy since the beginning of June about the future and fate of General Sikorski and the Polish Army in France. Most of the Polish Army had been in action either in Norway earlier that spring or later helping in the defence of France including Polish troops fresh from Norway. The Poles in London were receiving little, if any, news from the front in France and nothing of Sikorski. Nevertheless, the Polish Air Attaché, Colonel Kwiencinski, returned from a meeting with the British Minister for Air, having obtained a military aircraft for Retinger's use to go to Bordeaux to seek the whereabouts of Sikorski and to ascertain what the situation was in France regarding the Poles and the situation overall.

During the evening of 17 June Retinger received a telephone call from the British Air Ministry. He was told that his trip to France was to be the next morning at 02:00 hours, 18 June. Retinger was to board his aircraft at

Blackbushe Airport, Yateley, Hampshire, close to Camberley. From there his journey was to begin at four in the afternoon (16:00 hours). The aircraft was at the Retinger's disposal complete with pilot. Once in France, Retinger was to be afforded every convenience to locate Sikorski. The aircraft was obviously heavily armed; Retinger had to admit that he was uneasy having ammunition about him which was all too conspicuous.

Retinger's aircraft en route for France landed at the Channel Isle of Jersey to refuel. Later Retinger was to reflect that his was the last British military aircraft to use Jersey until its liberation in May 1945 following its occupation by German armed forces from June 1940. From Jersey Retinger flew into Bordeaux. At the airport chaos reigned. Nobody knew what was happening or what was about to happen. Retinger noted that he did not even have the means of transport to get from the airport but, luckily, he ran into Colonel Iżycki, later to become Commander of the Polish Air Force in the UK and together they bribed a French military driver to take them into Bordeaux itself. With Retinger travelled his pilot, Squadron Leader Biddle of the Royal Air Force. Retinger recalled that Biddle, just before taking him out to France, had just returned from a bombing raid over Germany and naturally was extremely tired. As soon as he sat in the French vehicle with Retinger, Biddle fell asleep.

Once in Bordeaux Retinger went directly to the British Embassy. It was not a pretty sight as hundreds of Britons were waiting, seeking to get away from France and return to the UK. After a bit of a struggle Retinger managed to get to one of the clerks approaching him in a state of complete panic. Retinger asked if he knew anything of General Sikorski and was told that the embassy had no idea of the whereabouts of Sikorski and all that they could think about was how to get out of France.

Retinger related that he was two or three hours in his search for the whereabouts of Sikorski before it occurred to him that in Bordeaux there had to be a Polish consul. After finding out the address of the consul, Retinger went directly there and found an old man who knew nothing and was also in a panic. When Retinger asked the old man about Sikorski, he answered that he cared only for his own life and not for some Polish prime minister. A quarrel broke out during which somebody recognised Retinger's raised voice. It was Aleksander Mohl, a Polish diplomat who had been engaged with the Polish Embassy in Paris.

From Mohl, Retinger learned that Sikorski was presumably in Libourne near to Bordeaux, where the Polish government-in-exile had been and with the Polish Air Force command. Mohl did not have details. He was the only man not panicked by events whom Retinger met whilst in Bordeaux. Retinger barely knew Modl but from that meeting a genuine friendship blossomed. Therefore, as a result of Modl's information he went to Libourne, once again having to bribe Retinger's driver to go there. The roads were choked with refugees from every part of France and some even from Belgium. Every mode of transport had been pressed into use by those fleeing the Germans, cars, horse-drawn vehicles, bicycles and many were on foot. Retinger even encountered a Gypsy wagon. The scenes were incredible; it seemed that some had pushed wheelbarrows all the way from Belgium about 500 miles away. Retinger recalled seeing some of the most bizarre things being transported by these wretched people as they fled their homes in the wake of the German Army's advance. He certainly saw a canary in its cage being carried (but surely one would not abandon a beloved pet and a memory of peacetime). For 300 kilometres the roads were so full of refugees that travel was virtually impossible.

Nobody in Libourne could tell Retinger where the Polish Headquarters were. Eventually Retinger met an acquaintance in the street who said that Sikorski was in the Under Prefecture (French administrative office). Without a word Retinger made his way to Sikorski's office. He found Sikorski alone. When he saw Retinger he could not believe his eyes. Sikorski asked Retinger what he was doing in France and, as it occurred to Retinger that it was approaching lunchtime, he made the humorous remark that he had come for lunch with Sikorski. At this point Professor Stanisław Kot, a friend to both Sikorski and Retinger, entered the office. Kot looked at Retinger and realised that their mutual presence in France had been an overlap from London. Kot shouted, 'you are the first ray of hope'. Sikorski asked Retinger why he had come.

Retinger explained that he had an aeroplane at his disposal to fly Sikorski out of France that evening to the UK to organise the evacuation of Polish forces from France to England. Without any hesitation Sikorski agreed on the condition that, within the next few days, he would meet with Churchill. After this Retinger did have lunch with Sikorski in what was described as a modest hotel where about twenty-five of Sikorski's closest aides could be found. They remained at their posts with the general and did not display the slightest trace of panic. Every one of this group were determined to carry on the fight against the Germans even if at that time they had no idea of how they might proceed to do so.

At 16:00 hours Retinger and Sikorski made for the airport in the same car in which the exhausted Biddle was still sleeping. Panic in Bordeaux was beginning to peak. Just to cross the bridge over the river Garonne took over an hour, such was the mass of vehicles and people all trying to do the same. By this time Biddle had finally awoken and was unsettled as he had orders to fly only during daylight hours. Finally, the airport was reached at about 18:00 hours and within a few minutes they were ready to start. Along with Retinger and Sikorski, there were also two or three people from Sikorski's immediate entourage.

Instead of following the coast as they had done previously on the inbound flight to France, in order to get to the UK in daylight the pilot flew straight across France. As they flew quite low it was possible for Sikorski's party to see very disturbing scenes as they crossed France. In the streets of Rennes, German troops were massing in large columns while enemy artillery shelled the areas around Rennes. From time to time, they saw skirmishes between French and German troops. This time they had to fly over Jersey as it was already occupied by the Germans. Finally, they arrived in the UK in darkness but still had to travel another two hours, this time by car to London where they were met at the Dorchester Hotel and welcomed by the British diplomat Sir Charles Peake and Victor Cazalet.[105]

Cazalet, who was destined to become Sikorski's liaison officer, was also a British Member of Parliament and a colonel of the British Army in addition to being a member of the British elite. He was also doomed to die with Sikorski just off Gibraltar on 4 July 1943. However, in spite of this perceived privilege, according to Sir Alan Lascelles Cazalet was all opinion or *doxa* and not *episteme* or knowledge. This followed an incident in 1942 when in the presence of Lascelles, Cazalet held forth about the future progress of the war and where it was going. Lascelles 'who knew too much' sat in silence but later confided to his diary that he considered his opinion of Cazalet was that he was '*doxa* all the way ... and damned little else'.[106]

Sadly, this was the British officer who was the link between the British government and Sikorski, who, according to Lascelles, knew little if anything which was worthwhile. In effect the Poles were kept out of the loop unless it suited the British to inform the Polish government-in-exile of anything which was significant in their relationship. It was no wonder that Sikorski spent much of his time from 1940 until his death in 1943 frustrated since anything like the reins of power within the Allies was kept from him. This sense of political impotence was increased once General Anders, on release from Soviet captivity in 1941, began to usurp Sikorski's authority as he began to consult with British officials from 1942, especially in the Middle East and about the war in that area.

Whatever the future held, Sikorski was now safe in London and about to enter negotiations with Churchill. Sikorski was already well aware that Churchill was no defeatist, unlike the British administration which had been replaced. Within a few weeks, Churchill would underline his determination to do all that it took to defeat Germany and her allies. In early July 1940, after making quite clear to the Vichy French government, the pro-German French government which had replaced the democratic French government following the Fall of France during May–June, that, if the French fleet anchored at Oran did not put itself beyond the reach of the Germans, he would order the Royal Navy to attack and sink this fleet. Churchill was ignored and so the Royal Navy attacked and destroyed the French fleet, killing just under 1,300 French sailors at the same time. It was a hard lesson for the French, but it rather imposed Churchill's determination to defeat the Germans no matter what had to be done. This was a man with whom Sikorski could work with and after his experience of working with the French it must have been a breath of fresh air to find a man who did not believe in defeat. Indeed, Churchill was about to lead the British in their own fight for survival with the Germans poised to invade the British Isles in the summer of 1940.

Sikorski's team contacted Churchill's office and a meeting between Sikorski and Churchill was arranged for the next day. On 19 June the two met and talks lasted for five hours. Retinger was not present at the meeting; the Poles were represented by Sikorski and Edward Raczyński, the Polish ambassador to the UK. Nevertheless, after the talks, Sikorski gave Retinger give a near verbatim report of what was said.[107] The problem with Sikorski was, as we shall see, that unless you were actually in a meeting with him, or minutes were taken and consulted, one could never be certain if Sikorski's version of events was a true record. This became apparent when he returned from visiting President Roosevelt in 1942.

Nevertheless, Sikorski told Retinger that Churchill only had a limited number of well-trained British soldiers while Sikorski indicated that he might be able to bring over from France 35,000 Polish soldiers and airmen. Admiral Nasmith-Dunbar VC and other naval experts were called into the meeting and with Sikorski and a long discussion commenced on how best to evacuate Poles to the UK. This discussion covered numbers to be evacuated as well as other military details which Retinger confessed to have forgotten. During the final discussion regarding evacuating Poles, Churchill revealed to Sikorski that he had 2,000,000 people in uniform but only 750,000 rifles and few artillery pieces. Churchill then questioned as to why the Poles wanted to come to the UK. Sikorski replied that every Pole wanted to fight the Germans since the German invasion of Poland, let alone the recent fighting in France in which the French had disappointed him and his countrymen in their hopes. Sikorski then asked Churchill if the British would fail them as well?

This was a heartfelt question and Churchill, with tears in his eyes (he often did – Retinger writes that he saw Churchill on three more occasions in tears) replied, 'I believe in you, and you can always rely on me. Britain will always keep faith with Poland'. At that moment neither Churchill nor Sikorski could have predicted the future, not even Yalta or the withdrawal of the recognition of the Polish government-in-exile.[108] These events were to happen in 1945, after

Sikorski's death and when Churchill was by then playing second fiddle to Stalin and to Roosevelt. One can only wonder what might have happened if Sikorski had lived. It was very likely that the AK would not have been wasted at Warsaw in the Warsaw Uprising. A more astute leader would have recognised that the Soviets had no intention of aiding the Poles in this venture.

Another point of conjecture might have been could Anders and Sikorski have learned to co-operate. Sikorski had the legal authority and senior ranking of the Polish Armed Forces while Anders had the charisma of the perception of having led the Poles out of Soviet captivity and from the Soviet Union. He also had the practical skills for dealing with Stalin and the Soviet government, having served in the former Imperial Russian Army; Anders spoke Russian. During his imprisonment between 1939 and 1941 there was a short period of laxity when he was given access to a library which consisted of works by Marx, Lenin and Stalin, all in Russian. Anders devoured these works and understood what the Soviet plans were for world domination, otherwise the World Revolution. If Sikorski and Anders had worked together properly, they would have been a formidable challenge to Stalin as it would have been more difficult to deceive them owing to Anders' linguistic abilities. But this never happened and later Churchill worked with Anders in the Mediterranean theatre of operations but there was no bond of honour between the two such as there had been between Sikorski and Churchill. The year 1940 was important for Churchill and he remembered those who had stood with him during the difficult summer of that year – Sikorski was one such man; another was the Free French leader, Charles de Gaulle. But as Retinger remarked as long as Sikorski lived, Churchill stood by his side.[109]

Indeed, with Churchill's patronage Sikorski was introduced to the powers-that-be and often the relationship was that of Churchill taking the role of an elder brother with his younger sibling. Churchill visited Polish troops, frequently saw Sikorski and was always extremely sympathetic towards him. Retinger testifies that he had on many occasions seen Churchill acting as host to Sikorski and other leading Poles at events or as a guest as Polish leaders held functions. As he had intended, Sikorski left London on 19 June. On the same day the evacuation of Polish troops from France began with aid from British armed forces and the Royal Navy.

Retinger made the statement that many Polish soldiers were rescued from France with the result being that 30,000 men were evacuated to the UK. He makes the claim that with young people escaping from Poland and volunteers from the Polish community in the USA this number rose to 80,000 Polish Armed Forces personnel under British command. Two years later this number was to increase to 210,000 people. In the period before the American entry to the war, the Polish force was third largest in the UK, the Canadians claiming second place and of course the British Army being the largest force present in the UK. The Polish Air Force acted as a sperate formation under British command.

Sikorski's absence from the UK was extremely brief and he only spent thirty-six hours in France and returned to London on 20 June. Before departing from the UK Sikorski sent another letter to President Raczkiewicz who was yet to sail for the UK. This letter was basically a report on what Sikorski had been doing while in the UK. Retinger reported to Raczkiewicz that relations between the exiled Poles and the British had been of a good and indeed fraternal nature.

However, it is not clear if Raczkiewicz actually received this letter owing to the movements from France to the UK and the chaos of June 1940 may well have held this letter somewhere until it was of little relevance, but Retinger's optimism should be noted. As Retinger's biographer observes, Retinger had been very close to Sikorski before the war. Their relationship grew closer with Retinger's responsibility in seeking and retrieving Sikorski from France. From that moment Retinger became the most trusted within Sikorski's inner circle. Sikorski needed allies like Retinger as being pushed to exile in yet another European capital was unedifying for the Poles. Sikorski, as he admitted to Churchill, had been let down badly by senior-ranking French political and military figures. This allowed for his leadership to be questioned once the Polish government-in-exile began to re-assemble in London at a time of a threatened German invasion.

Nevertheless, an undated Polish report but based on numbering in the 1940 Homeland file, possibly after September 1940 notes the popularity of Sikorski in occupied Poland. The report makes clear that Sikorski is the most popular figure in Poland despite his absence from that country. His popularity verged on nearly a cult but the report was anxious to ensure that this situation was not mindless foolishness. It was claimed that Polish society had looked at Sikorski's legacy as an opposition figure against the Piłsudski military regime. According to the report Polish society made their judgement for Sikorski by assessing his political and military talents in real time or, in other words, they were impressed with how he had dealt with the realities of invasion and annexation which had led to his establishment of a Polish government-in-exile. This was a popular move as was Sikorski's ability to work and establish alliance with both British and French governments. Many in Poland and elsewhere considered that these were the very blocks to rebuild a new Poland and be able to retrieve something from the wreckage of the defeat of the Polish Army during September 1939.[110] The popular support of Sikorski by Polish society should be noted. However, it should be remembered that, before the French capitulation during June 1940, Polish society thought that there was to be a swift end to the war with the complete defeat of Germany. It was also considered that Germany and the Soviet Union would eventually go to war.[111]

A German-Soviet war at times was a particular Polish obsession but the Poles were not wrong in their assessment of the German-Soviet situation. No doubt a long time watching the neighbours gave the Poles a real insight but when this war did come it didn't go the way that many Poles might have hoped for. The compilation of Polish reports obviously took time if only owing to the logistics of getting such material out from occupied Poland as so at times the conclusions might seem slightly dated.

Obviously, a report from September 1940 such as the above report did not reflect the fact that France had already been defeated and occupied. However, the facts about Sikorski taking the actions that he had before the Fall of France remained and it was seen in 1940 that in exile Poland had a good and faithful champion in Sikorski. A further example of slightly dated reports is one dated 13 July 1940 from General Dąb-Biernacki to Sikorski which discusses a 'new' Polish Army in France.[112] By then the French goose had been cooked and the British had also sunk the French fleet in Algeria less than ten days before Dąb-Biernacki's report to Sikorski. Some events just moved too swiftly for accurate reporting and, as already stated, did not go the way that many Poles might have hoped.

Even though the public face of the Polish government-in-exile was Sikorski and Raczkiewicz; Retinger was the trusted man who had Sikorski's back and so his reputation as *éminence grise* or 'grey eminence' (*szarej eminencji* in Polish) began. It should be clear that behind every major decision made by Sikorski and his government, Retinger had a hand. He was genuinely the power behind the throne and Sikorski's window on the world. The world of exiled Polish politics was murky; Sikorski needed at least one man in whom he could trust as he sought to salvage Polish honour from the debris of the French campaign and yet another withdrawal, this time totally from the European mainland, leaving a considerable number of Polish troops stranded there. Sikorski was fully aware that he was never first choice for the role of prime minister of Poland in exile or Polish defence minister but was largely in office owing to French sponsorship. He could rarely trust anyone in his Polish exiled circles; therefore, Retinger was important, as was Churchill's personal support for both Sikorski and for Poland. It should be noted that Churchill's support was more for Sikorski than Poland. For eighteen months Sikorski was to largely benefit from Churchill's approbation.

Chapter Five

Relocation in London, 1940

By 1940 Sikorski had made enemies on three fronts. First was the treatment of the pre-war Polish military Junta and its conduct during the September campaign. After the Fall of France during June 1940 Sikorski's belief that the inter-war Polish regime should have been prepared for invasion was weakened as France had collapsed after six weeks of fighting. In 1939 the Poles had fought for five weeks but much more had been expected of the French Army. Symbolically, the French had done worse as they had capitulated formally to the Germans; the Poles had refused to, but this was mere gesture. The Poles had been comprehensively defeated and were about to undergo a horrific ordeal as citizens from all backgrounds were to be murdered, enslaved and brutalised. The Poles may point to French collaboration in the form of the Vichy regime, seated in unoccupied France. The Poles were never offered such a facility by the Germans; it might have been a different story if they had been judging by the example set by those who collaborated with the Soviets. As for 'first to fight', well, they had to. The events of 1939 still remain largely mythical.

Secondly, Sikorski wanted to make overtures to the Soviet Union via Sir Stafford Cripps, a notable British left-winger with sympathy for the Soviet Union and newly-appointed British ambassador to the Soviet Union. This was to be an unofficial approach but it was hinted by Sikorski to Cripps that if the British government could offer its 'good offices' in the re-establishment of Polish-Soviet relations, the Polish government-in-exile might be prepared to 'recognise the Russian position in Eastern Poland'.[1] Given that the Soviet Union had invaded and annexed eastern Poland during September 1939 and was a close ally of Nazi Germany, it was obvious that this was a non-starter. In 1940 Cripps was sympathetic towards Stalin and his government; by the end of his tenure as ambassador in 1942 Cripps had had a reality check and was more wary of the Soviets.

Thirdly Sikorski's conduct during the French campaign had caused resentment in the Polish Army. As we have seen and shall see further, Sikorski had been heavy-handed towards those Polish officials and senior officers who arrived in France after the defeat of Poland during autumn 1939. There was also a suspicion that Sikorski was setting about making his own political future as and when he was able to return to Poland. This, of course, set him against those officials who had participated in the governance of Poland after 1926.

However, Sikorski had recognised a fact that many Poles refused to face up to by 1940. Poles understood that Poland was faced with two enemies: Germany and the Soviet Union. Few Poles accepted that only one could be defeated in the short term at least. Sikorski realised that Germany could be defeated but the Soviet Union was too big and so compromise was needed. Sikorski as the 'moderate soldier-statesman' realised the policy of 'one enemy': Germany.[2] This was a similar policy to that adopted by the British and American governments after 1941 when they found themselves at war with both Germany and Japan. This led to a decision on who was 'enemy number one' and, like Sikorski, the Allies decided that Germany was the greater of the two evils of that time.

Once the Polish Army reached the UK in the late summer of 1940 its morale was very low. It had been militarily defeated twice within a year and its numbers had been severely reduced as relatively few men had escaped from mainland Europe, despite a British-led naval evacuation of Polish personnel from France. Once again Polish troops considered that their officers had abandoned them, a trend begun in 1920. And again, a disproportionate number of Polish officers fetched up in the UK. Sikorski set out to find what had happened to the Polish Army during the French campaign.

During the sojourn of the Polish Army in France Sikorski actually had little choice but to obey French instructions and follow French interests. This provoked comment from within Polish elite circles. Once more it was considered that certain Polish officers had failed in their duty in France and Sikorski established a commission to investigate the actions of Polish officers during the French campaign.[3] Resentment by some Polish troops against their officers was such that they expressed a wish to join the British Army rather than serve under Polish officers.[4] Sikorski had a problem there. Once again it was perceived that Polish officers fled Europe with indecent haste with the result that there was a ratio of one officer to every two-and-a-half soldiers.[5] In fairness, even if many Polish soldiers had indeed been abandoned by their officers, not all officers escaped easily but still Sikorski had to deal with the aftermath of the French campaign and how it affected his army.

After the withdrawal from France, most Polish troops arriving in the UK were posted to Scotland. In order to restore the morale of Polish troops, two Sikorski loyalists, Generals Paszkiewicz and Kukiel, urged Sikorski to visit his men there and try to address the problems of Polish troops now languishing on the Scottish coast.[6] The poor morale had more to do with physical conditions rather than political considerations since many Polish troops were living in tents. Instead of going to Scotland himself, Sikorski sent Kukiel. This was a shrewd move by Sikorski as he needed to remain in London as a political storm was developing in exiled Polish circles in London and the last thing that Sikorski needed to do was to remove himself to the remoteness of Scotland in case of any attempted coup against him. There had been calls by former junta officers for Sikorski's replacement as C-in-C with Sosnkowski since, in their collective mind, Sikorski had failed in his duty in France.

On 16 July 1940, Lieutenant Colonel Kazimierz Stefczyk, head of the General Staff's First Bureau (Intelligence), warned Sikorski that junta officers were trying to implement a plan to regain power and did not care how they did so. Stefczyk reported that Sikorski was being blamed for all Polish problems since the invasions of September 1939 and that only Sosnkowski as a 'saviour and man of destiny' could save the situation. Sikorski was urged to do something without delay to counter the proposals of the junta.[7] Sikorski purged his administration and tasked Sosnkowski with re-organising the exiled Polish government.[8]

Sosnkowski quickly, probably rather too quickly, drew up plans for a new government which reduced it to just six ministers working with the prime minister and his deputy.[9] This would suggest a cabal rather than a Cabinet where views may be aired and debate encouraged. It was obvious that Sikorski, in line with other Polish military dictators, considered that he could rule rather than govern with a group of handpicked appointees. It quickly became apparent that Sikorski lacked the charisma needed to pull off such a trick. In short, he was no Piłsudski and furthermore lacked the corporate support of the Legionnaires for example. Sikorski always had to command and demand; he could never convince people just by being in their presence. Immediately, President Raczkiewicz demanded the instant dismissal of two Sikorski-ites, Stanisław Kot and Henryk Strasburger, while some of the minsters refused to accept their loss of office.[10]

Sikorski faced problems from within the army as an open letter from General Stefan Dąb-Biernacki accused him of running a dictatorship, tolerating a party clique and wasting the Polish Army in France.[11] Dąb-Biernacki, a lieutenant general and former inspector of the Polish Army, was a particular problem for Sikorski. On his arrival in France at the request of the Sikorski government, Dąb-Biernacki was arrested and imprisoned. He was later charged with dereliction of duty during the September campaign. He was further suspected of planning, from internment in Hungary, a coup against Sikorski's government. Eventually, Dąb-Biernacki was imprisoned in the Polish isolation camp at Cerizay, south-east of Nantes. This camp was controversial as it seemed to contain exclusively officers from the pre-war military junta who were considered to be no longer suitable for further service in the Polish Army owing to age, health, lack of qualifications and, quite simply but alarmingly, opponents of Sikorski.

The camp at Cerizay had been given to the Polish authorities by the French government who appeared to tolerate its use by Sikorski. Later, during May 1940, Sikorski ordered the establishment of what he chose to call a 'concentration camp' for 'provocateurs and dubious elements'.[12] It should have been that by May 1940 Sikorski and the Polish Army might have taken a break from playing at politics and presented a united front against a common enemy, Germany, whose armies streamed into France from 10 May. However, the lack of professionalism of the Polish Army was always foremost and so personal ambition became paramount rather than loyalty to the nation and its allies. It was only the Fall of France that thwarted Sikorski's own political ambitions and the removal of his political opponents. Sikorski's handling of Dąb-Biernacki backfired as he became a political martyr and a focus of opposition to Sikorski, continuing his activities once he arrived in the UK during the summer of 1940.

Dąb-Biernacki's letter was not an isolated incident but was part of a concerted campaign beginning in the winter of 1939–1940 by junta officials who wanted to remove Sikorski who refused to submit to such pressure and continued with his policies. After securing the support of Kot and Strasburger; Sikorski rejected Raczkiewicz's demand for his resignation, observing in a letter to Raczkiewicz that re-organisation was the prime minister's exclusive prerogative.[13] Raczkiewicz was determined to break up Sikorski's dual role and force a separation between the offices of prime minister and C-in-C Polish Armed Forces. He even offered the premiership to Sosnkowski who surprised Raczkiewicz by turning it down. It might have been the case that Sosnkowski surmised that, as a perceived leading 'Piłsudski-ite', he was unlikely to receive much support from a government based on socialists.[14] Sosnkowski advised Raczkiewicz to appoint Zaleski as premier.[15]

The appointment of Zaleski is an episode that ought to be remembered in the annals of the history of London at least as it produced possibly the only coup in the capital during the twentieth century. To begin with, Sikorski was dismissed on 18 July 1940. Raczkiewicz probably had room to sack Sikorski as Sikorski more-or-less refused to work with him. However, the political parties in exile rallied to Sikorski while Raczkiewicz was to receive a harsh lesson as to who was really in charge. Zaleski began to try to form a government and, while he was doing this, on the evening of 18 July the political crisis of Polish exile politics thus far peaked.

The Chief of Staff, Colonel Klimecki, accompanied by two other senior officers arrived unannounced at Zaleski's office at the Polish Embassy in Portland Place, London. Klimecki urged Zaleski to resign or other methods of persuasion would be used, including the 'most drastic'. As Klimecki was threatening Zaleski other armed officers gathered at the embassy.[16] This incident was a classic example of armed intervention in domestic politics and typical of how the inter-war Polish

Army intervened in Polish politics, even in the conditions of exile. Simply put, the Polish Army pulled off a coup d'état in central London.

Nobody batted an eyelid, but it did nothing to enhance Polish democratic credentials. It did, however, raise a question from Poles in Budapest asking whether it was true that Zaleski was prime minister and that Sosnkowski was his deputy and commander of the Polish Armed Forces. This was the subject of a rumour sweeping the Hungarian capital that not only had the above men accepted the posts but that Sikorski, Kot, Seyda and Stroński had all been dismissed.[17] Of course, by the time of the inquiry, events had moved on and Sikorski was back in office. However, it was a question that both Budapest and the entire Polish nation needed answering: was this the truth?[18]

Of course, it was not and the Polish Army had stepped in and prevented such a calamity from happening. Without doubt Churchill would have found it difficult to work with or trust the Poles had Raczkiewicz been successful in replacing Sikorski. Sikorski was definitely Churchill's man. The Poles needed to present a united face to the world and the only vehicle for this was the Polish Army, even if it did not have much respect for Sikorski: it certainly did not have any admiration for civilian politicians, especially those of Zalewski's stamp. Regarding Sosnkowski, he lacked the political astuteness of Sikorski and would have quickly led to Poland becoming isolated politically within the Allied camp. Furthermore, the President had forgotten that Churchill had given his hand to Sikorski and not to him. As long as Sikorski was present, so was Churchill.

The preservation of Polish unity was extremely important as, earlier in 1940, while the exiled Poles were still in France and it seemed unlikely that France would be defeated if attacked by Germany, there was a plot against the Sikorski government coming out from Hungary. At the beginning of March 1940 Sikorski was made aware of an attempt by former Polish junta figures seeking to establish a Polish government in Budapest. This information was contained in the so-called 'Whitehall Letter'. In this missive it was described how members of the ex-right-wing party ONR had 'swallowed their differences' with Colonel Beck's 'partisans'. The overall plan was the pursuit of 'reconciliation with the Germans under the aegis of Hungary'. An acting head of this movement, a 'Madame Wenda', was also mentioned. She was to act in the absence of her husband who was interned in Bucharest.[19]

This was the very thing which Sikorski had to prevent. At the time of the Budapest events Sikorski was still in France and did not even consider that he would be ousted from there. It was very unlikely that he and his followers ever considered that they would end up in exile in the UK. The British government was not prepared for the Fall of France as there had been little preparation made by the British to receive Poles in the UK. Only fifty-three visas had been issued and this only encompassed those for the Polish president, members of the Polish government and diplomats; 280 permits to land in the UK were issued for Polish clerical staff and their families.[20]

There doesn't seem to have been any intention of taking Polish troops at that time at least. It should be noted that, on the previous day, Sikorski had flown to the UK for a meeting with Churchill to discuss the evacuation of Polish personnel. It was agreed that about 90 per cent of the Polish military in France were to be evacuated but only 10 per cent of the Polish civilian population. It was at this meeting – Sikorski was in the UK for only forty hours – when Churchill declared to Sikorski that he was with him to the death or to victory.[21]

This indeed was a magnificent proclamation. It was needed and Sikorski, without doubt, was grateful for such support. However, dealing with the percentages to be evacuated, the 10 per cent mentioned would have been for the government, diplomats and their entourage. But those people would have been in a position both bureaucratically and physically to circumvent the situation and prevent being left behind in France. Polish soldiers, meanwhile, were doing their best to stem the German advance across France. This included Sikorski who had to be tracked down before he could be brought to the UK. It is not overly surprising that many members of the Polish Army were left in France after June 1940. Some were able to get to Allied territories, often to Gibraltar, to finally re-join the Polish Army while others worked with the French resistance movement in defying the enemy.

Nevertheless, France fell and so unity had to be maintained as even the UK was threatened with invasion and conquest by Germany. Polish troops were eventually evacuated from France but many were left behind for many reasons. The exiled Poles also had to maintain cohesion. This was indeed preserved. The UK was not defeated. However, the question of an alternative Polish government never went away and eventually it was an ally, the Soviet Union, which made it possible for a rival Polish government to be established and to eventually govern post-war Poland, albeit in the name of the Soviet Union.

Nevertheless, to return to the summer of 1940, given the location of the Polish coup events, the FO was remarkably very calm about the entire episode. Frank Savery remarked to F.K. Roberts at the FO of the manner of Polish officers, complaining about the 'Mexican behaviour of certain high Polish officers' but nothing else.[22] The Polish crisis had passed, and Sikorski was back in office within twenty-four hours of his dismissal. Indeed, within two days Roberts noted 'Savery rang. Polish crisis over'. Savery also noted that the success of the Polish military over the Polish civilian administration would only increase Sikorski's personal vanity and encourage him to interfere further in the running of the exiled Polish administration.[23] Sir Howard Kennard, the British ambassador to the exiled Polish government, was just as cutting of Sikorski, remarking to Savery after the Polish crisis:

> Sikorski's vanity is so colossal and unfortunately, he is encouraged to display it in certain circles here … I consider that something should be done to make him realise that he is not the only pebble on the beach … do not believe all that he tells you about Polish troops getting out of France etc. as he believes anything he hears and is most unreliable in this respect.[24]

This is not to suggest that the British government and the FO did not understand what was at stake within the Polish government-in-exile. British intelligence summaries reveal that the British authorities were well aware of the conflict between Raczkiewicz, and Sikorski. The FO wanted Sikorski to emerge as the victor as he commanded Poland's most valuable asset, the Polish army,[25] albeit in a truncated form after its losses in France. The fact that Sikorski's supporters seized power on his behalf on 18 July pointed not to legitimacy but to power. Sikorski may not have been the most popular Polish leader, but he did have the corporate support of the Polish Army and they had a monopoly of the means for violence as displayed to Zaleski and Raczkiewicz. The Polish president and his prime minister still knew their places vis-à-vis the Polish military. Sikorski in 1939 may have been a political nobody but by 1943 Churchill was able to remark to Stalin, the Soviet dictator, that 'if he (Sikorski) should go, we should only get somebody worse'.[26]

Churchill's remark revealed that there was a genuine lack of political and military talent amongst exiled Poles, even in 1943. This was due to the political immaturity experienced in Poland between 1926 and 1939 owing to the military junta not allowing for any experience beyond the military. Even that was somewhat stunted owing to the negative influence of Piłsudski and his successors. This legacy could not be shaken off within twelve months. Therefore, it made sense that Polish officers cut to the chase during the summer of 1940 and, using the threat of armed force, re-installed Sikorski.

The British authorities may have demurred slightly, but they continued to recognise the Polish government-in-exile as the official and only Polish government anywhere in the world. However, it was to begin a problem for Polish civilian politicians in exile; they were dependent on the support of the Polish military as 18 July 1940 had proven. With Sikorski in command, it was not an issue but any person wishing to succeed him as Polish prime minister would need to have the support of the Polish Armed Forces in order to survive the mess that was Polish exiled politics. Therefore, by 1940 it is easy to see that the Polish government-in-exile was essentially a military government, as had been the case in Poland between 1926 and 1939. Sikorski, or any other leader, could survive with the support of the Polish military. That support was necessary to maintain control and advance the Polish cause from the unenvious position of exile. A weak or divided leadership would doom the government-in-exile to oblivion. Sikorski certainly understood this as he began his policies of co-operation with the Allies. After June 1941 this included the Soviet Union.

After July 1940 Sikorski and his government began to settle down to the business of governing the exiled Polish community. He had the support of the British Prime Minister Winston Churchill, but immediately attracted British critics. One was Anthony Eden, the Minister for War and, later, Foreign Secretary. Eden considered Sikorski to be yet another 'Piłsudski-ite'.[27] Furthermore, Sikorski remained unpopular with the Polish Army, even if they were seen to support him. At heart, the Polish army remained favourable towards Piłsudski, and many were dismayed at Sikorski's negative attitude towards the inter-war junta.

Major Perkins, British Military Intelligence, accompanied Sikorski to Scotland on a visit to the Polish Army there. Perkins reported on the Polish military's hostility towards Sikorski and noted that many Polish soldiers were more attached to Sikorski's main military and political rival, General Kazimierz Sosnkowski. Three out of four Polish generals in Scotland were opposed to Sikorski. Perkins reported to Frank Roberts that the 'atmosphere on General Sikorski's arrival was distinctly frigid' but over the three-day visit there was a thaw and Sikorski concluded his visit 'reasonably popular'.[28]

This suggests that Sikorski was able to persuade his men that he was a good and decent leader. However, more than likely it was military discipline that held and respect for his office which prevented the open hostility that some had feared once Sikorski visited Scotland. Clearly Sikorski had to do something during the summer of 1940 and avoiding his men was not an option. He needed to go to Scotland and face down his opponents. This at least gave him a temporary breathing space.

The FO was aware of Sikorski's difficulties as a report on the political sympathies of the Polish Armed Forces in the UK discussed the notion that Sikorski was considered to be a 'symbol' to his men rather than a 'human being'. It was only Sikorski's rank in the Polish Army that commanded respect; it was not the man. The report continued observing that the Polish Army in Scotland knew little of the Polish government-in-exile. Scotland was remote compared with the seat of the Polish government-in-exile, London. A further problem was that those Polish politicians who had fetched up in London were second rate while the true leaders of Polish political parties had remained in Poland.

The only well-known figure was Professor Stanisław Kot, a close friend of Sikorski, a bitter critic of the inter-war junta and extremely unpopular with the

Polish Army. Frank Savery, the report's author, considered that overall Sikorski could depend on the loyalty of the army even if the rank and file detested him. He remained awkward in his dealing with ordinary troops who, in their turn, much preferred Sosnkowski over Sikorski. Jan Tarnkowski, an interpreter in the Polish camps, thought that it was a pity that Sikorski was represented in Scotland by General Kukiel, who was better known as a professor of history. Savery referred to Kukiel as being 'this respectable historian camouflaged in a military uniform, who, moreover, cannot speak any English'.[29] Furthermore he was only five feet two inches tall.

The reliance on Kukiel to represent Sikorski was a mistake as it increased the perception of Sikorski being remote, both geographically and personally. His visit to Scotland was evidence that, if he tried harder, he might have won his men over completely. But Sikorski had to keep close tabs on events in London as, not only was London the centre of Allied power, he also needed to keep his own countrymen in check. The events of 18 July 1940 are evidence of that. Furthermore, the pre-war Polish Foreign Minister, Colonel Beck, who was still interned in Romania, remained popular with the Polish Army.[30]

During October 1940, following rumours that Beck had escaped internment, Polish troops expressed their support for him. Despite being part of the defeated junta, Beck was still regarded as being symbolic of the alliance with the UK. The Polish government-in-exile certainly did not want Beck at large and feared that either the British or American governments might give him sanctuary in their respective countries. Therefore, it was suggested that, if Beck fell into Allied hands, he should be interned in Cyprus.[31]

There was a similar panic in early 1941 when Śmigły-Rydz escaped from internment in Romania. Sikorski told Eden that it was possible that Śmigły-Rydz might have crossed into Yugoslavia and that he had already instructed the Polish diplomats in Belgrade to help him, but he was not to be given any opportunity to contact the Polish Army. Sikorski requested that if Śmigły-Rydz came into contact with the Allies it would be preferable if the British government confine him to a British colony for the war's duration; Cyprus once more came into the frame.[32] A month later the FO learned that Śmigły-Rydz was still on the run in Romania. The FO confirmed that the British government would intern Śmigły-Rydz in Cyprus if he fell into their hands.[33]

By autumn 1940 Sikorski was struggling to survive in the hothouse of Polish exile politics. In losing much of the Polish Army in France during May–June 1940 he had lost much kudos within Polish military circles; only his rank saved him. His abortive attempt to reach accommodation with the Soviet Union and create a Polish Army from Polish prisoners of war and Polish deportees by then languishing in Soviet captivity caused more mistrust of Sikorski amongst Poles, especially from his own government. It should be recalled that, technically, a state of war existed between Poland and the Soviet Union while the secret nature of Sikorski's approach towards the Soviet Union alarmed his ministers and others.

As early as 19 June 1940 Sikorski had submitted an *aide-mémoire* to the British government discussing the possibility of raising a Polish Army in the Soviet Union. At the request of the Polish government-in-exile this document was never submitted but retained as information only. Ivan Maisky, the Soviet Ambassador to the UK, noted in his diary that:

> The ill-fated 'Polish Government' recently came running to London together with its president. Polish Premier Sikorski met with Churchill and assured him, first orally and then in writing, that the Polish Government did not wish to impede in any way the improvement of Anglo-Soviet relations.[34]

In a more telling confidence to his diary Maisky recorded this thought:

> In less official Polish circles the following notion is gaining ground: if the Germans hold Poland, Polish nationality will eventually be eliminated. If Poland goes over to the USSR, Polish nationality will survive or even develop. Hence the conclusion: 'Let it be a Soviet Poland, but still Poland!'[35]

Maisky was partially right regarding the future of Poland and the German attitude towards Poles and, indeed, all Slavs. Hitler was quite clear that he wished to see the Slav people eventually exterminated after the Jews. The American historian Catherine Epstein, in her study of Arthur Greiser who initiated the final solution in Nazi occupied Poland, notes that if Greiser had had his way, the Poles would have been slaughtered in the same way as the Jews. It was only, curiously, Himmler who stayed his hand. Without doubt, if Germany had been victorious in the Second World War, the Polish people would have also been exterminated along with other Slavs.[36]

Śmigły-Rydz had once warned that with the Germans one loses their life but with the Soviets (or Russians) one loses their soul, but Poland did survive even under Soviet oversight. Maisky never really took the Polish government-in-exile seriously and even in the privacy of his diary wrote this appellation in inverted commas, suggesting that he did not truly recognise it. He was certainly wrong about the Polish acceptance of the loss of territory to the Soviet Union. Śmigły-Rydz totally underestimated the Nazi will to commit genocide.

Nevertheless, Sikorski had made his approach to the Soviet government in writing. The existence of this document unsettled some unspecified members of the Polish government-in-exile. Sikorski's cabinet rounded on him for trying to enter into negotiations with the Soviets without consulting them. Furthermore, Sikorski by not consulting his foreign minister, was ignoring the terms of the amended Polish Constitution which obliged him to work with his foreign minister in such a situation.[37] However, Meiklejohn Terry noted that Sikorski certainly was willing to revise Polish frontiers which included a move westward to the present Polish frontier on the Oder-Neisse line as a matter of future defence.[38]

In 1939, the Germans had been able to invade eastwards into Poland and had captured nearly half the country in that direction before encountering any real geographic obstacle, the river Vistula at Warsaw. And even then, owing to three years of near drought conditions in Poland, the Vistula's waters had sunk so low that Germans merely waded across the river. It should be noted that Sikorski's plan regarding a revised Polish western frontier was not one based on compensation for the loss of territories to the east, but one based on compromise with the Soviet Union.

Sikorski wanted to remove the Germany ability to easily invade Poland from the west, taking advantage of the mainly flat Polish terrain. What he wanted was a ditch on the Polish frontier, the Oder-Neisse line with the river Neisse flowing northwards into the Oder. Sikorski, as Meiklejohn Terry noted, was not alone in this concept as it was not Polish communists in Moscow who saw merits in dealing with the Soviet government in this matter but in the first instance the idea had 'gained currency' with exiled circles in London and in the non-communist Underground.[39]

Sikorski's perceived judgements on the deployment of Polish troops during May and June 1940 and his attempts at rapprochement with the Soviet Union were clearly separate matters but they were to become part of a larger question within Polish émigré circles as many sought to remove or reduce Sikorski's powers. While Sikorski was to underestimate just how belligerent Stalin, who basically was the Soviet government, would be in negotiations as well as totally underhanded.

In 1940 Sikorski was unable to know that, by the end of 1941, the Soviet Union would eclipse Poland within the alliance fighting against Germany and would supplant Poland in the affections of the west, both at diplomatic level and in the minds of the British people. He also was not to know that, even before he and his compatriots had been driven from the continent of Europe during June 1940, Stalin had ensured that thousands of Polish officers and other leading Poles had been murdered by the notorious NKVD, the Soviet security service, during April 1940. No matter what, Sikorski was never to square that circle. Sikorski was to find that, despite the support of Churchill between June 1941 and until his own death in July 1943, he was doomed to play second fiddle to Stalin. And there was nothing which he could do about it.

Chapter Six

Settling In: London, 1940–1941

The situation altered in the UK at once when Winston Churchill took the office of Prime Minister during May 1940. With Churchill at the helm of state an air of realism took over in the UK. The concept of a swift victory was no longer considered. Instead, it was realised that a long war against Germany would have to be fought before a final Allied victory could be won.

This angered the Polish government as it swiftly became obvious that the British were not going to wage war against the Soviet Union with whom Poland remained at war while Soviet troops stood on Polish territory in eastern Poland, the so-called *kresy*. Nevertheless, the British and Poles were united in the war against Germany, but it was not an easy relationship between the two governments.

By July 1940, the UK government had discovered the internecine nature of Polish politics. It was to the UK's advantage to allow Sikorski to have his way and let him continue to pursue political vendettas as it had the effect of purging disruptive elements from the pre-war regime from the Polish Army.[1] This did nothing to unite the Polish Army. It also failed to remove disruptive, if not dangerous, officers from within the Polish Army. Part of the infighting within the Polish Army resulted in the cashiering of General Stefan Dąb-Biernacki who, in an open letter to Sikorski, dated 13 July 1940, with copies to President Raczkiewicz, Śmigły-Rydz and Piłsudski's widow, insulted Sikorski as C-in-C and Minister of War, accusing him of misconduct during the September and French campaigns. Furthermore, Dąb-Biernacki accused Sikorski of running a dictatorship and tolerating the excesses of a party clique.[2]

Dąb-Biernacki was dismissed from the Polish Army and sentenced to thirty months' imprisonment. The court martial which tried him supported Sikorski and observed that, in wartime, Dąb-Biernacki's actions were illegal and a custodial sentence was necessary to uphold discipline and morale in the Polish Army. Dąb-Biernacki's actions were not in isolation but part of a concerted plan by pre-war officials to remove Sikorski. It is credible to consider that, as Raczkiewicz was part of the pre-war regime, he might have been part of the plan to remove Sikorski.[3] He had already been thwarted from doing so earlier in the summer of 1940.

Sikorski was in no mood to play nicely with his political enemies and, within days, set up a commission to investigate the behaviour of Polish officers during the campaign in France.[4] This was reminiscent of his previous investigation of the conduct of Polish officers during the September campaign which many saw as a witch hunt as Sikorski sought out and isolated his political enemies. However, Sikorski was warned by three of his Cabinet members that, owing to the widespread discontent of Polish troops in Scotland, the British government was losing faith in the Polish military effort.[5]

Sikorski's problem was that, after persecuting members of the inter-war Polish junta over the failed defence of Poland during September 1939, the French Army had done no better defending their country in May 1940. Furthermore, France had formally capitulated to the Germans. Poland had never done so but, simply, both countries were defeated. Many Polish officers continued to blame Sikorski for the loss of the bulk of the Polish Army in France and hankered over replacing him with Sosnkowski. Lieutenant Colonel Kazimierz Stefczyk, head of the First Bureau, urged Sikorski to counter-attack before it was too late.[6] He did so but it merely smacked of politics as he replaced the 'Piłsudski-ite' General Inspector of the Army, General Stanisław Burhardt-Bukacki, with Kukiel following reports that Burhardt-Bukacki had tolerated dissent amongst the Polish Armed Forces in Scotland.[7] The FO was unimpressed by the appointment of Kukiel with Savery commenting, 'for the soldiers in general, he is simply a civilian who has been thrust into uniform, without possessing any qualifications for a high military post'.[8] However, the FO and the War Office (WO) were investigating the Polish Army and the exiled Polish community in regards of extreme nationalism and anti-Semitism.

The UK government was anxious that Sikorski should curb anti-Semitism and nationalism within the Polish Army and the exiled community as a whole. It was concluded by the British that the official Polish line regarding the anti-Semitism and nationalism were 'beyond reproach' but the implementation of polices regarding these two evils were being ignored by junior officers and lower ranks.[9] This was naïve as later it would be quite apparent that senior ranks were also capable of disregarding the rules as well. Nationalism was the other vice to be dealt with by Sikorski. There were many reasons for the lack of discipline and commitment within the Polish Army and much of it was due to the lack of purpose and direction – simply the devil making work for idle hands.

The most pressing problem was the large surplus of Polish officers arriving in the UK after the Fall of France for whom there was little or no employment as too few of the ranks had be able to escape from France. The question of unemployed officers gave Sikorski the opportunity to purge some from his ranks. He informed senior Polish officers that he intended to transfer a number of officers who were of 'no value to the army' to the reserve list. He also expressed a wish to place officers of undoubted uselessness in a separate camp on the Isle of Bute, off the south-west coast of Scotland. Sikorski stressed that this was 'not a penal settlement or a special fortress of politically inconvenient people' but merely a camp 'for those who I cannot use' The numbers given relate to 600–900 men.[10]

This is an incredible number and quite shocking that Sikorski felt that he had so many from within his ranks opposed to him to the extent that he needed them to be interned on a relatively remote island. At the end of 1940 Sikorski once more had to return to the question of the camp on the Isle of Bute and reiterate that the officers there were not being punished but were quite simply surplus to current requirements, but each case would be looked at with the view of seeking employment for them.[11]

The conditions on Bute were not severe but to many of the interned officers it became known as the 'Isle of Serpents' and was considered to be a 'penal settlement'. This was denied by Sikorski.[12] Leon Mitkiewicz, Chief of Military Intelligence, claimed that he had tried to convince Sikorski to close down the camp but failed to persuade him to do so.[13] The use of the internment camp on the Isle of Bute, and the July coup, tarnished the democratic credentials of the Polish government-in-exile while Sikorski was becoming increasingly viewed as yet another Polish military dictator. Savery urged the British authorities to prevent Sikorski from interning Poles on British soil, Poles of whom Sikorski disapproved.[14]

Sikorski's highhanded behaviour may have raised eyebrows in official British circles but, as long as he did nothing that harmed the British prosecution of the war against Germany, he was left very much to his own devises. Nevertheless, both Eden and Halifax trusted Sikorski so little that they debated whether he could be trusted to obey British orders in the event of a German invasion of the UK and the need to deploy Polish troops if this happened. Colonel Victor Cazalet, a Conservative Member of Parliament and British Liaison Officer to Sikorski, was entrusted to make it clear tactfully to Sikorski that, if the Germans invaded the UK, he and his men were under British orders. Cazalet successfully convinced Sikorski that this would be the case but wondered what promises Churchill had made to Sikorski for the present and for after the war.[15]

Despite some of Sikorski's more drastic measures which left him open to charges of running a mini military junta it should be recognised that he managed to, swiftly and effectively for the short term at least, close down an element of the Polish officer corps and prevent them from causing disunity within the exiled Polish Army. The interned officers were potentially dangerous and might have split Polish prosecution of the war against Germany. The ability of

Sikorski to deal with perceived renegade officers made him important to the British government as he was the single Polish leader with whom they could work, in 1940 at least.

After dealing with the immediate problems of the Polish Army, Sikorski began to consider how he might enlarge on his and his army's position in the UK. Prior to the outbreak of hostilities, the Polish and British governments had been in discussions concerning the movements of Polish forces if Germany were to attack Poland. A consequence of these talks was the arrival of a Polish destroyer squadron in British waters on 1 September 1939. This was followed by other Polish naval units during the autumn of 1939.[16]

From the outset of war the Polish Navy came under British command (the Admiralty) while, after the September campaign, the Polish Army in France fell under command of the French, a situation that lasted until the Fall of France. On arrival in the UK, the situation for the Polish Army altered radically as Europe was largely overrun by Germany. Everything had to be negotiated from new as many Europeans now retained token forces in the UK while the Poles still at least had a rump army but had lost many men in France.

Negotiations between the British and Polish governments were to be difficult and tedious as the Polish government-in-exile fought over every little detail. This was perceived by the British as being bound up with Polish honour and prestige, something that the British considered not to have any place at a time of peril with the enemy massing just over the Channel ready to invade the British Isles. British frustration is illustrated in official British documents in which it was commented that the Czech government (in exile) was less obsessed than the Poles with questions of prestige and was less likely to make extravagant demands. It was concluded that the Czechs would have been content with a 'good deal less than the Polish Government'.[17]

However, the Poles with 14,000 ground troops compared with 1,000 Czech troops in the UK during July 1940, were in a better position to negotiate.[18] Terlecki calculated the number of Polish service personnel available from the second half of July as being 28,000. This counted 11,000 ordinary ranks (ORs) and 4,300 officers as well as a further 1,000 cadet officers (officers in training). These were the available land forces. For the PAF, 250 officers and 2,000 airmen were already in the UK. Later in the Middle East, after the fall of France, the Carpathian Brigade was formed after leaving Syria. This consisted of over 500 officers and 4,000 ORs. The Polish Navy only had 150 officers and 1,500 ratings. In total 28,000 men and women. In contrast in 1940 in the UK there were 4,000 Czechs, 2,000 French, 1,000 Dutch, the same thereabout of Norwegians and 500 Belgians.[19] These numbers were to alter, especially in the case of France, as the war progressed. The French case should also be noted as the Allies were able to exploit imperial French territory, especially North Africa which was eventually used as a springboard back into Europe via Italy.

Even if the Poles, namely the Carpathian Brigade, fought bravely in North Africa and later Anders' Army distinguished itself in the Italian campaign, Poland was always going to be a sideshow owing to its lack of available territory which could be used by the Allies to prosecute the war. Of course, once an ally reached Polish territory, it was that perennial enemy of Poland, Russia or the Soviet Union. The Soviets merely regained territory stolen from Poland during the autumn of 1939 following the dual German-Soviet invasion of Poland during September that year.

Even in 1940, despite the large number of Polish troops available to the British, Poland had a weak hand. Churchill had plenty of troops but little to arm them with. However, by the end of 1941, he had twenty-five divisions, fully armed and ready on the south coast of the UK alone. Poland was always going to be a second-rate power within the alliance. The entry of the USA and the Soviet Union into the war against Germany in 1941 confirmed this.

It was really only the solemn word of Churchill to Sikorski which kept Poland relevant. This became more difficult for Churchill after summer 1941 and once Sikorski was dead. After July 1943, following the death of Sikorski, this undertaking was lessened but did not prevent Churchill from taking up the cudgels for Poland, often in defiance of Stalin and occasionally against his great ally President Roosevelt. Churchill had a similar relationship with the Free French commander, General de Gaulle, who needed defending against Roosevelt who took a personal dislike to him and sometimes, it might be said, that Churchill needed to defend de Gaulle from de Gaulle!

Sikorski, from the very beginning of his exiled premiership, demanded that Poland be treated as an equal within the alliance against Germany. In November 1939 he requested that Poland be represented in the Supreme War Cabinet.[20] This was refused, citing precedents from the First World War when only the UK, France and, from 1918, the USA, had been permanent members of the Supreme War Council while other countries such as Belgium and Romania had only been invited to attend meetings on a need-to-know basis.[21] The question of Polish representation on the Supreme War Cabinet was partially resolved during spring 1940 when Colonel Mitkiewicz was reluctantly accepted by the British and French governments to represent Poland in the Allied Military Mission.[22]

Within six weeks of Mitkiewicz's appointment, a British senior officer, Lieutenant General Sir James Marshal-Cornwall, complained that the Polish General Staff had attempted to use the Allied Military Committee as a source of information. The Polish General Staff was told that the correct procedure for securing intelligence concerning Polish troop movements in France was via the French High Command and nowhere else.[23] This was, of course, before the Germany invasion of France. This lack of formality in Polish approaches towards officialdom was to become a vexing feature of the Anglo-Polish wartime relationship. The Polish government-in-exile, in spite of its posturing, never became an equal ally and was treated as a minor ally in the same manner as Belgium, Holland and Norway.[24]

The Poles, who saw themselves as 'First Allies', could not understand why they were treated as just another ally, especially as most of the exiled governments represented in London could hardly be accused of fighting too hard against the Germans. In contrast, the Polish contribution had been vast, if unsuccessful. At least the Poles had fought the Germans once invaded and had contributed to the defence of France as well as being willing to contribute to the defence of Finland following the Soviet invasion of that country in November 1939. Polish troops and sailors also took part in the partially successful Norwegian campaign of April-June 1940. A further contribution was that of the Polish Air Force during the latter stages of the Battle of Britain. Away from the glamourous fighter pilots, Polish sailors served on the precious convoys supplying the UK with its essential needs while Poland also co-operated with intelligence work. However, overall, the Polish effort was largely political, and this interested Churchill as he sought to demonstrate the international nature of the alliance arrayed against Germany. Sikorski agreed with this concept as he stated to Churchill that the re-organisation of the Polish Army on British soil was important from a political point of view in addition to the martial advantage that the British Army might derive from the re-establishment of the Polish Army.[25]

After July 1940, an element of stability returned to internal Polish politics. This provided an opportunity to rebuild the Polish Armed Forces.[26] On 5 August 1940 the Anglo-Polish Military Agreement was signed. The preamble established that the UK and Poland were committed to prosecuting the war to a successful conclusion.[27] Despite the unspecified British fears of allowing a Polish Army to remain on UK territory, the UK government recognised the autonomy of the 'Army of the Sovereign Polish Republic'. In principle, the British authorities allowed Polish land forces to operate as a single operational force led by a Polish commander. However, the overall deployment of Polish Armed Forces on a fighting front depended on the British who would use such forces as and when they were needed. Simply, the Poles were not independent in anyway and were wholly dependent on the largesse of the British or otherwise.

Nevertheless, the Anglo-Polish Military Alliance was generous to the Poles. The rules and regulations were set out under which Polish armed services were to operate. Polish service personnel swore allegiance to the Polish Republic and Polish soldiers, unlike Polish airmen, were subject to Polish military law rather than the British equivalent. The only exception was if a Polish soldier broke British criminal or civil law.[28] The subjection of Polish service personnel to the British penal code was important as Polish officers were still in the habit of fighting duels. To the Polish mind it was a question of honour being satisfied but the British view was a more mature 'murder was still murder'.[29] Under the terms of the agreement the Polish government-in-exile was permitted to complete its re-organisation of Polish land forces by mobilising Polish citizens resident in the UK as well as drafting volunteers who had arrived in the UK from overseas. The most important element of the treaty was the recognition by the UK government of Polish Armed Forces being an arm of the sovereign Polish Republic.

Nevertheless, many problems remained. The most glaring one was the surfeit of officers. A consequence of this imbalance was a disagreement between the British and Polish governments regarding rates of pay for the Polish Army. The question of the British Treasury bankrolling the Polish Army caused the British government to take an interest in the Polish Army to ensure that British money was not being wasted. This was an element of civilian oversight that the Polish Army had never experienced. Senior Polish officers were not happy as previously the Polish military had been allowed to conduct its own affairs with no question of having to answer to civilian politicians.

Anthony Eden, then Secretary of State for War, understood the need for the surplus of officers ready for the task of re-building post-war Poland and its army but, in the short term, the British government was unwilling to finance the Polish Army in all of its ventures and so demanded a reduction in its wages bill. Eden noted that the so-called 'cadres' received a salary which discriminated against the remainder of the Polish force. This concerned Eden as he feared that the differences in salary would weaken the cohesion of the Polish Army and ultimately damage its fighting potential.[30] The question of salaries was agreed in January 1941 when the British government agreed an annual credit to the Polish government-in-exile for the sum of £3.5 million (about £161 million in 2023) which was to be used to pay members of the Polish armed services. There was no recommendation on how this money should be distributed. It was left to the discretion of the Polish government-in-exile.

Sikorski tried to explain to Churchill that the surplus of officers had forced him to form cadre units as well as an officers' legion but claimed that when the time came to re-build the Polish Army it would experience a shortage of officers. Sikorski only reached agreement with the British government when he convinced Churchill that Poles living in Canada should be drafted into the Polish Army to try to fill its ranks.[31] Any attempt to recruit Poles from North America, however, was problematic. Sosnkowski, not a great fan of Sikorski, previously, in a memorandum to Kot, saw, that owing to the Piłsudski cult in the USA, Sikorski's inter-war anti-junta stance would ruin any chance of securing recruits from the USA.[32]

Overall, the Polish government-in-exile was undecided how it should proceed in efforts to re-establish its army during 1940. Notes prepared for Sikorski's attention suggested two possible alternatives to recruiting in North America. The first choice was not only to consider North America but also target those Poles living in Argentina and Brazil. It was suggested that perhaps Sikorski might broadcast to the USA and give a pro-ally and pro-Polish message. The second selection considered the possibility of organising an expeditionary Polish Corps from Polish troops in the French Mandate of Syria while the Polish Ambassador in Ankara, Turkey, directed intelligence and propaganda against the Soviet Union.[33]

Both of the two 'alternatives' were risky. The question of recruiting Poles from neutral states as proposed risked spreading the war and was it even legal to do so? The promotion of anti-Soviet propaganda from within Turkey was highly dangerous as the country was already a hotbed of intrigue and espionage. The Poles also lacked British support for such activity while the diplomatic status of the Polish ambassador to Turkey might well be compromised. Indeed, Stefan Werner, a Polish diplomat in Ankara, complained to Kot, that it was very difficult to operate in a neutral country where there were no declared enemies (or friends). Werner considered that the only people that he could trust were American correspondents in the country.[34]

The only practical proposal was the idea of forming an expeditionary corps of Polish troops in Syria. After the Fall of France those troops, commanded by General Stefan Kopański, left the French Mandate of Syria rather than surrender to the collaborative Vichy regime and marched into British-held Palestine. From there Kopański's men formed into the Carpathian Brigade which was later to serve with distinction in North Africa, including Tobruk.[35] The question of anti-Soviet intelligence work and general agitation was not viable as the British government considered the Soviet Union to be neutral, something that the Polish government-in-exile failed to comprehend.

The British government was cautious in allowing the Polish Army to expand. This was pragmatic as the British had their own concerns. Churchill wrote to Sikorski during January 1941 asking him to postpone a planned trip to the Middle East and on to the USA. Churchill told Sikorski that he did not want to face a possible German invasion in the spring (1941) without the leader of the largest allied contingent being present. Churchill flattered Sikorski's ego by declaring Poland to be the 'first ally in the war', adding that the sentiments expressed were his personal wishes.[36] Churchill was very good with flannel when it suited him, and he equally would deny a person if the circumstances merited it.

There was indeed another side to the British attempt to forestall Sikorski's proposed trip to North America. The FO resented Sikorski's American venture, claiming that he might 'embarrass either his hosts or themselves or both'. Eden doubted that the USA would even welcome Sikorski's visit.[37] Churchill did, however, try to assure Sikorski that the US government would welcome a visit from him, and that President Roosevelt would be happy to receive him. Churchill also urged caution as he informed Sikorski that the American administration hoped that any recruitment of American Poles would be carried out with the 'fullest consultation' of the Americans. At this point Churchill was still sounding out the Canadian attitude towards any trip by Sikorski to that country.[38]

The most important aspect of Sikorski's attempt to recruit Poles living in North America was who was to underwrite the entire venture and under what circumstances should Polish citizens be recruited. It was quite clear that American Poles were very hostile to Sikorski and his Soviet policy even before he arrived in the USA.[39] And this was even before he had tried to enter into relations with the Soviet government as was the case after June 1941. Sikorski was in a bind no matter what he tried to do.

From the very beginning the Polish government was hampered in its attempt to recruit Poles from North America. The US government was the most hostile and insisted that no American Poles were to be recruited into the Polish Army. It was similar in Canada as the Canadian government was clear that Poles in Canada who held British citizenship were not be recruited into the Polish Army but instead enlist in the Canadian armed forces. Furthermore, the Canadian Army accepted no financial liability for the Polish recruitment drive.[40]

The Canadian government had, since the outbreak of war, been consistently polite but reserved in its dealings with the Polish government-in-exile relating to the question of the recruitment Poles' for the Polish Army. A memorandum from the Canadian undersecretary for external affairs reveals that the Canadian government considered Canada to be a 'country of immigration' and that immigrant communities should look to Canadian concerns first and not to their former homelands. It was suggested that if the Canadian government encouraged the formation of contingents of men to serve in non-Canadian forces it might suggest that Canada was putting the concerns of other countries before their own. However, if one looks at the Canadian government's attitude towards French recruitment it becomes quite clear just how accommodating the Canadians could be.

The principal Canadian objection to Polish recruiting was the definition of the war. In a memorandum to the Canadian prime minister, the Canadian undersecretary for external affairs pointed to the immediate Anglo-French objective of the war being the territorial integrity of Poland but its occupation by Germany and Soviet Union and the emergence of the Soviet Union as a power in the region meant that even the British government refrained from making demands for the restoration of Polish territory at the end of the war.[41] This was a dangerous position for Poland as it was quite clear that, very early in the war, it was obvious that Poland was unlikely to receive the return of pre-September 1939 territories while the question of independence was left in the air. Simply Sikorski had very little power or influence with the Allies and was only consulted when it suited Allied war planning when he was expected to fall into line.

Sikorski remained upbeat and was convinced that his force of 16,000 men in the UK and 6,000 from the Carpathian Brigade, in Egypt, was enough to build on with the recruitment of Poles in Canada.[42] Sikorski considered that it remained in his interests, and Poland's, to pursue a recruitment programme in the Americas. His main interest was to continue to try to raise a cadre army from which he hoped to build an army that would defend a future Poland from a possible predatory Soviet Union. To this end, working against the objectives of the British government, Sikorski continued in his attempts to recruit from the New World. His attempt to recruit in Canada was a failure. For the Polish Navy, only thirty men were recruited; South America only realised fifty volunteers. The situation was no better for the Polish Army as only 300 men were recruited with another 350 expected. The PAF attracted ninety recruits in North America with a further forty-two men recruited in Latin America. Overall recruitment into the Polish Navy from the Americas should be seen as a failure as a British Cabinet paper reported that discipline and morale in the Polish Navy was very high, except for the thirty-eight recruits of American nationality enlisted in Canada who had failed to 'settle down' under Polish naval discipline and had been returned to Canada for demobilisation.[43]

The major flaw in Sikorski's American recruitment drive was that young Polish Americans during 1940 and 1941 were not interested in the war and considered it to be a Polish matter.[44] He also failed to understand that he was not trying to recruit young Poles but young Americans who were unlikely to volunteer to fight for a country which their forefathers had already rejected. Therefore, by the end of 1941, it was obvious that the only viable source of recruitment for the Polish Armed Forces was from the Soviet Union where Poles were being released from Soviet captivity following the German invasion of the Soviet Union during June 1941. Polish-Soviet relations had been resumed at the end of July 1941.

Despite these very obvious setbacks for Sikorski and his plans for an expanded military it was not all gloom and doom. At the end of 1940 he received a Polish report from Helsinki. This report concerned Poles arriving from Wilno (Vilnius). In 1940 Wilno was occupied by the Soviet Union as it was a Polish city prior to the 17 September 1939 invasion and so it was certain that the people in the report must have escaped from Wilno. Sikorski learned from this source that Poles still in Poland were aware of the establishment of a Polish army and government in the UK. Furthermore, Poles had faith in the British and knew that both Berlin and Leipzig had been bombed by British aircraft. These events had been received with 'great joy' in Poland. The ability of the British to fly bombers over Germany had caused alarm to the German authorities.[45]

This report no doubt gratified Sikorski and his government as it was clear that they were making the right moves and were known to their compatriots in occupied Poland. Events in 1941 were about to alter radically for Poland. The Polish report originating in Helsinki reminds us that Finland had been defeated in March 1940 by the Soviets following the Winter War of November 1939 to March 1940. The Finns had been obliged to sue for peace and had lost territory to the Soviet Union. The year 1941 saw Finland take part in the invasion of the Soviet Union but only to try to recover lost territories from the Soviets. The Finns were never part of the ideological war against the Soviet Union as waged by Germany.

Chapter Seven

The Polish-Soviet Treaty, June–July 1941

When Germany invaded the Soviet Union on 21 June 1941 it bought relief for the British. It was unlikely that they were to be invaded that summer as the Germans and their allies were totally committed in their offensive against the Soviets. It also broke up the infernal alliance between the Soviets and the Nazis. With the Germans preoccupied with the new war against the Soviet Union, the British were able to take stock and plan for the future. However, as the Germans ran deep into the Soviet Union it became obvious that, if they remained unchecked, the Middle East and North Africa might be imperilled before the Red Army could counter-attack and stem the German advance.

It was to this end that Churchill overturned all of his previous anti-communist work and sought an agreement at least with the Soviets. There was only one man who would do: Stalin himself. His word was law and Churchill needed to reach out to him and begin negotiations. This also meant doing something about the current situation of hostilities between Poland and the Soviet Union. There had been no fighting since 1939 but the Soviets had behaved disgracefully towards Poland and worse was yet to come. Sikorski had two ideas regarding a treaty with the Soviets: he wanted the swift release of Poles held by the Soviets and the building of a Polish military force. He tried to push through an agreement with the Soviet government using the failed format of the July 1939 talks. Under pressure from the British government, he was forced to abandon this plan.[1]

It should be noted that the Poles, technically at war with the Soviet Union since September 1939, could do little, if anything, about their relationship with the Soviets but did at least maintain observation of what the Soviets were up to and how it might affect Poland. One such operational post was Portugal, one of a handful of neutral countries in Europe. The Polish government maintained an embassy in the Portuguese capital, Lisbon, and, as with all such situations in wartime, exploited their host's hospitality for espionage purposes and intelligence gathering. Portugal was sympathetic towards the UK during the Second World War and even allowed for Portuguese islands to be used by both US and UK forces from 1943.

By the end of 1941 the Polish government had realised that the war was to be a long haul. It was also obvious to most, except, it would seem, Stalin, that the alliance between Germany and the Soviet Union was only a short-term arrangement. Hitler had every intention of destroying the Soviet Union and all Slav people, including the Russians. The exiled Poles had begun to weigh up the pros and cons of Hitler and Stalin. Quite often, the Poles had been more sympathetic towards Germany rather than Russia especially since 1917 but eventually a line was drawn in the sand in early 1939 with Poland falling out with Germany and entering into an alliance with the British and French governments. With France fallen and the UK held at bay, the Poles began to look at the situation between Stalin and Hitler and who was worse. A Polish memorandum of late 1939 concluded that Stalin was better for Europe than Hitler.[2]

This conclusion opened up some interesting territory as Stalin had been considered the worst of dictators as far as the Poles had been concerned. Stalin had done nothing to disprove the Polish attitude: prior to the outbreak of war he had ensured that Poles living in the Soviet Union were persecuted, often sent to labour camps, or Gulags as they were termed, that were basically concentration camps. Frequently Poles were executed following trumped-up charges and a travesty of a trial. The Polish Communist Party was destroyed by Stalin in the late 1930s which made it all the easier to introduce communism or, more accurately, Stalinism to Poland after 1943 as Moscow-trained Polish Stalinists took the lead role in that country, albeit under Soviet tutelage. Part of the assessment of Stalin being better for Europe than Hitler stemmed from Hitler's clear statements made in his infamous work *Mein Kampf*.

Situated in Lisbon taking advantage of their protected the status in a neutral capital, the Poles were able to note what the Germans had been doing – Lisbon was a hotbed of espionage – and in a letter to Sikorski, presumably from the Polish military attaché to Portugal, Molotov's visit to Berlin was duly noted. This visit was considered in the light of other visits in which Hitler had seen Mussolini, Franco and the French arch-traitor Pétain. Molotov's visit was just another one. It was considered by the author of the letter that these were just the first steps towards a 'New Europe' or a 'European Union' which was eventually going to translate as world domination.[3]

Equally, prior to the German invasion of the Soviet Union, there was an assumption that Germany eventually would be defeated. However, the exiled Poles considered that a defeated Germany would still throw up concerns for Europe. It had already been assumed that there would be a parting of the ways between Nazi Germany and Stalinist Russia as it was quite obvious that the pact between the two dictatorships could never last. A swift glance over Hitler's diatribe of *Mein Kampf* and other discussions and speeches made by him and other senior Nazis made it quite clear that the Nazi vision was that of an eastern empire at the expense of the Slavs, including Russia. Stalin was clearly deluded as he tried to ignore this even at the point of German forces invading the Soviet Union.

The Poles considered that, once Germany was defeated, there would be a 'rise of Russian Communism in neutral states'.[4] It should be considered that some states would be endangered by the power of the Soviet Union, militarily or politically. There was a clear example as Finland had been attacked by the Soviet Union during the winter of 1939–1940. This no doubt caused the author of this paper to argue that the examples of Austria, Czechoslovakia, Poland and Denmark illustrated that small states were too weak to 'impose a recognition of their desire for peace'.[5] Of course, these states in February 1941 had all been victims of Nazi aggression. Later, Czechoslovakia and Poland were to be annexed by the Soviet Union after 1944. A remedy was suggested: a return to original frontiers, in some cases those of 1934, might be necessary while a European federation, both military and economic, would be necessary. Furthermore, the importance of physical barriers was mentioned.[6]

Sikorski, in a speech published in the Polish military journal *Bellona*, during February 1941, continued to warn against the dangers posed by the Soviet Union. He also pointed to the folly of trying to ignore the fact that the inter-war Polish frontiers were too open to an enemy attack as witnessed in September 1939. Furthermore, Sikorski called for reform within the Polish Army so that it could be mobilised earlier and ready to deal with any encroaching enemy. Sikorski was explicit in his condemnation of Communism or 'Bolshevikism' [*sic*], writing 'the growing waves of bolshevikism bring not only extermination to Poles and Czechs but also a complete annihilation of our European Christian-Latin civilizations'.[7]

In an interview in 1999, the senior Polish politician Radek Sikorski (no relation to General Sikorski) told this author that part of the 'Polish Return to Europe' was to remove itself from the Byzantine tradition to that of the Latin.[8] At the time Poland was on the cusp of receiving NATO membership and was negotiating membership of the EU. What Radek Sikorski meant was that Poland was trying to remove itself from the backward and eastern looking of the communist system and to embrace democracy and its more open and transparent organisations.

The implications of General Sikorski's words, spoken and written, along with those of Radek Sikorski's observation are very important. Nearly eighty years after the end of the Second World War it had become quite clear that the assessment of the situation in February 1941 was bang on. The Soviet Union did indeed annex east-central Europe: Austria and Denmark were spared this. Austria was occupied in part for a decade after the war, but it is interesting to note that the Soviet Union was allowed to annexe Slavic lands but not states perceived as being western and democratic, including two who had been enemy states during the Second World War – Finland and Austria. Since the reported demise of the Soviet Union, many countries such as Poland have joined NATO and the EU and, more controversially, three former Soviet republics, Latvia, Estonia and Lithuania, have all followed this example.

The question of NATO membership has become all important since February 2022 with the invasion of Ukraine by Russia. Ukraine, a former Soviet republic, had sought NATO membership and been rebuffed. Vladimir Putin, the Russian dictator, seeks to prevent further NATO expansion eastwards as he deems it a threat to his country while claiming that Ukraine is part of Russia. Baloney!

The question of neutral states being able to protect themselves from a determined aggressor has been revised since the invasion of Ukraine. Both Sweden and Finland, Cold War neutral states, sought NATO membership after the Russian invasion of Ukraine. It is quite clear that Putin would not have dared to invade Ukraine if it had been part of the NATO alliance.

It is obvious that Putin remains determined to prevent further NATO expansion and only attacks, thus far, states that do not enjoy military protection from that source. Finland, of course, recently became a member of NATO. Material support from NATO to Ukraine has rather caught Putin short in his war against Ukraine. Therefore, the Polish assessment was more accurate than perhaps it was meant to be.

The mention of a revision of physical barriers is imaginative as it should be remembered that, until the German Army reached Warsaw during September 1939, there had been few geographic barriers to prevent German armour and mechanised infantry from advancing rapidly into Poland. Once the Polish Army was able to get behind the river Vistula and other natural obstructions it was able to fight back properly. Of course, the Soviet invasion of eastern Poland in September 1939, the stab in the back, undid the good work which the Poles were beginning to undertake.

If, as the Poles rightly suspected, war would break out between Germany and the Soviet Union, the question should have been just who would come out best. Anyone acquainted with the history of east-central Europe knew that it was impossible to invade Russia successfully and to held its territories to any depth owing to the vastness of the terrain. Without doubt this was a consideration which Sikorski entertained while reflecting on the tenacity of a people such as the Russians to hold their own land. Furthermore, the murderous nature of the Nazis made it impossible to expect any mercy which left the Soviet people nothing expect to fight to survive once Germany invaded their homeland.

Even if Stalin was a vile dictator and a murderer and did not keep his word, it was possibly in Sikorski's calculations easier to negotiate with him. Of course, by 1940 it was quite impossible to try to reach any agreement with Hitler. This was why Sikorski and most of his compatriots plumped for Stalin and the Soviet Union even before the country was invaded by Germany. It was obvious that war was to break out between the two countries and when it did both Sikorski and Churchill had something to work with. The question of post-war Europe was just that – something to be settled at war's end.

Within two days of the German invasion of the Soviet Union Sikorski announced that this would be advantageous to Poland. He held the opinion that the Soviets would have to acknowledge the importance of Poland 'as a real force in the development of the conflict'. This was due to the fact that 'in the depths of Russia' between 200,000 and 300,000 Polish prisoners of war were detained. Sikorski considered that the Soviet government needed aid from across the world as well as favourable international public opinion. However, the Soviet Union was met with a lack of confidence owing to the German invasion and, of course, the previous Soviet co-operation with Nazi Germany. It was possible according to Sikorski that he and his government might be instrumental in persuading world opinion to be more favourable to the Soviets.[9]

Basically, Sikorski saw an opportunity for he and his government to influence events. However, he was thwarted as Churchill had also seen the opportunity that the invasion of the Soviet Union represented and sought to preserve the Soviet ability to defend itself. The main thing was that there was no chance of a German invasion of the UK during the summer of 1941 if the Germans and their allies were distracted on the Russian Front. It was not certain whether the Soviets could hold out during that summer.

The British feared that a German breakthrough in the Soviet Union might well imperil British assets in the Middle East. The British concern was that the Germans would be able to cross the Caucasus mountains and head towards British Palestine. Churchill had to try to ensure that the Soviets were well supported and to have as many allies as possible. He also needed to try to shut down difficult relations such as the situation between Poland and the Soviet Union. It was already known that Sikorski wanted to improve relations between the two countries and so Churchill also saw a further opportunity for his Soviet policy.

Therefore, Churchill set out to obtain a peace treaty and restoration of relations between Poland and the Soviet Union. This was something that Sikorski had considered during the previous year, but it had borne no fruit and the reasons for this failure were to be the same objections put forward in 1941. The difference, however, was that Churchill earnestly wanted a new agreement between the Polish government-in-exile and the Soviet government. Churchill was determined that the Poles were not going to be permitted to stand in the way of such an ambitious project, one which was to prove to be instrumental in the defeat of Germany. Even though the wartime alliance with the Soviet Union did not last much beyond 1945, if that, it need not detain us regarding events in 1941.

Ivan Maisky gives an immediate account of how the Soviets viewed the British and their reaction, especially that of Churchill, to the invasion of the Soviet Union. On the evening of 22 June 1941 Churchill broadcast a speech in support of the Soviet Union. Maisky considered that it might have been guarded when Churchill mentioned communism for the sake of the USA or the Conservative Party but, as Maisky wrote, 'On the whole, Churchill's speech was bellicose and resolute: no compromises! War to the bitter end! Precisely what is most needed today.'[10]

Maisky was correct in his assertions. Such a speech was necessary; it gave the green light from Moscow for British missions to arrive in the Soviet Union.[11] However, regarding Polish-Soviet relations, Maisky is reticent as he only mentions the Polish-Soviet Treaty on 30 July 1941 when he signed the treaty on behalf of the Soviet government and so the agreement also became known as the Sikorski-Maisky treaty. In his diary Maisky wrote, 'Today at long last we signed the Soviet-Polish Treaty! I can hardly believe it'.[12] Maisky sounded exhausted and exasperated; he may well have been as the treaty had been the result of protracted negotiations and bullying of the Polish government-in-exile by the FO and the British government, principally Churchill himself.

Maisky recorded a statement which Sikorski made in French to him regarding the treaty. Sikorski said that:

> He was delighted that we were signing the treaty. He came to the conclusion long ago that Poland could not balance between its neighbours in the west and in the east for ever. It had to choose either with Germany against Russia, or with Russia against Germany. Sikorski himself had always thought that Poland must be with Russia against Germany.[13]

This was very much against conventional Polish thought – neither country was trusted but Poles seemed to have more empathy with Germany, especially nationalists who clearly favoured Germany. De Gaulle, the Free French leader, noted that Sikorski wished to reach an agreement with the Soviet Union which was a risky venture in itself.[14] Simply, Sikorski, by putting his signature to the treaty, had signed his own death warrant.

Not only had Sikorski passed his own death sentence, he had also swept himself out of history. Nevertheless, even though Maisky relegated the treaty which bore his name to a trivial incident of that day, 30 July 1941, it was an important part of the jigsaw that was the Second World War and needs examining in more detail. From early on Sikorski had been pragmatic in his attitude towards the Soviet Union. In 1940 he had even considered a revision of Polish frontiers which meant that on the whole the Soviets would be allowed to retain their theft of Polish lands taken in 1939 while in cahoots with the Nazis.

Sikorski considered that post-war Poland should receive compensation and receive lands taken from Germany. However, this idea infuriated any Pole, including President Raczkiewicz, who were natives of eastern Poland.[15] After 1941 when the full horrors of the 1939–1941 Soviet occupation of eastern Poland became obvious, Sikorski's plan became untenable. By the end of 1945 with the complete Soviet annexation of Poland, eastern Poland was lost forever. The Soviets got away with grand theft.

Nevertheless, Sikorski's 1940 plan does show him to be a visionary as he was willing to consider a western frontier along the river Oder which formed a line of natural security for Poland vis-à-vis Germany rather than the wide-open terrain which formed the traditional invasion route east and west and always through Poland. Given that the Germany which faced Poland between 1945 and 1989 was East Germany, a hardline Soviet-friendly state, there was little threat from Germany. Since 1999, Poland and the now re-united Germany are NATO allies. Today, there is little fear from the west. The main threat to Poland today is from Russia. Polish NATO membership is a stumbling block to any Russian hostile intentions towards Poland.

Sikorski often considered future Polish defence policies. Strategic plans for a future Poland were all-important to Sikorski for his vision of post-war Poland.[16] A speech made by Sikorski in January 1941 concerned the need at least to explore the questions of new frontiers to try to gain the strength to prevent another war in twenty years' time.[17] Furthermore, Sikorski's plans for the entire region of east-central Europe were very similar to those of Piłsudski before 1921 which called for a collective east-central European bloc to be created. Even if this federation of nations was aimed at Germany, it would have had the effect of limiting Soviet influence in the region.[18] It is without doubt that Sikorski would have approved of Polish NATO membership and of that of the EU. It was the ideal which he sought but, in his lifetime, it was not on the table.

Sikorski's accommodating attitude towards the Soviet Union after June 1941 was not shared by senior members of the Polish government-in-exile, notably Zaleski and Sosnkowski. A basic requirement of Sikorski's opponents was Soviet recognition of the pre-war Polish frontiers, Soviet withdrawal from eastern Poland and the creation of a Polish Army in the Soviet Union under Polish command.[19] Furthermore, Sikorski lacked support for his Soviet policy from the Polish Underground Army and the Polish underground political parties.[20] This was a bitter blow for Sikorski as it was clear that Sosnkowski was using his position as head of the Polish underground military to agitate against Sikorski who realised that, to prevent a split within the Polish government-in-exile, in 1940 he had to proceed with caution and be seen to be defending Polish interests.[21]

By spring 1941, the Polish government-in-exile was aware that a German invasion of the Soviet Union was imminent. This was due to the massive German military build-up in the eastern zone of German-occupied Poland. It became a matter of trying to assess the date of the German operation. The Polish underground erroneously predicted 15 April 1941. This report had been made towards the end of March 1941.[22] This meant that the predicted date may well have been correct as an anti-German coup in Yugoslavia was attempted during April 1941 which had seen German resources deployed in the Balkans and the invasion of the Soviet Union delayed for several weeks. Churchill informed Sir Stafford Cripps, the British Ambassador to the Soviet Union, that three out of five panzer divisions had been ordered to move from Romania to Poland but in the light of the 'Serbian revolution' the order had been countermanded.[23]

Later, on 8 June 1941, a coded message from Poland reported a build-up of German forces in eastern Poland. Churchill had earlier thanked Sikorski for his memorandum relating to the possibility of a German attack against the Soviet Union. At the time Churchill had been discussing with British commanders the intelligence coming out of Poland.[24] The co-operation between the British and the Poles regrading intelligence work should be noted. However, what Sikorski really wanted if war was to break out between Germany and the Soviet Union were the Polish troops held in Soviet captivity since at least 1939. Sikorski considered that there were 300,000 Polish troops held by the Soviets. Cripps left his meeting with Sikorski with the distinct idea that if war did happen the Soviet government would release those Polish troops.[25]

There was further correspondence regarding the prospect of a German invasion of the Soviet Union, this time between Sikorski and Raczkiewicz. In a letter dated 19 June 1941, Sikorski sent Raczkiewicz a report regarding the chances and concerns which Sikorski had if Germany was to invade the Soviet Union. He told his president that the Germans had massed 130 motorised divisions and 2,000 frontline aircraft along the German side of the German-Soviet partition line across eastern Europe. The main jump-off point was Poland and possibly Romania. It was noted that there had been a recent visit to Munich by General Ion Antonescu. It seemed that the Germans held out the prospect of the recovery of Bessarabia from the Soviets if Romania took part in the invasion of the Soviet Union.[26]

In his briefing to Raczkiewicz, Sikorski mentions that this would have to be voted on in Romania. However, this was basically a fiction as Antonescu was not only prime minister of Romania but also its foreign minister and defence minister. Indeed, his title was *Conducător*. Basically, like Hitler, Mussolini or Franco, he was dictator with a local title to try and dress up for foreigners what was really meant and he could do just as he pleased, especially regarding Romanian participation in the coming invasion of the Soviet Union, Operation Barbarossa. Antonescu, holding three of the most important offices of Romania, dominated that country during wartime but was executed by firing squad in 1946 for his war crimes. In 1941 Sikorski was concerned that Barbarossa might be successful. Sikorski realised that, if the Soviet Union was defeated, there was a distinct possibility that Germany might turn again to its attention to an invasion of the UK. Sikorski noted that the British were counting on victories against the Germans in Ukraine and Baku.[27]

A few weeks later Sikorski continued on the theme of German war aims in a speech delivered on 2 July 1941. He told his British audience that 'Hitler, anticipating that the war can only be decided by the conquest of Great Britain and unable to starve her, attacked Russia in order to crush her military forces and to capture food stocks and raw materials before the United States actively intervened'.[28]

The prediction of American intervention was astute, but it was largely the Germans shooting themselves in the foot. Following the Japanese attack on the US naval base at Pearl Harbor, Germany declared war on the USA on 11 December 1941. This was an unnecessary move and condemned Germany to defeat on the battlefield and elsewhere as the Americans could supply both the UK and the Soviet Union as well as begin to move American resources including fighting personnel to wherever the war warranted them. Prior to this there had been American supply to the UK under the authority of President Roosevelt. Hitler's declaration of war made life politically much easier for Roosevelt and most definitely for Churchill.

According to Sikorski, Hitler hoped for a quick and complete victory over the Soviet Union. This would apparently have led to a revolution there and allowed Hitler to introduce his own government, not only in minor Soviet capital cities but also in Moscow and Kiev. If Hitler was successful, Sikorski reiterated that the UK would be endangered once again while, at the same time, Hitler could offer the world a compromise peace which Sikorski considered to many Germans 'would amount to no more than an armistice'.[29] This was something that the Germans might not value as it failed to define a complete victory for Germany and suggested that Germany was unable completely to defeat their foes and so would have to settle for second best.

Sikorski was farsighted in his observations, especially that of a German victory over the Soviet Union being very dangerous for the war in the west.

What he needed was for the German Army to get bogged down in the Soviet Union and waste its energy there. This was exactly what happened until the Soviets were in a position to counter-attack the Germans and their allies and eventually push all the way to Berlin. Sikorski added that he was to speak to Cripps that evening.[30] It should be noted that the exiled Poles were working with Romanians also in exile, notably Viorel Tilea, the exiled Romanian ambassador. At the beginning of March 1941, the Polish government-in-exile was aware that German troops were gathering on Romanian soil and that Antonescu had been in talks with Göring. It was observed by the Poles that Romanian society preferred Antonescu to the extreme Hitlerite Iron Guard.[31]

After a revolt by the Iron Guard during January 1941, Antonescu destroyed it, using the Romanian army; Iron Guard leaders fled to Germany. As the Polish evidence is dated 1 March 1941 these events were very recent news at a time when it was difficult to ascertain what was happening in Europe. Even more intriguing is that, given that Antonescu had destroyed the pro-Hitler Iron Guard, the Germans still trusted him to support them for the invasion of the Soviet Union. Again, the Poles were able to point to the fact that the Romanian King Carol and his entourage had little influence and that most Romanians had great faith in Antonescu.[32] Simply, the senior Nazi officials went to the most influential Romanian political actor and sought his support.

After Germany invaded the Soviet Union and Churchill had broadcast his speech in support of the Soviet Union before the Soviet government had even made any request for aid, Sikorski felt compelled to respond.[33] The problem was how the exiled Poles could be prevented from offending the Soviet government. This was to be a problem for the remainder of the war as the Allies had to keep the Soviet government happy in the face of what the Soviets at least considered to be severe provocation by the Polish government-in-exile. It was not; the Poles were basically trying to hold the Soviet government accountable for its crimes in occupied Poland between 1939 and 1941 and then, after 1943, trying to prevent Soviet annexation of Poland. Therefore, Churchill ordered that Sikorski's speech be heavily amended. Sir Alexander Cadogan recorded in his diary that Sikorski wanted to give an 'impossible speech' and the FO had to deal with the matter.[34]

The censuring of Sikorski's speech to Poland clearly illustrated and defined the limits of his autonomy vis-à-vis his government, the British and the Soviets. Polish relations with the Soviet Union were to be micro-managed by the British government. The British government, especially Churchill, meant to maintain its policy of Germany being enemy number one and sought any ally to prosecute this effectively.

Churchill suspended his previous anti-Communist rhetoric and prepared to co-operate with the Soviet government which was basically Stalin with his henchmen, Vyacheslav Molotov, the Soviet foreign minister and Lavrenti Beria, the head of the Soviet security service, the notorious NKVD; Stalin even told a British official that Beria was his 'Himmler', the head of the Gestapo. Beria and Heinrich Himmler were as grotesque as one another. The British appeasement towards Stalin and the Soviet government not surprisingly dismayed the Poles but Tendyra notes that the British government swiftly realised that an Anglo-Soviet alliance, desired by London, depended on an improved relationship between the Polish government-in-exile and the Soviet government.[35]

In his broadcast to Poland on 23 June 1941 Sikorski hinted at a cessation of hostilities between Poland and the Soviet Union. There had been no fighting since October 1939, but a state of war remained between the two countries. Sikorski linked any cessation of belligerence to the release of all Polish prisoners, civil and military, from Soviet imprisonment and the cancellation of the August 1939 Nazi-Soviet Pact. Sikorski considered that this would restore the situation between Poland and the Soviet Union regarding frontiers as laid out in the 1921 Treaty of Riga.[36]

The British government was aware that many exiled Poles did not want any rapprochement with the Soviet Union and would do their best to wreck any attempt to do so. This was in part due to a belief amongst some in the Polish government-in-exile that the Germans would very quickly drive the Red Army out of Soviet-occupied Poland and the Polish eastern borders would no longer be worth discussing.[37]

British officials concluded that Zaleski and senior members at the Polish Foreign Ministry were willing to sabotage any attempt to reach an agreement with the Soviets.[38] Eden had to wait until 4 July 1941 for an official Soviet response to Sikorski's initiative. Cripps was instructed to raise the Polish question in Moscow but Maisky had already given his assessment and therefore that of Stalin of the Polish government-in-exile, which was that the Polish government was reactionary and profoundly hostile to the Soviet Union.[39] It was obvious that many Poles would be hostile towards the Soviet Union but at least Maisky could see a positive side to Sikorski even if he only made this public in the 1960s by then beyond reach of Stalin and Beria, both dead since 1953, writing that Sikorski was a good soldier but a bad politician surrounded by 'ultra-reactionary figures'.[40]

However, as Bethell notes that by June 1941 the Soviets had committed so many grave crimes against Poles it was difficult for them to forgive or to forget Soviet atrocities committed in Poland and elsewhere. Even if it was in Polish interests to try to work with the Soviet government it was quite impossible for many Poles to try to remove the Soviets from being enemies of Poland to becoming allies. For many Russia was the eternal enemy and considered to be untrustworthy at best, an issue that was to divide Poland over the coming years.[41] The Polish refusal to trust the Soviet government was totally justified as, within two years, the discovery of the mass murder of Polish officers and others was made. This rent Polish-Soviet co-operation. But in 1941 Sikorski was forced by circumstances to press on with re-establishing Polish-Soviet relations.

On 4 July 1941 the Soviet government, via Maisky to Eden, finally replied to the Polish proposals and it was not good. The Soviets proposed the creation of Polish, Czechoslovak and Yugoslav committees based in the Soviet Union and the raising of military forces of those countries to fight alongside the Red Army against Germany. All Polish PoWs – Maisky discussed a figure of 20,000 rather than that of 300,00 as Sikorski had previously claimed – were to be released. Of course, this was far less than Sikorski's estimate. The Soviet government was willing to hand over these 20,000 men to the Polish authorities. For the first time the Soviet government made mention of an 'independent, national Polish state' based on 'ethnographical Poland' to be decided on post-war. This was the basis on which the Soviet government was prepared to sign a treaty with the Polish government-in-exile.[42]

Discussion of national committees was dangerous. It was an indication that the Soviet government was preparing to extend its reach into east-central Europe in anticipation of establishing Soviet-friendly regimes in the area after the war. Basically, the Soviet government was preparing Soviet-friendly puppet governments staffed with traitors and collaborators. It was entering talks with the Polish government-in-exile for tactical reasons only.[43] Sikorski rejected the question of national committees as well as questioning figures relating to Polish PoWs in Soviet custody. But, according to British minutes of Sikorski's meeting with Eden, Sikorski indicated that the frontier question need not be discussed during any forthcoming negotiations. He merely wanted the Soviets to renounce treaties concluded with Germany in 1939. Sikorski also demanded the release of all Polish PoWs, and deportees to the Soviet Union, reinstatement of Polish diplomatic representation in Moscow and the creation of a Polish sovereign army in the Soviet Union.[44]

The Soviet government, in reply, refused to accept that the invasion of its country by Germany rendered all agreements with that country null and void and so denied that the pre-September 1939 between the Soviet Union and Poland could be restored. Basically, the Soviet government did not want to renounce the Nazi-Soviet pact of August 1939 owing to the secret protocol of the agreement which dealt specifically with the partition of Poland between Germany and the Soviet Union.[45] An official Soviet renunciation of the treaty would have weakened the Soviet claim over eastern Poland. Even so, the annexation of this territory by the Soviet Union was illegal and remains so.

Nevertheless, the British put Sikorski under pressure to come to terms with the Soviets. Sikorski made it clear to his ministers that, if they wished to continue to enjoy the full support of the British government, it would be better if the questions of the Polish eastern frontier and the Treaty of Riga were not mentioned as this would not be useful and they were unpopular issues in the UK. Instead, suggested Sikorski, it might be fruitful if the Polish government-in-exile continued to press for the official annulment by the Soviet government of the Soviet-German treaties of August and September 1939.[46]

At the same time, Sikorski had to try to prevent attempts by his own government to sabotage talks with the Soviet government. In addition to trying to balance his policies between the British government, the Soviet government and the Polish government-in-exile, Sikorski had to try to convince the Polish military underground and political authorities in occupied Poland that he was heading in the right direction. It was a thankless task. Many Poles considered that Sikorski should not even be talking to the Soviet government as they could not understand why the Soviets were suddenly the good guys, owing to the virtue that their former partners in crime had attacked them.[47] It was a valid point but one's enemy's enemy is always going to be your ally and that was the point that Poles missed. But that would be to pursue the British view of how to defeat Nazi Germany. As history tells us the Poles gained nothing by entrusting their futures to the Soviet Union and to Stalin.

During the second round of negotiations held on 11 July 1941 both Maisky and Eden brushed aside Sikorski's attempt to raise the question of pre-war Polish borders. Eden pushed for a quick conclusion of negotiations between the Poles and the Soviets.[48] A difficult meeting was concluded with an agreement by both sides to work together. A statement was issued which defined the four points on which progress could be made was submitted by Maisky.

1. The Soviet Union to declare null and void its 1939 treaties made with Germany concerning Poland.
2. Diplomatic relations to be restored.
3. Both governments to declare their readiness to fight against Germany.
4. A Polish Army under Polish command to be created in the Soviet Union.

There was no mention of the pre-war Polish-Soviet frontier or release of Polish PoWs or political prisoners.[49] The Soviets were giving little away and the Poles were getting even less. There was some hope, nevertheless, as Anthony Eden, the Foreign Secretary, in a note to the Polish government-in-exile made it quite clear that at the time of writing, 4 July 1941, the British government had not recognised the Soviet annexations of 1939, including that of eastern Poland. It was noted that the German attack on the Soviet Union of June 1941 had rendered these land grabs null and void. For his part, Sikorski continued to reach out to the Soviet Union and attempted to normalise relations with the Soviet government. He also requested the release of all Polish prisoners of war held in the Soviet Union as well as all Polish citizens detained by the Soviets. The British government was in full support of any reconciliation between the Polish government-in-exile and the Soviet Union.[50]

It would soon transpire that the reality was that the Poles would have to do all the running with the Soviet government doing just as it liked regarding captive Poles. In October 1941 Sikorski's close confidant and advisor, Professor Stanisław Kot, sent a letter to Molotov's deputy A.J. Wyszyński (Vyshinski), which documented the plight of Poles still held captive within the notorious Soviet Gulag system.[51] The Gulags were concentration camps where Poles and others were held and used as slave labour by the Soviet government. As we shall see, the Soviets were unwilling to free Poles from captivity and, even when Poles were released, they received very little help or assistance to get to points where they could meet with Polish officials or organisations which could receive them and point them in a direction of benefit to themselves and the war effort, principally the Polish Army.

Another reason for the lack of Soviet aid was that many Poles were in pitiful conditions due to ill-use and starvation at the hands of their captors. The Germans were not the only people using concentration camps. This was something that the Soviets were desperate to keep secret and, of course, the question of the missing Polish officers, missing since April 1940 would also come up. The Soviets had a lot to hide and were determined to keep their grubby murderous secrets just so – secrets.

By mid-July, the talks were stalling; there had been no movement regarding the Polish eastern frontiers or the question of those Poles deported to the Soviet Union. Both Maisky and Sikorski threatened to quit the talks. Sikorski could ill afford to do this as he would have lost everything, and the Soviet government would have cleaned up. Furthermore, Sikorski and the Poles would have been abandoned by the British. It was becoming clear that the British favoured the Soviet Union as, on 12 July 1941, a pact of mutual assistance was signed by the British and Soviet governments. On the 18th the Czechoslovaks and Soviets concluded the Soviet-Czechoslovak Treaty of Friendship. The Poles could see that they were in danger of becoming isolated within amongst the Allies.

In securing a pact with a major ally and a treaty of friendship with a minor ally, but one whose homeland was in central Europe, the Soviet government gave Sikorski little room to manoeuvre. The treaty between the Czechoslovaks and the Soviets revealed the lack of unity within the Slavic world. However, it should be remembered that Czechoslovakia had had no historic dealings with the Russians or Soviets while the Poles had had centuries of antipathy towards Russia and anything that came from there. But Czechoslovakia had suffered aggression at the hands of Poland during October 1938 when Poland invaded and annexed the disputed territory of Teschen, which, legally, was Czechoslovak territory granted by the Great Powers in 1920. The Polish timing was foolish since the action looked craven as it was carried out at a time when the British and French governments were trying to prevent war between Czechoslovakia and Germany owing to German expansionism in the region. Sikorski knew that, in the face of history, he needed to continue with negotiations with the Soviets or else he would be powerless to help his compatriots still detained in the Soviet Union.

After a meeting with Eden on 18 July Sikorski agreed to a weakened version of the proposed treaty between the Poles and the Soviet Union. This version made no reference to the Polish eastern frontiers but did obtain an agreement from the Soviet Union that the treaties relating to the partition of Poland between the Soviet Union and Germany were invalid. This was obviously the case anyway, owing to the German-Soviet war and so, in effect, the Poles gained nothing. Sikorski agreed to the treaty on the promise of a note from the British government stating that the Anglo-Soviet declaration contained nothing that would affect Polish-Soviet relations and that the British government would not recognise any territorial change made by force against Poland.[52]

Again, Sikorski had been duped. The British side of the agreement was so ill-defined that it was rendered meaningless. Dealing with the Soviet government or, quite simply, Stalin was basically expecting gangsters to keep their word. Talks with Stalin and his regime were akin to negotiating with Hitler and the Nazis during 1938 and the British were hoodwinked in both cases. Nevertheless, Sikorski had to try to convince his own government that the proposed treaty served Polish interests. In a Cabinet meeting Sikorski tried to explain that, if the Polish government-in-exile did not meet British demands, the British might well cut the Poles adrift by withdrawing their good offices of friendly mediation between the Polish government-in-exile and the Soviets. This would have dire consequences for the exiled Poles and for Poland in general.

General Sosnkowski continued to press for the restoration of eastern Poland. Zaleski, the Polish foreign minister, claimed not to oppose a good treaty with the Soviet government but was against a bad and hasty one which undermined Polish integrity in the rush to get it signed off. Furthermore, Zaleski resented the fact that Sikorski had unilaterally negotiated the treaty without any reference to the Polish government-in-exile.[53] Sikorski was not bothered by Zaleski, a mere civilian, but was concerned by Sosnkowski's opposition as he considered him to be a dangerous rival.

Sikorski tried to remove Sosnkowski from London. Sikorski first tried to remove Sosnkowski to Moscow as ambassador and Chairman of the Polish Recruiting Commission in the Soviet Union once Polish-Soviet relations were restored. Sosnkowski was unfazed and continued to demand that the Soviet government should recognise Polish reservations in relation to the proposed treaty.[54] The British security services were already aware of the rivalry between Sikorski and Sosnkowski and made the following observation:

> Sikorski is vain and anxious to be in the limelight while Sosnkowski is a quiet modest man whose honesty cannot be doubted. Sikorski is jealous of him and as long as Sikorski remains Prime Minister, Sosnkowski will be kept in the background.[55]

An interesting but damning report and why was it compiled in the first place?

Eden correctly deduced from his meetings with Sikorski during July 1941 that Sikorski was reluctant to sign an agreement with the Soviets due to opposition from his own people.[56] Eden insisted that the agreement would give the Poles 'a very good deal'. He also offered to include a British note to the effect that the British government would not recognise territorial changes made in Poland since August 1939. However, Eden insisted that this was not a guarantee of Polish pre-war frontiers. This rendered the note worthless. Nevertheless, the War Cabinet endorsed the note on 24 July 1941.[57] The tabloid *Daily Sketch* of 23 July 1941 considered the Polish-Soviet agreement would be signed no matter what and that this would turn enemies into allies. It was noted that there would be no definite recognition of pre-war Polish frontiers 'as had been previously arranged'. This was to be decided after the war at peace conferences which will follow the cessation of fighting. The *Daily Sketch* argued that to have met with Polish demands before war's end would have only created 'dissatisfaction amongst other Allied countries who also have territorial claims'.[58] A most obvious case would be that of Czechoslovakia demanding territory back from Poland after the annexation by Poland of Teschen during October 1938.

The British considered that their work was done and that the Poles should sign the agreement with the Soviet government. To this end Eden began to pressurise Sikorski to accept the Soviet terms. Eventually Sikorski took drastic action to get the pact signed. He did not believe that Poland had anything to gain by being neutral in the Russo-German War; he also recognised that the UK government would make every effort to aid the Soviet Union in this war.

He also feared that if the Poles tried to hinder this or continued to desire the defeat and occupation of the Soviet Union by Germany, the Polish cause would disappear and be forgotten.[59] Therefore, on 24 July 1941, Sikorski summoned Zaleski and Sosnkowski and told them that the pact was to be signed.[60]

Following this meeting Sikorski, still full of bluster, put forward once more the requirement that the treaty had to be signed. He lied to his Cabinet by claiming that the British note guaranteed the Polish pre-war frontiers, but he was truthful when he asserted that if the Polish government-in-exile rejected the treaty it would be isolated and leave Moscow to establish its own puppet Polish government and army. Sikorski concluded his argument by stating that the balance of power at the end of the war would be more important than the 'unrealistic Bolshevik promises at the present time'.[61] Sikorski was of course right but he never dreamt that the Soviet Union in 1945 would be a superpower with only the USA as a rival.

The following day, prior to dinner with Eden, Sir William Strang, assistant undersecretary of state for Europe, and Polish political figures loyal to himself, Sikorski decided to hold a vote on the treaty. Sosnkowski, Zaleski and Marian Seyda, the Polish justice minister, certain that British and Polish officials were going to pressure them to agree to it, resigned.[62] Sikorski took full advantage of Sosnkowski's resignation and removed him from the post of C-in-C of the Polish underground army even though Sosnkowski had only resigned his ministerial post. Sikorski had removed a difficult and potentially dangerous opponent, but Sosnkowski remained popular with the Polish Army and the military underground. His removal threatened to split the army and cause further divisions in Poland.[63]

After receiving news that Cripps had secured a 'universal amnesty' for all Polish citizens in the Soviet Union, Sikorski finally signed the treaty on 30 July 1941. Sikorski had further weakened Raczkiewicz's office by ignoring the president's constitutional prerogative to sign the pact. By signing the treaty Sikorski prolonged Allied support for the Polish cause but it came at a personal price. He had made enemies of Sosnkowski and Zaleski, men who already detested him. Sikorski had also belittled the presidency by signing the treaty without presidential authority. However, he demonstrated that political power belonged to him and not the president thus reviving images of the inter-war military Polish military junta. But crucially Sikorski had failed to secure an Allied guarantee for pre-war Polish frontiers. This failure caused a loss of personal prestige, especially with the Polish Army. In the homeland, Poles living in occupied Poland considered that Sikorski, given the circumstances, could have done no better but sign the treaty with the Soviet government.[64] However, many Poles saw Sikorski as a traitor for signing the agreement.[65] And so the Polish plots against him began in earnest.

Sikorski's loss of prestige with the Polish Army did not bypass the FO as, from 1942, British officials began to negotiate with another Polish commander, General Władysław Anders. General Anders had been released from cruel Soviet captivity during the summer of 1941 and had been made commander of Polish troops in the Soviet Union from where he would lead them to Iran, Iraq, the Middle East and, finally, to Italy where, as II Polish Corps, they would distinguish themselves. Sikorski's apparent triumph in securing an agreement with the Soviet government was a pyrrhic victory as it marked the waning of his influence within the Allied camp who began to prefer Anders.

By the of 1941 the Polish diplomatic mission in the Soviet Union had already got the measure of Anders. It was reported that Anders was of average intelligence but was politically very ambitious.[66] What Sikorski's diplomats had underestimated was the lengths to which Anders would go to achieve supremacy within western exiled Polish circles. It was to become a tragedy for all and so preventable if only there had not been so many very visible egos competing for a single prize, that of supreme leader of the Poles. Meanwhile, in Poland, the Soviet government was beginning to prepare the ground for imposing its own rule on Poland. A report from Poland noted that, owing to criticism of Piłsudski and his regime, a void was being created. This was coupled with the influence of the pre-war Polish military junta which was condemned as being anti-democratic. It was noted that the Soviets would fill the political vacuum being created in Poland with the denigration of Piłsudski and the successor regime.[67]

While it was true that Piłsudski and his successors were not democrats, equally they were hardly tyrants in the class of Stalin and his dreadful regime. Given the horrors visited on Russia since the Bolshevik revolution of 1917, it was pure cant espoused by the Soviet government that Poland had been ruled between 1926 and 1939 by military dictators. But the Soviet government was able to split Polish opinions in occupied Poland and chip away at support for Sikorski and his government-in-exile. Nevertheless, in 1941 Sikorski was considered by many in occupied Poland as representing the nation in much the same way that Churchill represented the UK and Roosevelt the USA.[68]

It is interesting to note that Sikorski was considered to be representative of Poland and not President Raczkiewicz. Without doubt, the Soviets knew that their regime was not popular and presumably understood that Sikorski's continued willingness to work with it would no doubt be his downfall, especially in the face of opposition to Sikorski's Soviet policy from within the Polish Army and émigré circles in the USA. It was a policy which continued to weaken Sikorski's authority within Polish circles even though the British government demanded that he maintained a good relationship with the Soviet government. It was never going to be an easy balancing act for Sikorski while the Soviets ensured that it was almost impossible for him to please everyone involved. Simply, the Soviets had no interest in Sikorski. They were preparing a Stalinist Polish puppet government for when the Germans were driven from Poland. Unfortunately, Anders, in his disloyalty to Sikorski made the Soviet task that much easier. Indeed, it was a tragedy waiting to happen.

Chapter Eight

Conflict in the Army, Anders vs Sikorski

The agreement between the Soviet government and the Polish government-in-exile may have formally ended the state of hostilities between Poland and the Soviet Union but it enlarged internal conflicts within the exiled Polish community in the UK and beyond. By unilaterally negotiating and signing the treaty, ignoring Raczkiewicz's prerogative to either sign it or not, Sikorski ensured that the agreement was identified only with him. As the agreement failed to protect pre-war Polish frontiers, it was considered by many Poles that the entire episode was nothing but a paper exercise in which the Soviets gained everything. Sikorski was blamed as he was perceived to have caved in under British pressure and exposed Poland to Soviet aggression. The fact that there was little that Sikorski could have done, and that Poland was perpetually under Soviet threat, meant nothing to his opponents.

Even before the German invasion of the Soviet Union, Sikorski received reports on the situation within the Polish Army which should have been cause for alarm. It was quite clear that he was no longer universally supported by the army. The inter-war Polish military junta, *Sanacja*, was beginning to increase its influence once more. A report concerning the situation within the Polish officer corps from early June 1941 considered that until recently many Polish officers had been on the whole apolitical. However, owing to ever increasing *Sanacja* agitation, there had been a shift away from this situation and it was clear that many officers were beginning to criticise Sikorski and his government. Many officers disapproved of interference by Sikorski and his government into the military and felt that the army was being micro-managed.[1]

The Polish Army was not accustomed to oversight by civilian governments. It was not a common thing in many armies at the time, but the inter-war Polish Army had been almost a sacred cow and not subject to scrutiny in any form. That had been its undoing by September 1939. Left too long to its own devices, the Polish Army had been unable to perform its only role in Polish society, the defence of the state from within and without. The consideration that most Polish officers in this report had been previously apolitical is frankly nonsense. The Polish Army had been a hive of politics and the most influential body in inter-war Poland – indeed senior Polish senior officers ran the country, albeit poorly – but, nevertheless, the Polish Army ran Poland after 1926. It was quite clear that the reality was that Polish officers were seeking an alternative leader to Sikorski and preferably one who detested the Soviet Union.

One figure to emerge as Sikorski's greatest enemy was General Anders who abhorred the Soviet Union and all that it stood for. However, Anders, even if he hated the Soviets, did at least understand them. He spoke Russian and had served in the former Imperial Russian Army before 1917. Furthermore, during his time in Soviet captivity between 1939 and 1941, which was often brutal, he had also experienced times of near humanity from his gaolers. During one of these periods, he had been given access to a library which was comprised largely of the works of the likes of Marx, Lenin and Stalin, all in Russian. Anders devoured these texts and learned much about his enemy. He found that his newly acquired knowledge was to be to his advantage when negotiating with Stalin and Molotov. The greatest folly of Sikorski was not to have used Anders as an ally and work with him during talks with Stalin. Anders should have been an equal, perhaps in the role of a consultant, and perhaps further mistakes in Polish wartime foreign policy could have been avoided.

Without a doubt if Sikorski had lived and Anders had been surer of his position within the politics of the exiled Poles, the tragedy of the Warsaw Uprising would have never happened. Sikorski would have forbidden such a foolhardy adventure and Anders is on record condemning it. In an interview in 1967 he said:

> starting in the Czarist officers' school of cavalry and ending in the French Military Academy, I was instructed not to attack without any chances of victory. It is not advisable to undertake the action without any chances. This should be applied particularly when a large number of civilians may be drawn into such an action.[2]

If there had some more experienced and better trained Polish officers at Warsaw and in London perhaps the AK might have been saved and the future of Poland and east-central Europe quite different.

During August 1941 Polish prisoners in the Soviet Union were being steadily released. There had been no guarantee from the Soviet Union concerning guaranteed liberty of Poles captive in the Soviet Union but an 'amnesty' had been announced. Many Poles were insulted by this, as it implied that they had committed crimes, but it was just a measure used by the Soviet Union to supply cannon fodder for the Red Army. There were to be several amnesties proclaimed for prisoners held by the Soviets before the war finished. Sikorski wanted the term 'amnesty' replaced with that of 'released'. He was ignored.[3]

On 2 August 1941 Sikorski nominated General Bohusz-Szyszko as head of the Polish Military Mission to Moscow. He was charged with trying to conclude a draft Polish-Soviet military agreement and to organise the enlistment of Poles in the Soviet Union into the Polish Armed Forces. Initial reports from both Bohusz-Szyszko and Sikorski's close friend and, by then the Polish government-in-exile's provisional envoy to Moscow, Józef Retinger, confirmed overwhelming support for Sikorski from the majority of Poles in the Soviet Union.

Bohusz-Szyszko also reported the indignation expressed by Anders and other senior officers regarding the behaviour of Sosnkowski and his anti-pact colleagues. Sikorski had written to Anders offering the post of commander of Polish Armed Forces in the Soviet Union. Anders had not been Sikorski's first choice which had been Lieutenant General Stanisław Haller but, at the time, summer 1941, he was missing. Later, it became clear that he had been murdered, along with thousands of Polish officers by the Soviet security forces, the NKVD, at Katyń.[4] Anders, nevertheless, denounced those who had opposed the Sikorski-Maisky treaty, declaring 'everyone without exception' (Poles in the Soviet Union had put their misfortune behind them and) supported the pact.[5] This state of harmony did not last long.

There were many reasons why Sikorski wanted to free those Poles in Soviet captivity beyond wishing for the liberty of his compatriots. In 1941 it was estimated that 1.5 million Poles were held captive by the Soviets, of whom 200,000 were military personnel. It was from those numbers that Sikorski wanted to build a huge Polish Army and use them on those fronts deemed necessary to aid the war against Germany. Sikorski also realised that, to maintain good relations with the Soviets, he needed to retain some of his men in the Soviet Union. Furthermore, Sikorski was aware of the enormous propaganda value, especially in the USA, of a large Polish contribution to the war in the Soviet Union.[6]

Nevertheless, Sikorski was cautious. Probably remembering the 1940 French campaign and the loss of much of the Polish Army in France, in addition to being extremely distrustful of the Soviet leadership, during September 1941 Sikorski warned Anders not to allow Polish forces to be annihilated on the Russian Front and insisted that the Polish Army should only fight for Polish interests.[7] Indeed, Sikorski wrote the following to Anders.

> that Poland upholds now and will uphold in the future the full independence of her political line, and that in no case will she agree to become a tool of the policy of any Power. She desires to preserve her independence in the political field, and to secure the place which is due her in post-war Europe … . We wish to co-operate closely and loyally with the USSR,

> during this war and after it. However, we do not wish to go further than that. Realising that the New Poland will be basically from that of yesterday, we shall nevertheless oppose the transplanting of communist ideas on our soil. Neither do we agree to disappear in the Pan-Slav melting-pot.[8]

Brave and correct words. However, Sikorski was then unable to anticipate just how the Soviet Union was able to counter-attack the Axis powers in late 1941 and then, by 1943, go onto the offensive and drive all the way to Berlin by April 1945. Anders was issued detailed instructions from Sikorski who considered that Polish forces should only be deployed on the Russian Front once an entire Polish division had been established and had reached combat readiness. Sikorski had calculated that such a division would not be ready until spring 1943.[9]

Sikorski was determined that Polish units were not to be scattered throughout the Russian Front. Sikorski's orders to Anders should be contrasted with the friendly and trustful manner when he entrusted the Carpathian Brigade in the Middle East to the British Commander, General Sir Archibald Wavell.[10] Sikorski even hinted that the Polish Army might have a role in establishing a democratic system of government in Poland post-war.[11] One can speculate what the Polish Army of that time might have assessed as democracy after fighting a major war.

Anders was a good choice for command in the Soviet Union. Having undergone the same trials and hardships endured by his compatriots in the Soviet Union between 1939 and 1941, a bond had been established between Anders and other Poles, including those he was destined to command. Sikorski could not begin to comprehend what had been endured as he had not suffered the collective experience of hundreds of thousands of Poles formerly in Soviet captivity and their understandable antipathy towards the Soviet Union. It followed then that the newly released Poles would have been unlikely to have accepted an 'outsider', one who had so far spent the war in the relative comfort of the UK. However, although few soldiers in Sikorski's headquarters in London shared his commitment to the Polish-Soviet Pact, Anders did initially.

The state of harmony between Anders and Sikorski did not last long and it was basically Sikorski's error which caused the rupture. Sikorski's mistake was to send Kot to Moscow as ambassador. Kot was the antithesis of everything that Anders held dear. Kot was entirely anti-junta and had told Anders to remove all ex-junta officers from the Polish Army being established in the Soviet Union.[12] Unsurprisingly, Anders ignored him. The FO commented during 1942 on Kot's political activity in an assertion that 'M. Kot ... a man of very great energy, has got his men into every cranny of the Middle East. He is certainly preparing a big future for the Peasant Party (Kot's party) after the war'.[13] And that was the problem. Kot was certainly preparing a post-war Poland which allowed him to be in a powerful position. The British were also aware that Kot was partially to blame for the Polish Embassy being allegedly involved in espionage against the Soviet Union.[14]

Kot and, therefore, Sikorski were beginning to attract dissent from within the Polish Army being raised in the Soviet Union, something of which Kot was conscious. In a written complaint to Sikorski concerning Anders refusing to remove 'Piłsudski-ites from his entourage, Kot brought up his discontent with the appointment of Captain (*Rotmistrz*) Jerzy Klimkowski as Anders' adjutant.[15] Klimkowski was later to head an extreme right-wing group of junior officers which caused grave concern to both British and Polish governments. Anders, in dismissing Kot's call to dismiss all officers who had served in Piłsudski's Legions, claimed that he was trying to establish a new Polish Army following the principle that all differences of opinion should be set aside; all would be accepted if they were willing to unite in the common cause of regaining Polish independence and liberty. After the war Anders was deeply critical of Kot. He noted that Kot did not speak Russian or understand the country: Anders was fully conversant in both. In September 1941 Anders told Kot to stop interfering in military matters. By October 1941 their relationship had gone from bad to worse.[16]

As the German Army advanced deep into the western territories of the Soviet Union Sikorski and Anders agreed a plan to evacuate the Polish Army from the Soviet Union in the event of a collapse of the Russian Front.[17] Sikorski was cautious with the question of the withdrawal of the Polish Army from the Soviet Union as he feared that Stalin might stop further recruitment of Poles there. However, it was considered that if President Roosevelt spoke up for the Poles Stalin might allow the evacuation of the Polish Army in view of the vast amount of American war material being provided for the Soviet war effort.[18] Even so, Sikorski was limited in what he could actually do regarding his army in the Soviet Union as everything was bound up in the recently signed Polish-Soviet military treaty.

As might be expected, it was not long before disagreements began between the Polish and Soviet governments in relation to the Polish Army. During October 1941 Anders refused to allow the partially equipped 5th Infantry Division to be sent to the front. This immediately damaged Polish-Soviet relations. The Soviet government claimed that the Polish government-in-exile was acting with ill-will.[19] The Soviet government, as the Soviet people fought for their very survival, would not or could not understand the Polish caution. Unity was also breaking down between Anders and Sikorski who received a grievous blow to his Soviet policy when Anders decided to move his military units from the Soviet Union to the disposal of the British in the Middle East. This suited both the British and Soviet governments. Stalin was nervous of having a large build-up of Polish Armed Forces on Soviet soil while the British Middle East Command was happy to receive the transfer of Polish troops to Iraq as the British had an acute manpower shortage in the region. Sikorski had been outfoxed by Anders since he no longer had much leverage with Stalin. He was aware that without a decent-sized Polish force fighting alongside the Red Army, the Soviets would do as they pleased once they arrived in Poland.[20]

The British attitude towards the Poles was quite obvious by the end of August 1941. Churchill wrote to Sikorski regarding a letter concerning the estimated strength of Polish forces which could be raised in the Soviet Union. Churchill confirmed that the question of equipping this force was to be discussed at a coming conference between the USA, the UK and the Soviet Union to be held in Moscow. However, what Churchill really wanted to discuss was the question of Polish liaison officers at different British headquarters. Earlier that month Sikorski had raised the matter of the establishment of a Polish military mission at the British General Headquarters, Middle East.

Churchill had no problem with that but wrote:

> I shall hope, however that you will not press for the appointment of liaison officers at General Headquarters, Home Forces. I am advised that the liaison between your Headquarters in London and the War Office is complete and cordial, and that to serve the needs of the Polish Corps in the field a Liaison Headquarters of some size and importance had been established to keep necessary contact between the Polish Army Corps Command and the General Officer Commanding-in-Chief, Scottish Command. It would therefore seem that the appointment of liaison officers at General Headquarters, Home Forces would be unnecessary. But there is another aspect of this question. If you were to have liaison officers at General Brooke's Headquarters, we should almost certainly be faced with similar requests from some or all the other Allied contingents. This would be embarrassing.[21]

Indeed, it would have been embarrassing. Ever since co-operation with the Poles had been thrust on the British the relationship had been difficult. The Poles genuinely failed to understand that they were of little or no importance to the British. The Poles were to be of some value to the British in 1941 as they were a reinforcement to the British in the Middle East. The Poles perpetually tried to expand their influence into the war even before the German invasion of the Soviet Union.

Biggar, Scotland, 31 August 1940. General Sikorski (1881–1943) attends a mass with Lord Hamilton (1903–1973), President Raczkiewicz (1885–1947) and other dignitaries. (*Marta Piskorowska*)

Biggar, Scotland, 31 August 1940. Raczkiewicz and Sikorski giving a speech at the mass. (*Marta Piskorowska*)

Fife, Scotland, 23 October 1940. General Sikorski and Prime Minister and Commander-in-Chief Winston Churchill (1874–1965) reviewing Polish soldiers, probably from the 2nd Rifle Battalion, 1st Polish Rifle Brigade. (*Janusz Jarzembowski*)

Fife, Scotland, 23 October 1940. General Sikorski with Winston Churchill and commanding officer. (*Marta Piskorowska*)

Possibly Scotland, c.1940. General Sikorski (on the right) is escorted by Anthony Eden, then Secretary of State for War, with both Polish and British colleagues, visiting Polish troops. (*Janusz Jarzembowski*)

Scotland, c.1940. General Sikorski visiting a Polish barracks after inspecting a catering facility. (*Marta Piskorowska*)

Perth, Scotland, November 1940. General Sikorski reviewing Polish troops. (*Marta Piskorowska*)

Newport, Scotland, 15 December 1940. General Sikorski decorates Norwegian Major General Carl Gustav Fleischer (1883–1942) with the order of Virtuti Militari for bravery. He coordinated Allied forces which included Polish troops in the battle for recapturing Narvik on 28 May 1940. (*Marta Piskorowska*)

Saint Geverout, France, 27 November 1940.

Scotland, April 1942. General Władysław Anders (1892–1970), commander of the Polish II Corps (1943–47), visiting the 1st Polish Armoured Division with divisional commander Major General Stanisław Maczek (1892–1994). (*Janusz Jarzembowski*)

Blairgowrie, Scotland, 1942. Polish 1st Corps. From left to right: General Sikorski, King Peter II of Yugoslavia (1923–1970), Colonel Franciszek Skibinski (1899–1991) and President of the Republic of Poland Władysław Raczkiewicz (1885–1947). (*Janusz Jarzembowski*)

Blairgowrie, Scotland, 1942. Another photo of the visit by King Peter showing, from left to right: a Polish officer, Raczkiewicz, Sikorski and an officer from Yugoslavia, standing on the new British Infantry Tank Mk IV Churchill II. (*Janusz Jarzembowski*)

Blairgowrie, Scotland, spring 1942. General Sikorski beginning his inspection. He had ordered the formation of a Polish Armoured Division in September 1941, with its core from 10th Armoured Cavalry Brigade and 16th Tank Brigade. (*Janusz Jarzembowski*)

Gullane, Scotland, January 1943. General Sikorski visiting the Divisional Artillery regiments on a British Universal Carrier belonging to the 1st Motorised Artillery Regiment. (*Richard Szcawinski*)

Jever, Germany, late May 1945. The division had withdrawn from Wilhelmshaven on 22 May after accepting its surrender to the German night-fighter airfield at Jever, prior to an occupational role in post-war Germany. Visiting the division, from left to right, stands: Lieutenant General Anders, a Polish officer and General Maczek. From 21 May, Maczek had been promoted and returned to the UK, with Brigadier General Klemens Rudnicki (1897–1992) succeeding him. (*Janusz Jarzembowski*)

In April 1941 Churchill informed Sikorski that his wish to send General Bohusz-Szyszko to the Middle East on a Polish military mission there was not possible. General Sir Archibald Wavell regretted that General Kopański, the senior Polish officer in the Middle East, had already nominated Colonel Orski as Polish liaison officer in the theatre. Churchill observed that there were already Polish officers in the Middle East who could be employed as liaison officers if the mission was later increased in size. The question of transport difficulties was cited as to why the numbers in the Middle East had to be kept as small as possible. In conclusion Churchill did offer a solution as he wrote:

> In these circumstances, I should be grateful if you would be content to send General Bohusz-Szyszko to take charge of the Polish Military Mission at General Wavell's Headquarters with instructions that he should draw any additional officers that he may require for his staff from Polish officers in the Middle East.[22]

The question of transport was a perennial one for moving to and from the Middle East and was fraught with danger. However, Churchill was not against having Bohusz-Szyszko sent to the Middle East. It was just a question of how he was to be employed. In the event, Bohusz-Szyszko was sent to Moscow after the German invasion of the Soviet Union but the question of Polish participation in the Middle East was never dropped. Eventually, it was Anders and his army which was to make its name, not in the Middle East but in Italy as the Middle East campaign expanded into the Mediterranean campaign and the eventual invasion of Italy in 1943. But, before those glory days, Anders' forces trained and re-trained in the Middle East, notably in Iraq and Palestine before heading to Italy. Polish troops were often treated as reserve troops as it was considered that British and American troops should take the lion's share of the fighting. This made sense owing to numerical superiority and wealth of equipment, especially once the USA engaged fully in the war. The Poles were often on the fringes of the fighting – not because their soldiers lacked courage but opportunity. If Polish forces could be based in areas such as Palestine it would allow British troops to go to the fighting fronts in North Africa for example.

Regarding the upcoming conference in Moscow, it would seem that even the British were unprepared for Beaverbrook's attitude towards the Poles which left them bereft of anything meaningful. The British attitude towards foreign contingents should be noted. Many knew that they had little to offer, save the French who had vast overseas territories and fighting personnel, Churchill always had to be more cautious in his approaches towards de Gaulle and his followers. France was also 'old Europe'; Poland, despite being an old European nation but wiped from the map between 1795 and 1918, was not seen as such.

The British appeared to do little to aid Sikorski as he tried to make the Polish case in the Soviet Union. At the end of September 1941 the Anglo-American mission led by Lord Beaverbrook, the Canadian newspaper publisher and British Minister of Supply, and Averell Harriman, arrived in Moscow to discuss war aid to the Soviet Union. The USA was yet to enter the war so the fact that it was an Anglo-American initiative was enterprising and illustrates that the Americans understood that the Soviet Union needed to be kept in the war against Germany. There was nothing to suggest that Poland would even be considered. The Polish government-in-exile failed to gain representation at the meeting in Moscow because it was believed that the western powers would protect Polish interests. They were wrong as Beaverbrook disliked Poland and the Poles and did nothing to aid them.[23] It was left to the UK and the USA to provide extra equipment for a second division which the Soviets were refusing to equip.[24]

The meeting was a disaster for the Polish government-in-exile as it was clear that they were not of any real relevance to the Allies and exposed their weakness to the Soviet government. Sikorski appealed to Churchill to modify the outcome of the conference. Otherwise, Sikorski claimed, Poland was left at the mercy of the Red Army. A senior FO official, Sir William Strang, noted that Beaverbrook had failed 'to take a sympathetic line with the Poles'.[25] This was underlined by Cripps, who wrote in his diary that Beaverbrook had caused a lot of harm.[26]

By November 1941 Polish fears of being short-changed by the Harriman-Beaverbrook meeting were borne out. They were not supplied by the Soviets and stated that 'our position in relation to the Soviet government had thereby been weakened'.[27] Earlier, during September 1941, Sikorski told Churchill that the formation of a Polish Army in the Soviet Union was entirely dependent on all supplies, including arms and military equipment, coming from the UK and the USA.[28] Molotov had already stated that the Soviet government had no objection to the British arming all Polish troops over and above the first Polish division already established in the Soviet Union. But this was unrealistic since Polish troops had already been evacuated to the central Volga region and away from easy British access.[29]

The removal of Polish troops to Uzbekistan and other regions was attributed to the Soviet military authorities by both Kot and Anders. They claimed that Anders was ordered by the Soviets to direct the overflow from Polish camps to these remote areas.[30] The British War Cabinet told Eden to tell the Soviet government that the UK government preferred Polish forces to be placed to the left of the Russian line, as near as possible to the Persian (Iranian) frontier to equip the Poles easier.[31]

Earlier, Sikorski had asked the Soviet government for the exact location in the Soviet Union of the Polish Division. General Sir John Dill, Chief of the Imperial General Staff (CIGS), considered that, from the British point of view, it would be best if the Poles could be concentrated in the Caucasus to defend Soviet oilfields from the invading Germans. Furthermore, it would be of 'inestimable value' to the British as a means of reinforcing the British Army in the Middle East overland rather than having to ship them to the area. This had been Sikorski's idea, but he had asked the British to put it to the Soviet government in case Stalin became suspicious.[32] This was not unreasonable since Stalin was notoriously distrustful of all, notably Poles, with whom he came into contact with.

Sikorski wanted a working relationship with the Soviet government or, to be more realistic, with Stalin who was the Soviet government. To this end, Sikorski resolved to go to Moscow to prevent any further deterioration in Polish-Soviet relations. He still wanted to move his forces to the Caucasus and needed Soviet backing for this.[33] While Sikorski was trying to get his plan approved by the Soviet government, prominent Poles, both civilian and military, were urging that the Polish Army be evacuated to Persia (Iran).[34] By visiting Moscow Sikorski hoped to bolster his authority amongst Poles everywhere. This was necessary owing to the continued criticism of his perceived pro-Soviet approach in diplomacy.[35]

Sikorski was running a grave risk. A failed trip would reinforce the perception amongst many Poles that he was a washout amongst the Allies. However, Sikorski had some remaining credit with the Allies as he still had troops in the Soviet Union whom he was anxious to have moved to a more suitable place to be supplied. Sikorski was supported in this by the British who sought reinforcements for the Middle East. If Polish troops were relocated on the Soviet-Iranian border it put them in striking distance for the British.[36]

Nevertheless, the initial British interest in Sikorski's scheme was limited. Following a meeting between Churchill and Sikorski, Churchill realised that Sikorski's motivation for the redeployment of Polish troops was to fight for the British and not for the Soviet Union. Churchill encouraged Sikorski to raise the question of moving Polish troops to the south, ideally Iran. But this time he insisted that Sikorski should present the idea to the Soviets as his own.[37]

Before going to Moscow, Sikorski visited the Middle East where he saw the situation there and discussed it with General Sir Claude Auchinleck, recently appointed C-in-C, Middle East. He also took the chance to visit the Carpathian Brigade who were fighting in Tobruk. It was a very visible sign of Polish troops fighting in North Africa. Previously Sikorski had been hurt by the jibe that Polish troops fighting in North Africa were mercenaries and fought only for British and not for Polish interests. During the summer of 1941, General Stefan Kopański, commander of the Carpathian Brigade, had hoped that the brigade would be deployed in Syria and eventually Turkey or the Balkans. This might have bought the brigade closer to Poland.

Sikorski argued that every enemy of the UK was a foe of Poland. This led to the Carpathian Brigade being deployed in Libya to fight both the Germans and Italians. The prospect was that an Allied victory in North Africa would pave the way for an Allied invasion of Italy, a return to the European mainland but not the most direct route back to Poland. This was significant as it was clear that Sikorski was placing the concerns of the wider alliance and the war first and not continuously pursuing a relentless project of Poland first. It was a clear shift in Polish policy regarding Italy since, previously, Sikorski had been reluctant to move Polish troops to Egypt for a war against Italy as he had considered that this did not serve Polish interests.[38] Eventually he decided that Italy, being an enemy of the UK, was also an enemy of Poland.[39]

Sikorski's Middle East policy was part of his plan to try to deflect some of the criticism directed by the Soviet government at the Polish government-in-exile. The Soviets frequently accused the Poles of bad faith and being unwilling to fight. Sikorski asserted that his presence in the Middle East suggested the opposite, raised the profile of the Polish contribution to the war effort and 'guaranteed its continued development'.[40] Sikorski not only had to impress the Soviet government but also exiled Polish circles. Therefore, he wanted to capitalise on the success of his visit to Tobruk and his men there and demanded that the Polish government-in-exile should exploit the trip fully with the words 'It might sober up … those hysterical émigrés in London and that group of (Polish) political madmen … who are trying to muddy the waters in New York.'[41]

While in the Middle East Sikorski wanted to tighten the rein of the shambolic command structure and settle the various rivalries in the area. The importance of the Middle East was paramount. He needed to ensure that this was understood by Poles in the area, especially with the imminent arrival of large numbers of Polish troops. Sikorski wanted to reduce the activities of those who had been aligned to the pre-war Polish junta, especially those currently serving in the Polish Army. He was equally concerned that a large number of pre-war civilian officials were also arriving in the area and were in cahoots with the Polish Consul at Tel Aviv, Henryk Rosmarin. It was alleged that they were involved in working against Sikorski. Before leaving Cairo, Sikorski issued strict instructions stressing the apolitical character of the armed forces and the necessity of quashing political intrigue which undermined the unity of the Polish Army and poisoned its morale.[42]

What Sikorski had not appreciated was that, if anything, he was undermining morale and unity as he was perceived to be perusing a pro-Soviet policy. It was often claimed that Sikorski neglected the very real concerns of Poles emerging from Soviet camps where they had endured extremely harsh conditions and had seen their comrades die as a result of the brutality meted out by their Soviet captors. Later, in 1943, it was to become quite clear how ruthless the Soviets had been in their ill-treatment of Polish captives.

Sikorski arrived on 30 November 1941 in Kuibyshev whence the Soviet government had evacuated as the Germans advanced on Moscow in 1941. Stalin had decided to remain at the Kremlin rather than evacuate to Kuibyshev. Sikorski was the first Allied leader to visit the Soviet Union following the German invasion and was accorded the full honours due to the head of an independent state by the Soviet government.[43] However, it did not take long before the Soviet government began to show ill-will towards its Polish visitors.

On 1 December 1941 it was made clear by the Soviets that the questions of Polish citizenship and frontiers were open to interpretation.[44] The following day the Soviet newspaper *Izvestiya* published an account of a meeting held in the town of Saratov presided over by two Polish communists, Stefan Jędrychowski and Wanda Wasilewska. From this meeting a manifesto to the Polish nation was issued. It was clear to Sikorski that the Soviets had a potential rival to the Polish government-in-exile, albeit a future Polish puppet government, but a massive problem for Sikorski. There were further developments of which Sikorski was ignorant as, on 28 December, a handful of Polish communists had been parachuted into Poland, tasked with reconstructing the pre-war Polish Communist Party (KPP). The party had been destroyed during the 1930s on Stalin's orders but a decade later a new party, the Polish Workers' Party (PPR), was to replace it. The Soviets also began to parachute Soviet partisans onto Polish territory.[45] It was obvious that the Soviet government was going to provide its own solution to the problem of post-war Poland – simply a Soviet-friendly Polish state.

Sikorski, accompanied by Anders and Kot, met Stalin at the Kremlin on 3 December 1941. Owing to Stalin's aggressive manner the meeting went badly for the Poles. Sikorski had gone to Moscow with the idea that he was in a strong position to negotiate with the Soviet government. He was wrong. Sikorski had failed to recognise Poland's position within the Allies and with whom he was trying to negotiate. Poland was a minor ally while the Soviet Union was a major player in the alliance waging war against Germany. Sikorski may have had the moral high ground in his dealings with Stalin, but this cut no ice with the Soviet dictator who only understood strength and guile. Sikorski had neither. The Poles should have been better prepared for negotiations with Stalin as they knew of his shenanigans since Kot had had a very difficult time with Stalin on 14 November.[46]

Sikorski and Anders raised with Stalin the question of the appalling conditions of Polish camps on the Volga and the slow process of establishing further military divisions in the Soviet Union. Stalin merely said that if the Poles did not want to fight then they should leave the Soviet Union. Stalin further stated that the Soviet Union would liberate Poland and return it to the Poles. Anders may have wanted the Poles out of the Soviet Union but neither man would have liked the idea of the Soviets freeing Poland; and to which Poles did Stalin mean to return the country? Stalin continued with his browbeating and quickly Sikorski found himself defending the British government from Stalin's verbal onslaught as well as backing down to many of Stalin's demands. At one point Sikorski even raised the possibility of moving both the Carpathian Brigade and I Polish Corps, stationed in Scotland, as well as several PAF squadrons to the Soviet Union. Once faced with Stalin, Sikorski was totally intimidated by the man.

Finally, Stalin agreed to an expansion of the Polish Army to seven or eight divisions, about 96,000 men. He also agreed to the transfer of these men to the south and to provide provisions for them. He did agree to the transfer of 25,000 Polish troops as reinforcements for the Middle East as well as the transfer, as agreed earlier, of Polish naval and air force personnel. All Poles were to be released from Soviet captivity while Polish delegates were to have access to civilian Polish deportees. The Polish government-in-exile also received a 100-million-rouble loan to take care of its people.[47]

The next day Sikorski and Stalin signed a 'Declaration of Friendship and Mutual Assistance'. Stalin also offered to settle the border question, face to face. Luckily, Sikorski had enough nerve to decline. Sikorski considered that the frontiers should be settled at the end of the war and that December 1941 was far too early to predict the balance of power at war's end.[48] Cripps noted that Sikorski had found negotiating with Stalin to have been exhausting as, on 7 December, Cripps visited Sikorski and found him in bed 'recovering from the feast that he had had in Moscow'.[49]

Kot claimed that, after visiting Polish troops in Central Russia, Sikorski had planned to raise the frontier question with Stalin and the Soviet government but illness, the arrival of Eden in Moscow and possibly the successful Soviet winter counter-offensive prevented him from raising the question.[50] Sikorski should have pursued Stalin on this matter as Sikorski's enemies considered that his failure to do so or to settle the matter earlier with Stalin was a lost opportunity to close this loophole in the Polish-Soviet Treaty.[51] Stalin further goaded Sikorski with a proposal that perhaps an agreement might be reached 'as soon as the Polish army goes into action'.[52]

This was unfair on Sikorski as if he had allowed under-armed and virtually untrained Polish troops to be sent to the Russian Front where, without doubt, they would have been swallowed up and lost, he would lose the little integrity that he still held amongst émigré Poles. Stalin's view was obvious: either Polish troops were made available for the service on the Russian Front or Polish borders would be subject to revision and without doubt in favour of the Soviet Union. Anders maintained that the only way to save the Polish Army in the Soviet Union was to evacuate to Iran.[53] It was just after the Sikorski-Stalin talks that Sikorski began to feel threatened by Anders.

Chapter Nine

Anders

Once Sikorski began to feel threatened by Anders, he decided to tackle the problem head-on and accused Anders directly of being a rival for power. Sikorski observed the necessity for unity in both the civil and military arms of the Polish diplomatic corps.[1] Anders replied that he and his men 'are all Poland's men' and that in this respect Sikorski could rely totally on them.[2] However, Anders failed to explain what he meant by 'Poland's men'. Nor did he express anything like unreserved support for Sikorski. Simply, his reply was ambiguous.

Anders' attitude was, however, noted by the Polish press attaché in the Soviet Union, Ksawery Pruszyński. According to Pruszyński, the Polish Army was definitely interfering in politics and incredibly, given Anders' antipathy towards the Soviet Union, accused him of currying favour with the Soviet government. Pruszyński claimed that Anders' disloyalty towards Sikorski would lead to the Polish authorities being split in three stages:

1. A division between the Polish Army in the Soviet Union and the Polish Embassy there.
2. A split between the Poles in the UK and those in the Soviet Union.
3. A rupture between Anders and Sikorski.

Pruszyński recommended that Anders be removed from the Soviet Union so that Sikorski's Soviet policy be protected. He was ignored.[3]

Sikorski's opponents wanted to replace him with somebody who at least was perceived as protecting Polish interests. The most likely candidate was Anders. However, his supporters failed to recognise the extent that the Allies were willing to back the Soviet Union to keep it in the war against Germany. Writing after the war, the veteran British politician Harold Macmillan explained British war policy as being 'first things first'. This meant 'deal with Nazi Germany first. That is enemy number one'. Any question of war with the Soviet Union was due to 'much wishful thinking'.[4] The Poles, of course, were doing the 'wishful thinking'. The USA echoed this policy of enemy number one as Roosevelt, even after the Japanese attack on the US naval base at Pearl Harbor, never wavered from the 'Germany-first strategy'.[5] Prior to the Japanese attack at Pearl Harbor there had been no state of war between the USA and Germany, but Hitler and Mussolini declared war on the USA on 11 December. The position of the Polish government-in-exile was that it was completely dependent on the UK and should follow British wishes. Polish territorial claims were of no interest to the UK government unless they furthered British war aims. They did not. Sikorski's opponents failed to understand this.

To add to Sikorski's woes, the British also began to undermine him by consulting with Anders. In a visit to Moscow made by Anders between 14 and 16 August 1942, he met Churchill in an apparent summons from the British prime minister. At the beginning of August 1942 Anders made an unauthorised appeal to Stalin for the continuation of the recruitment of Poles into the Polish Army. This was completely contrary to Sikorski's orders.[6] Anders in his meeting with Churchill told him of his views of Russia and the Russians: 'there was no justice or honour in Russia and there is not a single man in the country whose word can be trusted.' Churchill distanced himself from Anders' statement, declaring such talk to be dangerous if it was made public and that no good would come of antagonising the Russians. Anders understood and issued strict orders to the Polish Army against any derogatory talk about the Russians.[7]

Anders' continuous insubordination made Sikorski's position very difficult. Sikorski lost even more popularity with the Polish Army while Anders' reputation as a defender of Polish interests grew. It should be considered that Anders, however, only had to deal with the welfare of his troops; Sikorski had to manage both global and Polish interests, not the easiest of balancing acts. Furthermore, Anders' actions gave the British a choice of Polish leaders which meant using either Anders or Sikorski as and when the situation suited the British and their ambitions. This was something Sikorski feared as he assumed that Anders would make unacceptable concessions to the British. To try to head this off, Sikorski sent his Chief of Staff, General Tadeusz Klimecki, to directly settle the situation regarding Anders and local Polish and British commands in the Middle East. Sikorski proposed the formation of a group in the area. It was planned that this would be the nucleus of a future Polish Army in the region. It was proposed that it would be reinforced by additional Polish troops coming from the Soviet Union. Frank Roberts at the FO remarked that such a formation 'will presumably make the Poles potential masters of whichever country they were placed'.[8] The British rejected the plan as being ill-conceived.[9]

On arriving in Egypt, Klimecki quickly established that Anders continued to ignore Sikorski's orders. Indeed, Anders was not even supposed to be in Cairo, far less discussing Polish military details with the British authorities there. Anders had even been as bold as to submit his own proposals relating to the future of the Polish Army in the Middle East and in the Soviet Union to General Sir Alan Brooke (CIGS) and General Sir Henry Maitland Wilson, commander of the newly-formed Persia and Iraq Command (PAIC).[10] This alarmed both Sikorski and Klimecki.

Klimecki's task in Cairo was to preserve Polish unity within the Polish forces in the Middle East and ensure their rapid arming. He also insisted that this force should be located in the best possible location for their concentration. Klimecki had already wished to secure the transfer of 3,000 troops, in addition to the 8,000 already agreed, as reinforcements for the PAF and parachute units in the UK. Anders opposed both of Sikorski's plans, claiming they drained his own force.[11] Anders' proposals were far more convenient to the British government as he continued to advocate the evacuation of the Polish Army from the Soviet Union to Iran. The Polish troops could then be used to reinforce the British in the Middle East.[12] Klimecki feared that Brooke would press Sikorski into accepting Anders' plan and so reported to Sikorski that a combat-ready Polish force was in British interests and not those of Poland. Sikorski was not interested in fighting for British imperial interests as he saw it.[13]

The ultimate Polish war aim was the liberation of Poland and therefore any deployment of Polish troops which did not reflect that was avoided by the Polish government-in-exile. To further this ambition Sikorski sought to convince the Allies of the need for an offensive in the Balkans. Sikorski considered that the Polish Army would have a role to play in this proposed campaign. The purpose of a Balkan operation was to separate the German forces in the east from those in the west. This would have allowed the Allies, including the Poles, to advance from the south deep into Europe and reach Poland from that direction. Sikorski's plan called for the preservation of his army for Polish war aims and not for British interests.[14]

A compromise was reached with the British government and a Polish formation was formed. Even though it was actually a corps, it was called an army as that was more prestigious for the Poles. Overall, it was a concession between Sikorski's plans for a second Polish corps and the more modest ideas of Anders. The main strength of the new Polish establishment was its artillery and anti-tank capacity. This suggested a defensive role; the armoured units which Sikorski had hoped for were to be modest. Nevertheless, Sikorski approved the plan on 1 September 1942.[15] But what else could he had done? It was unlikely that he would or could have opposed it as it would have been political suicide for him in the arena of inter-allied military politics. His role was already limited but an absolute decision to co-operate with the Allies would have simply led to Anders becoming the dominant Polish political actor in the west.

The fact that the corps was called an 'army' suited Anders as he wished to call the corps the 'Polish Army in the East' (*Armia Polska na Wschódzie* – APW). Sikorski, conscious of the positive effect the creation of a new Polish Army would have in Poland, agreed.[16] The appointment of Anders as Supreme Commander of APW was political. He was appointed over General Zając, who already had a command in the area. However, it was a close choice professionally. Both men had had divisions merged into single formations and both were lieutenant generals. Anders had a technical superiority owing to an earlier promotion. Neither man wanted to relinquish command of his men whose loyalty they enjoyed, and both were ambitious. Anders was appointed because Sikorski was politically too weak to prevent it. Anders also enjoyed a comfortable relationship with the British government as well as with some of Sikorski's more vocal opponents.

Anders had to be commander of APW. Had he not been appointed Sikorski would have experienced further political problems. There were definite tensions within the Polish Army between Sikorski and Anders and between Anders and Zając. Anders did not fully trust Zając because he believed that Zając owed allegiance to Sikorski and not to himself.[17] The FO also noted that although the relationship between Sikorski and Anders had been good in the Soviet Union, politically they were quite different. Anders had a reputation as being a 'political-soldier'. This was in an army in which Piłsudski's influence still ran deep with a large number of officers being anti-democratic. Sikorski's arguments with Piłsudski were noted and it was anticipated that there was to be friction within the Polish Army. Nevertheless, a later document suggested that even though Sikorski was not personally popular he still commanded loyalty from the majority of Poles in Poland and abroad.[18] It is interesting that the British were aware of how the Poles chose to operate and that Sikorski had had a poor relationship with Piłsudski who, as will be recalled, died in May 1935. The FO was nothing but thorough in this matter.

The concept of loyalty to individual commanders was a tiresome feature of the inter-war Polish Army. British officials were distressed to observe that the Polish Army continued to be deeply politicised even after all the trauma that Poland had suffered since 1939. A British intelligence officer, Major Bryson, reported that 'every general officer in the Polish Army has his own group who look to him to lead in any further struggle against rival factions.'[19] Anders certainly did nothing to try to persuade the British that this was not the case as he tried to replace Zając with Michał Karasiewicz-Tokarzewski, the former leader of the military underground and present commander of 6th Infantry Division. The same report noted that Anders was very popular and was considered by Polish troops as their best general. Amazingly, Bryson considered that Anders had no political ambitions.[20] It should be recalled that Sikorski back in 1940 did not trust Karasiewicz-Tokarzewski and removed him as head of the underground army.

However, two things united the APW: the desire to fight Germany and their collective hostility towards the Soviet Union. Some of the antagonism towards the Soviet Union stemmed from traditional Polish antipathy towards Russia but the universal experience of Soviet captivity of Anders' men had increased Polish bitterness towards the Soviet Union. By 1942 there was a deep reluctance amongst Polish troops to serve alongside the Red Army. Bryson reported hearing Polish officers state that they would rather be shot than 'fight side by side with the Bolsheviks'.[21] This caused British officials to consider that only Anders had the ability to hold the Polish Army together and convince it to fight on the Russian Front if that became necessary.[22]

The APW resented any attempts by the Polish government-in-exile to improve relations with the Soviet government if it meant making concessions to the Soviets. Anders made some limited attempts to curb anti-Soviet agitation from within the ranks of the Polish Army which did not go unnoticed by the British.[23]

However, Anders was part of the problem in the relationship between the Soviet government and the Polish government-in-exile as, during September 1942, he started a row with the Soviet government with orders he issued to his army. Anders ordered his men to avenge the graves of Poles scattered from Africa to Siberia. Clearly, he was referring to those not only killed in action by the Germans but also those who had died as prisoners, often slaves, at the hands of the Soviets. He furthered this by adding that the cities of Lwów and Wilno, both cities claimed by the Soviet Union and Poland, awaited the return of Polish soldiers.

Anders' order was published widely, in the Polish weekly military newspaper *Zew* (Appeal) and in other newspapers. Anders claimed that his message had been misinterpreted but the damage was done.[24] However, Anders was indeed running to an agenda. He sought to remove Sikorski and so tried to make it more-or-less impossible for Sikorski to maintain a correct relationship with the Soviet government. That would be to assume that the Soviets even wanted to have anything like decent rapport with the Polish government-in-exile.

In the Sikorski story there is an episode which many Poles refuse to acknowledge happened: the conspiracy by the Polish Army in the Middle East against their Supreme Commander and Prime Minister General Sikorski. The conspirators were known as the *Klimkowszczyna*. This was the largest group in the APW opposed to Sikorski, basically, a group of 400 young officers serving under Anders' command. The *Klimkowszczyna* was led by Anders' aide-de-camp Captain Jerzy Klimkowski, from whom the group derived its name. The

Klimkowszczyna had no political agenda beyond the immediate removal of the Polish government-in-exile as headed by Sikorski.

The *Klimkowszczyna* believed that by their passivity Sikorski and his government were betraying Poland to the Soviet Union and the western powers. The *Klimkowszczyna* wanted the Polish government-in-exile to make way for younger and more energetic men. Most members of the *Klimkowszczyna*, including its leader, in common with many junior officers serving in the wartime Polish Army, were politically sympathetic to the extreme nationalist right.[25] This was not surprising as, after 1926, there was a definite move by successful Polish military governments to persuade Polish youth of the right of their causes in the use of various youth movements linked to the Polish military. Therefore, it was inevitable that a group such as the *Klimkowszczyna* arose from young officers in the Polish Army as they would have been youngsters during the inter-war period subject to strong anti-Soviet propaganda from 1926 by the Polish military junta.

It followed therefore that, after over a decade of anti-Soviet propaganda and then suffering Soviet captivity, some young Polish officers reacted with fury towards what they perceived as Sikorski's pro-Soviet policy. This might have been the case but for the problem with Klimkowski's biography. As leader of the *Klimkowszczyna*, Klimkowski should have been a leading anti-Soviet agitator but, as American historian Harvey Sarner noted, this might not have been the case with Klimkowski. Sarner observed that after the war Klimkowski was one of the first Polish officers to return to Poland from the west and was actively encouraged by the communist authorities to blacken Anders' name and reputation. In 1959, Klimkowski published a memoir, *Byłem Adiutantem Andersa*, recalling the times that he spent serving under Anders, published in Warsaw which certainly did smear Anders. This was in contrast with many Polish officers who had served in the Polish armies in the west or serving the underground which remained loyal to the Polish government-in-exile, who once they became known to the Soviet authorities, or to Polish collaborators who served them, frequently suffered for their loyalty to their country. But Klimkowski was allowed to publish a memoir which was published by the Polish Defence Ministry. This was very irregular, until one looks deeper as Sarner did.

Jerzy Klimkowski would appear to have been a traitor twice over with Poland being the victim. Despite many people 'knowing' that Klimkowski collaborated with the NKVD which included a plot to arrest Anders in July 1942 in order to prevent him leaving the Soviet Union there is no evidence to prove this allegation. Soviet documents point towards Klimowski spying for the NKVD and reporting to an NKVD major. Sarner asserts that rumours relating to Klimkowski were enough to deepen further political divisions within Polish communities in the Middle East and the Soviet Union. At the same time, they undermined Polish creditability in the west.[26]

Sikorski was concerned that Klimkowski was being controlled by the NKVD and that the Soviets were causing 'real damage' to the unity of Polish Armed Forces. Furthermore, Sikorski sent this particular communique via British channels as he feared that the Soviets had compromised Polish communications in Iran and could read all messages sent from and to the Poles at that source.[27] The British were also aware that the Soviets were steadily eroding Polish unity. A report from the British 30 Military Mission to the War Office stated that the NKVD was 'quietly but steadily' pursuing a programme of propaganda against the evacuation of Polish troops from the Soviet Union as well as sowing discord between the UK and Poland.[28]

A memorandum from the British Minister of State, Cairo, noted that the *Klimkowszczyna* (not named as such) had been established as a political movement to promote Anders as head of state in opposition to Sikorski. The movement was described as 'run largely on German lines, with a totalitarian youth movement to ensure a strong Poland after the war'. The leaders of the group were described as Klimkowski and Colonel Okulicki, deputy chief of staff, with active support from the commanders of 5th and 7th Divisions. Major Bohin, commander of the Carpathian Lancers, was reported as being disgusted with the entire affair but concluded that it was possible that younger cavalry officers were prepared to support Anders. The British report suggested that Anders may not have been aware of the true intentions of the *Klimkowszczyna.*[29] Tokarzewski is of course Karaszewicz-Tokarzewski whom Sikorski had totally distrusted since the fall of Poland. The FO suggested that perhaps Sikorski might go to the Middle East to deal with problems relating to Poland and to check that Anders was not involved in any conspiracies.[30]

This was not the first time that the British had noticed extreme Polish nationalist groups in the Polish Armed Forces serving in the Middle East. It was first reported by the British to Sikorski as early as September 1940.[31] This would suggest that conspiracies against Sikorski had little to do with his Soviet policy as Anders and his men in 1940 were still in Soviet captivity and not known to the Allies. The plots against Sikorski had everything to do with post-war power in Poland.

It is unlikely, given that Tokarzewski was involved, that Anders knew nothing of the *Klimkowszczyna*. Anders certainly knew Klimkowski and had done for at least ten years. In a postscript to a report to Sikorski, dated 25 September 1941, Anders asked for promotion for the then Lieutenant Klimkowski. Anders stated that in 1939 Klimkowski was in his Army Group and was a well-known soldier. Anders felt that he could vouch for Klimkowski as a soldier as he had known him for ten years.[32] That is since 1931. There is further evidence that Anders knew of Klimkowski's activities and attitude as a letter in the Polish archives in Kensington, from Klimkowski to Anders, points out all of Sikorski's mistakes, as Klimkowski saw them, since 1940. Klimkowski argued that a new government was needed to rectify these perceived errors.[33]

The question is: did Anders actually see this letter? If he did how seriously did he take Klimkowski? What is probable was that Anders was willing to tolerate Klimkowski. Nevertheless, the British authorities considered that Klimkowski was Anders' 'evil genius' who was to be seen, by whom is not clear, and warned that the British military authorities were not going to tolerate any disturbances by him.[34] This should have been sufficient warning to Anders that he had to do something about Klimkowski. But it may well have been that Anders was more willing to do something about Sikorski instead.

There were other groups within the Polish officer corps who held political agendas, but all remained united in their hostility towards Sikorski's Soviet policy. Within Anders' command there were at least three other groups of conspirators working against Sikorski. General Tokarzewski-Karaszewicz discussed removing Sikorski from the offices of prime minister and C-in-C. Colonel Adam Koc, the inter-war Polish finance minister, was involved in this conspiracy. In 5th Division, Colonel Jerzy Grobicki formed an illegal organisation of Polish nationalists and anti-Soviet elements. A further group, headed by a Colonel Krogulski, considered that the Sikorski government was not sufficiently robust in negotiations with the Soviet government. This group indulged in nationalist propaganda to defend the concept of pre-war Polish frontiers. Some Polish officers allegedly went further and argued that Poland could only be restored with assistance from Germany.[35] This was blind bitterness against the Soviets and totally delusional.

Initially Sikorski was unconcerned with the activities of Klimkowski. Anders had promised to remove him but did nothing. Klimkowski remained his aide-de-camp and commander of 12th Lancers. Little was done about Klimkowski until the death of Sikorski in July 1943. Sikorski had had Klimkowski removed to the USA as part of the Polish military mission there but, as he spoke no English, Klimkowski quickly became isolated.[36] But his ability to cause mischief did not need Klimkowski to be present in the Middle East. His malevolent influence was enough and there were senior Polish officers from Anders down who had a beef with Sikorski and were willing to see him removed from office one way or another.

After Sikorski's death, APW authorities arrested, tried and imprisoned Klimkowski on various charges. Sarner asserts that Klimkowski was caught in possession of secret materials which had gone missing from Anders' headquarters.

He was tried, stripped of his command and sentenced to a jail term of one year and seven days. After the war he returned to Poland. The allegation that Klimkowski was caught with secret documents suggests the possibility that he was working for the NKVD even though there is no evidence that he remained in contact with it once he left the Soviet Union.[37]

The above story jumped ahead of the chronology. Therefore we now need to rewind slightly to examine the relationship between Anders and Sikorski because, as an astute reader will have already noted, Anders was Sikorski's *bête noire* and the author of his destruction by doing little, if anything, about the lack of loyalty to Sikorski and the legitimate Polish government. Indeed, one could cry treason when Anders' relationship with Sikorski is examined. This we shall now do.

Chapter Ten

Sikorski and Anders, a Toxic Relationship

By 1942 the APW was the most important asset of the exiled Poles but tainted by the large number of anti-Sikorski-ites within it. This placed Sikorski in a predicament as he tried to please everyone: his own army, the Western Allies and the Soviet government. It was an impossible task and he eventually satisfied nobody. Furthermore, as the war proceeded it was clear that Polish participation was not important. The Americans were making up the numbers necessary to fight the Germans in the west and the Soviet Union was totally committed in fighting the Germans on the Eastern Front. The Americans provided valuable equipment to fight the war on both fronts. As active Polish participation in the war began to recede, the Polish Army reverted to its favourite hobby – politics.[1]

The Polish Army's keenness for politics meant that any professionalism that it might have had began to suffer. Sikorski sought to impose senior appointments on Anders but failed. He furthered this by trying to transfer thousands of Anders' best troops to the UK. This was at a time when the APW suffered a manpower shortage. Furthermore, both Sikorski and Kot were trying to prevent Anders from appointing General Bohusz-Szyszko as commander of 5th Rifle Division. Sikorski seemed unable to prevent this while Anders ensured that he got his way. Anders' continued insubordination made a bad situation worse.[2] What is not clear is why Sikorski did not order Anders not to appoint Bohusz-Szyszko and let that be an end to the situation. The most obvious answer is that Anders did not care for Sikorski. Anders knew that geography meant that he could do as he pleased, owing to the vast distance between the Middle East and London. The only person that Anders had to please was Churchill and ensure that the APW remained relevant to the British war effort.

The British government observed the conflict between Anders and Sikorski and concluded that it was linked to the question of leadership in post-war Poland. Hankey reported that it was almost certain that Anders wanted to return to Poland at the head of his army and take power at the expense of the political parties.[3] This suggests that the FO was already alert to the probability that the Polish exiled military leadership had no intention of restoring democracy to Poland. Democracy had been absent in Poland since 1926 and the military leaders in exile since September 1939 were interested in power for themselves with the restoration of a post-Piłsudski fascist-style dictatorship. This was possibly why Sikorski attempted to remove men from Anders' Army in order to reinforce his own force, I Polish Corps.

This caused some members of APW to conclude that Sikorski was preparing paratroopers in his corps to be the first Polish troops into power to seize power after the defeat of Germany. Indeed, Major Bryson wrote of the APW:

> they regard the parachutists especially as Sikorski's praetorian guard, and while admiring the latter as soldiers would be loath to see them get the first footing in Poland if the result were that Sikorski remained in power.

Nevertheless, the British government concluded that the Polish remained united as long as they continued to fight Germany.[4]

Sikorski's position was weakening. The Polish forces which numbered about 116,000 men were wholly dependent on their allies and therefore subservient to the aims of the Allies. This was made clear to Sikorski when he submitted his plan for an offensive in the Balkans to Churchill and Roosevelt. The British prevaricated while everything that Sikorski had laid out ran contrary to American planning. In 1943 American service chiefs presented Roosevelt with a paper which opposed operations in the Balkans beyond air and sea supply to local resistance units and aerial bombing. The Americans were opposed to anything which might retard the date and scale of the invasion of western Europe. Furthermore, from 1942, the Allies increasingly saw eastern Europe as a Soviet sphere of influence and considered that good post-war relations with the Soviet Union were essential.[5] Yet again Sikorski had been told that whatever Poland wanted or needed was irrelevant to the Allies unless it coincided with Allied war policy.

Sikorski's position was further weakened when his Soviet policy suffered a devastating blow. On 16 January 1943 the Polish Embassy in Kuibyshev received a note from the Soviet government. The note tersely informed the Poles that all inhabitants of the Soviet-occupied areas of eastern Poland, including ethnic Poles, were now Soviet citizens.[6] This obviously was a massive shock for all Poles, whether in exile or otherwise.

It was the most obvious indication that the Soviet government were not going to return eastern Poland after the war. It was clear where the eastern Polish frontier was going to lie. Furthermore, there was nothing that the Polish government-in-exile could do about it. The western governments were unlikely to do anything about it. It also concurred with the pre-1921 British idea of where the Polish eastern borders should be, the so-called Curzon Line.

The Soviet statement was timely as it coincided with Allied advances in North Africa and the probability of a Soviet victory at Stalingrad.[7] However, Sikorski intended to alter Polish policies which was summed up in the statement 'Poland has entered upon the path of political realism with determination'.[8] Basically, Sikorski recognised that Poland could not afford two enemies and so had to choose one over the other. Like the British and Americans, he plumped for Germany as the main enemy. The Polish relationship with the Soviet government would have to be left until war's end. By then, of course, it was all too late: Sikorski was dead, and the Red Army had overrun much of east-central Europe. It had already begun its advance westwards by early 1943.

During spring 1943, Colonel Victor Cazalet, Sikorski's British liaison officer, made his assessment of the Polish Eastern Frontier. Cazalet was acutely aware of the problems which beset Sikorski regarding relations with the Soviet government which mostly lay with the Polish eastern frontier and that, since the partition of Poland between Germany and the Soviet Union in 1939, it was going be a huge problem at a peace conference. One of the main problems was the Soviet deportation of 1 million Poles to the Soviet Union. Many of them were not even residents of eastern Poland but had fled there as refugees from other parts of Poland at the time of the German invasion on 1 September 1939.

By this point of the war, it was clear that the Soviets were already demanding the incorporation of nearly half of the pre-September 1939 Poland into the Soviet Union and, unless there was a settlement, there could not be a satisfactory settlement of borders to the west of this. Cazalet wondered if there could be a settlement which both satisfied Soviet security concerns and was acceptable to the Polish people. Cazalet was well aware that the Soviets, especially, were being deliberately vague in their demands regarding the future of Poland and what Stalin actually meant 'when he declared he was in favour of a larger and stronger Poland than before 1939'.[9]

Cazalet was right to question Stalin's and the Soviet government's intentions. The Soviet government certainly wanted security as it was all too often that an invasion of Russia or the Soviet Union from the west came via Poland. Poland was merely the terrain through which an enemy passed. The Soviet logic was that if the Soviet Union controlled Poland they controlled that invasion route eastward. And, of course, Soviet-style communism could be exported westward as the Red Army advanced towards Germany. It was not necessarily all about security. It was also about Soviet aggression and duplicity and, above all, opportunity. Equally, what would the Poles accept regarding ceding territory to the Soviet Union? It was an unlikely scenario that the Poles would give up land to the Russians, given the history of antipathy between the two countries while there was only a vague notion of receiving territory taken from Germany as compensation for that annexed by the Soviet Union. But, overall, the Soviets, even if they said 'liberation', were annexing all land they entered in east-central Europe.

Cazalet offered some suggestions to the questions which lay before the Allies in connection with Poland. He prefaced any suggestions by saying that it all depended on how sincere the Soviet government was in trying to settle the Polish Question. Cazalet considered that the Polish people should be presented with the situation with the Soviet Union as a complete picture rather than in dribs and drabs. Cazalet was well aware that the Soviets could not be trusted. He also pointed to Stalin's words regarding that he was in favour of a larger and stronger Poland than before 1939.[10] But Cazalet knew that Stalin could not be trusted and was an indefatigable liar and cheat. Simply, Stalin and the Soviet system had no honour, but the British and Americans had to work within these parameters.

This meant that the complete Soviet annexation of eastern Poland would have to be accepted. There was nothing the Allies could do about it. Nevertheless, Cazalet raised the questions of population transfer and compensation given to Poland for the loss of eastern Poland. He also made an interesting observation that a future Poland 'must include as few minorities as possible'.[11]

In his briefing paper, Cazalet could only see a bleak future for the relationship between the Soviet Union and post-war Poland. He realised that it was unlikely that anything could be agreed between the Soviets and the Polish government-in-exile. It was clear to Cazalet that it was likely that the Red Army would finish the war beyond Poland and that this would lead to large-scale guerrilla warfare between the Poles and the Soviets. He observed that the argument that the Poles would lose in such a situation would not have an effect on them as Poland as a nation would prefer to go down fighting rather than submit to 'foreign or alien rule'.[12]

The problem for Poland was, as Cazalet highlighted, that the Polish government-in-exile could not afford to give away any territory 'without forfeiting all its authority both abroad and in Poland'. There were two cities that it seemed in 1943 Poland certainly could not cede: Wilno (Vilnius) and Lwów (L'viv). These were Polish cultural centres as dear to Poland as Winchester and York are to the English. Cazalet considered that the situation in eastern Poland was to be the most difficult to settle as there were such mixed populations while the Poles consistently claimed the upper hand in the relationship between Poles and Lithuanians and Pole and Ukrainians. The problem was that nobody was certain what the Soviets really wanted. Despite Stalin's private assurances made to Sikorski during December 1941 that he wanted larger and stronger Poland, Cazalet remained suspicious. He considered that Stalin merely wanted Poland to become a Soviet satellite state. But this could not be clear until the end of the war.

Overall, what Cazalet wanted to avoid was a war later between the Soviet Union and Poland. Such a war he considered would have serious repercussions. Opinion in the UK would be divided, small nations would support Poland, which was seen as a small nation. In the USA most people would support Poland. Cazalet thought that Americans would see such a war as being that of 'Christianity against Bolshevism'. He considered that the American 'latent fear or hatred of Bolshevism will find ample justification for their emotion'. It was under these circumstances that Cazalet wondered what chance there was 'of winning the peace or planning a new world'.[13]

Cazalet was not wrong in his assessment of the situation between the Soviet Union and Poland during March 1943. His assertions were made a mere month before the discovery of the mass graves at Katyń which wrecked the entire situation between the Polish government-in-exile and the Soviet government. As Cazalet suspected, Stalin had no interests regarding Poland beyond it becoming a vassal state of the Soviet Union. The Soviet government had no interest in being a loyal ally to Sikorski and his followers.

This was the situation with which Sikorski had to deal. He tried to deal with it alone whilst it might have been easier if he had shared his burden perhaps with Anders who at least understood the Soviets and their world; he might have lightened his load. If he had tried to explain his problems to Anders, he might have found solutions and possibly an ally. Instead, Sikorski chose to alienate Anders and so added to his long list of woes and probable enemies.

It should be considered that, by 1943, Sikorski was not only dealing with external enemies, most notably the Soviet Union. He also had internal enemies, his own officer corps, and notoriously II Polish Corps. Most of Sikorski's internal enemies were not enamoured with his Soviet policy. Many of them considered Sikorski was giving away too much to the Soviets. Nevertheless, Sikorski had to try to fight for a new Poland in the face of Soviet aggression against that country even if it was disguised as liberation as the Red Army advanced across Europe towards Germany.

The prospect of the Red Army advancing across Europe was so alarming to the Polish government-in-exile that, even before the delivery of the Soviet note on 16 January 1943, regarding eastern Poland, Sikorski sought support from the American government. He flew to the USA and arrived in Washington DC on 1 December 1942. This was following a potentially fatal accident in Montreal, Canada, when all the engines of his aircraft failed. Sabotage was swiftly detected, but not the perpetrators.[14] Sikorski was received by Roosevelt but gained nothing.

Despite his failure in the USA, on his return to London Sikorski claimed that his trip to Washington DC had been a success. The British government swiftly found out that he was lying while the FO's informant suggested that the information supplied should be burnt.[15] British intelligence contacts asserted that, according to Polish sources, Sikorski's visit was a total failure. Lord Halifax, British ambassador to the USA, on checking Sikorski's claims that Roosevelt had agreed to the creation of buffer states against the Soviet Union, discovered that it was 'pure fiction' on Sikorski's part.[16] Furthermore, Sikorski also angered other exiled governments located in London whom he falsely claimed to represent when he visited the USA.[17]

While Sikorski was wasting his time in the USA, in the Middle East Polish troops, equally whiling their time away doing nothing and stuck out in the desert, had little idea of the wider aspects of the war. Instead, they concentrated on their parochial view of life and meddled in politics. The *Klimkowszczyna* continued to demand the removal of Sikorski and his government in addition to the transfer of Polish power from London to the Middle East where the majority of Polish troops were based.[18] In April 1943 Eden suggested that there was a need to give Polish troops in the Middle East 'employment'.[19]

By the beginning of 1943 both the British and Polish authorities realised that Klimkowski's group posed a greater threat than thought previously. A major concern was that the *Klimkowszczyna* appeared to believe that Germany posed a lesser threat to Poland than the Soviet Union did, and that Poles should co-operate with anti-Soviet Germans.[20] Sikorski was sufficiently alarmed at this to declare to his ministers that unless this movement of 'madmen and traitors' was stamped out 'we will squander everything that we possess … including our honour'.[21]

General Kopański, Klimkowski's immediate superior, believed that 'beyond seizing power, this group had no political programme'.[22] However, the very existence of the Klimkowski conspiracy casts doubts on Anders' loyalty to Sikorski.[23] This cannot be cast aside lightly as Sikorski was Anders' prime minister and supreme commander. Both offices demanded loyalty and respect. Nevertheless, Anders continued in his disloyalty and disrespect for both Sikorski and the senior posts which he held. On 18 February 1943 he wrote and suggested to Sikorski that he should resign in protest at Soviet violations of agreements made with the Polish government-in-exile. If Sikorski did this, according to Anders, the world would be alerted to the Soviet government relating to its handling of Poland.[24]

This was grossly insubordinate and cunning. Perhaps Anders knew that the world did not care about Poland in its one-sided relationship with the Soviet Union. But he almost certainly thought that, once Sikorski had resigned, he might be able to fill his shoes and dominate the political agenda of the exiled Polish government. Anders also recommended that President Raczkiewicz should form a government which would be anti-Sikorski in nature. Anders was taking this action as he considered that the British supported him. He based this on the fact that local British officials in the Middle East, including Richard Casey, Brigadier Way of 26th Military Mission and his military advisor, Colonel L.R. Hulls, agreed with his policies.[25]

However, views of local British representatives did not reflect those of the British government. The British continued to support Sikorski as the only viable Polish leader regarding the British government's relationship with the Soviet government. The FO regarded reports from Way and Hulls, both of whom were considered as being anti-Soviet, with caution.[26] Frank Roberts, at the FO, described Hulls as 'fanatically pro-Anders, anti-Sikorski and anti-Soviet', yet Sikorski's attempt to persuade the British to remove Hulls as their representative to the Polish Armed Forces failed.[27] Sikorski had in the past complained to Eden that he considered Hulls to be a bad influence on Anders while the FO considered that Hulls should be spoken to. Hulls, however, denied Sikorski's allegations and claimed that they were linked to internal Polish politics. Eventually, the whole incident was allowed to lapse.[28] And, of course, Sikorski was the legally recognised political and military leader of the Polish government-in-exile and that counted no matter the machinations of Anders and his followers.

Anders continued in his double-dealing. In an 'off the record meeting' with Casey in Cairo he launched an unacceptable tirade against Sikorski. Anders claimed that Sikorski had a propensity for party politics and was a 'one man government'. Anders also claimed that Sikorski had a dubious political entourage and was unsuitable for the dual role of prime minister and supreme command.[29] Anders may have been largely correct in his assertions, but it was not for him to comment on the subject publicly and certainly not to representatives of a foreign power.

Without doubt Anders had political ambition He was also blind to the reality of his position. While it is true that he stood in good stead with the British authorities in the Middle East and was popular with a majority of exiled Poles, the fact remained that Sikorski continued to enjoy full support from the British government. There is no evidence that the British government had even contemplated replacing Sikorski, not even in the face of a deeply hostile Soviet government who wanted him replaced. The British government refused to tolerate any situation which threatened the unity, discipline and fighting capacity of the APW. The British raised with the Polish government-in-exile the question of the situation with the APW in Iraq. Sikorski was urged by the

British to go the Middle East and assert his authority over Anders or recall him to London to review the situation in the Middle East. Either way Sikorski was to bring Anders to heel.[30]

Sikorski tried to take the sting out of matters by stating that 'politics was not the business of military commanders'. In a private letter to Anders, he urged him to 'dismiss conspirators from his entourage and from the army'. Sikorski also observed that Anders' call earlier for a demonstrative resignation would only confirm the Allies' view that the Poles are rash romantics.[31] Churchill's response to a report submitted by Casey concerning Polish in-fighting and anti-Soviet activities confirmed Sikorski's fears. Churchill was furious with the ingratitude of the APW and noted:

> here we have all the elements of instability which led to the ruin of Poland through many centuries in spite of the individual qualities and virtues of Poles. In my view, no countenance should be given to subversive movements in the Polish Corps … we have armed and are feeding these Polish troops and they begin their usual Polish fissiparous subversive agitation.[32]

Clearly by 1943 Churchill was beginning to lose patience with elements within the exiled Polish ranks.

What Churchill could see but the likes of Anders refused to see was that, between 1942 and 1943, Sikorski was the only Polish leader who could chart a course between his government, the Allies and the Soviet government. He was the only Polish leader who had any idea of the problems between the Allies governments and how to conduct the war against Germany. Even then Sikorski only had a limited knowledge as he was not privy to many decisions; the Poles as with all of the minor allies remained on a 'need to know basis' regarding all elements of war policies. Anders had even less knowledge of what was going on. During April 1943 Eden considered that Anders did not fully appreciate the international background in relation to the difficulties faced by the Polish government-in-exile.[33]

Eden was spot on with his analysis of the situation facing Sikorski who was also his own worst enemy as he failed to share responsibility with others. This failing led to misunderstandings with other Polish groups. The consequence of this was that senior military officers such as Anders and Sosnkowski reacted with lack of insight regarding Allied military-politics. The Allies interpreted such behaviour as disloyal. Furthermore, it fed into the perception of the Polish romantic tradition of futile gestures in the face of reality. This was damaging as it appeared that there was disunity within exiled Polish political and military circles – which there was.

Sikorski tried to conduct a damage-limiting exercise. He was well aware that not only were Polish schisms damaging relations with the Soviet government, but German propaganda took advantage of the difficult Polish-Soviet relationship. Nevertheless, Sikorski squandered the chance of bonding with Anders and his men. If Sikorski had tried to make an ally of Anders, perhaps even giving him a deputy role working alongside one another, instead of delivering stern lectures on an apolitical army, things might have been better for Poland. Sikorski could have put the question of politics in the Polish Army aside for another time and accepted that politics was part of that army and tried to have made alliances within what was basically his own army and not that of Anders as widely touted then and eulogised today. Anders' formidable knowledge of Russia and the Russian language should have been the best confederate of Sikorski: it was not to be.

The above course would have been acceptable to the British government as the minister of state in Cairo reported on a 'off the record' talk with Anders, that the Polish government-in-exile was out of touch with the Polish Army in the Middle East. The British minister stated that Sikorski needed to take in the views of this army, or nothing would come of any meeting between Sikorski and Anders. However, it should be noted that the minister was certainly wrong when he claimed that Anders (and his army) were apolitical, and that Anders was a 'soldier first and last'.[34] This may have been true, but it failed to understand the role of a Polish soldier in Poland and its political undertones.

This leaves the argument that if Sikorski had at least tried to share his responsibility and co-operated with Anders he might have found solutions to the problems facing the Polish government-in-exile. If Anders had been privy to these problems, he might have been able to act as a bridge between the Polish government-in-exile and the Polish Army in the Middle East. This certainly would have reduced tensions between the two and have made Sikorski's leadership task easier, but he failed to do so. Once the Soviet Union was able to go over to the offensive after 1943, with no domestic allies of any real value, Sikorski found his duties as prime minister and supreme commander irksome and even more demanding.

Chapter Eleven

Katyń and the End of Sikorski's Soviet Policy

Sarah Meiklejohn Terry makes the observation that for the Poles in exile 1943 was a turning point. The spring and early summer of that year certainly were owing to two events: the discovery of mass graves containing the remains of thousands of Polish officers in the Katyń forest in the Smolensk area during April and, of course, the death of Sikorski off Gibraltar on 4 July. Katyń totally wrecked any progress which Sikorski may have made with his own government and with the Soviet government.[1]

And, of course, Sikorski's death spelt the end of his policies concerning relations with the Soviet Union. For Stalin, it was very convenient as he already had a puppet government in waiting for when the Soviet Union would be able to annex Poland. Not that this meant that the Soviets were responsible for Sikorski's death. They didn't need him dead. There were enough Polish collaborators ready to do Stalin's bidding. It was just much easier as dead men cannot oppose you as Robert Conquest observed when considering Stalin's killings of the 1930s that 'members of an alternative Government have at least got to be alive'.[2]

British historian Simon Sebag Montefiore adds to the history of Stalin's cynicism in relation to the sinking of a barge on the Volga river. The barge contained a group of Trotsky's specialists and all drowned. 'Death solves all problems,' he is said to have replied to a furious Trotsky. The time of the incident was 1919. 'No man, no problem,' continued Stalin. Montefiore notes that this was the Bolshevik way.[3] This is a reference to how Stalin dealt with those whom he considered to be a threat to him domestically as early as 1919 and at a time when it was assumed that Trotsky would eventually succeed Lenin. At the time, Trotsky was seen as the action man of the Russian Civil War as he sped from one front to another. Stalin was a relative nobody at the time. In 1920 Stalin even blotted his copybook by not allowing reinforcements to the Red Army during the Battle of Warsaw; politically, he suspected the order to reinforce the Soviet forces at Warsaw. The Soviets lost at Warsaw and lost the Polish-Soviet War. This stalled the spread of Soviet-style communism for a generation and much of the blame should lie with Stalin. No wonder he sought to make amends by the end of the 1930s and largely at the expense of the Poles.

By 1943 the Soviet Union was about to gain the upper hand on the Eastern Front. The Red Army was on the verge of beginning its relentless advance westward which would only cease on arriving in Berlin during April 1945. Whether Sikorski lived or died was irrelevant to Stalin as he was certain of being able to annex Poland and install a Stalinist Polish government there following in the wake of the Red Army as it 'liberated' Poland. Liberation of course was actually annexation by the Soviet Union.

On 13 April 1943 German radio announced the discovery of mass graves containing the remains of Polish officers in Katyń woods. In the Polish archival record this is picked up from a report made from the Polish Embassy in Washington DC which refers to the German radio report. The Germans reported that the remains of several thousand Polish officers had been found in the Smolensk area. Initially it was reported that the Polish officers had been taken from the Soviet camp at Kozielsk and had been murdered by the 'Bolsheviks'. It was recorded that General Smorawiński's remains had already been identified. Such was the severity of the German revelations that Colonel Włodzimierz Onacewicz, the Polish Military Attaché in Washington DC, asked Sikorski for instructions of how to proceed with such information. Onacewicz had heard the message in person while the censor was trying to keep it from the general public. However, Onacewicz feared that secrecy in this matter would be impossible and he considered the horrific effect that it would have on the Polish diaspora.[4] The reference to General Smorawiński is to General Mieczysław Smorawiński, captured by Soviet forces during September 1939 and murdered in Katyń in April 1940.[5]

Onacewicz was quite right to be worried at how this extremely disturbing news would be received by Poles all over the world. It certainly spelt the end of rapprochement by Sikorski with the Soviet government. What is interesting is that Stalin and the Soviet government and subsequent Soviet governments denied Soviet involvement at Katyń. The Germans made the claim that Soviet security services were responsible for this atrocity. For nearly fifty years, until 1990, the Soviet Union claimed that the mass graves were the work of the Germans. Historian Robert Conquest notes that Soviet claims are linked to a conference of Gestapo and NKVD officers on action to be taken against Polish nationalism. The conference was held in the winter of 1939–40 at the ski resort of Zakopane which at the time was occupied by the Germans.[6]

However, the mass graves were found in what had been Soviet-occupied territory. The burial sites appeared to date from April 1940 when Soviet forces occupied the area. Even though Katyń was to prove to be the final break in Polish-Soviet relations, before April 1943 the Soviet government had been conducting an unrelenting campaign against the Polish government-in-exile.

Prior to that date, the Soviet government had been acting in a hostile manner in negotiations between Tadeusz Romer, the Polish ambassador to the Soviet Union, and Molotov, the Soviet foreign minister. Molotov ignored all the concerns of Romer concerning the poor treatment of Poles in the Soviet Union and the future of Poland. Molotov merely delivered an ultimatum to Romer.[7]

However, no matter the Soviet denials and claims of Polish treachery from the very beginning it was obvious who had committed the crime uncovered in the Katyń forest. The German invaders could count and presented their evidence. The problem for the Germans was that the evidence was extremely inconvenient for the Allies who did not want to know that their Soviet ally was every bit as murderous as the Nazis. The Germans also worked from Soviet sources as, on 17 September 1940, the official Soviet military journal *Red Star* reported that, in the period after 17 September 1939 (the Soviet invasion of eastern Poland), the Red Army captured about 181,000 Polish troops who included about 10,000 officers, both from the Polish regular Army and the reserve. It was established that, during November 1939, three camps for Polish prisoners of war were set up at Kozielsk, to the east of Smolensk, Starobielsk, in the Kharkov area and at Ostashkov, in the Kalinin region. Ostashkov camp held mainly Polish police and military police.

The Poles had figures but, as it turned out, they had underestimated just how many officers were murdered by the Soviet authorities. The narrative continued. At the beginning of 1940 the authorities of all three camps told their inmates that the camps were to be closed and they would be able to return to their families; lists were being drawn up to determine where prisoners would like to go after being freed. At the time the prisoners were numbered as follows: at Kozielsk there were 5,000 prisoners of whom 4,500 were officers; at Starobielsk there were 3,920 prisoners, including about 100 with the remainder officers including nearly 400 doctors; at Ostashkov there were 6,570 prisoners, of whom 380 were officers.

The massacre of the Polish officers and other Polish elites began on 5 April 1940 and continued until mid-May 1940. They were murdered in daily groups of between 60 to 300. Prisoners from Kozielsk were taken to the Smolensk area. By June 1940, from the three camps in question, there appeared to have been only 300 survivors to be transported to Griazov in the Novogrod area.[8] These were facts that the Polish government-in-exile had established and, from the time of the Polish-Soviet Agreement, Polish officials negotiating with Soviet officials, including Stalin and Molotov, pursued the question of the missing Polish officers. They were stonewalled at every turn by the Soviets.

The future commander of the wartime Polish Army which fought alongside the Red Army, the controversial Zygmunt Berling, gives compelling testimony regarding Soviet actions between 1939 and 1940. At the time he was a newly-retired lieutenant colonel of the inter-war Polish Army but was later made general by the Soviets. He had been close to Anders who grew to loathe him and is seen as a traitor and hero in equal measures in Poland today. By 1944 the Soviets did not trust him, and it would seem that in many ways his work with the Soviets was a matter of survival and that he was not really a true believer in communism. However, Berling was not one to endure the hardships which the likes of Anders and many other Poles did so stoically up to their deaths or liberation.

Regarding the interest of the Soviet authorities in the lives of their Polish captives once they were released Berling, made it quite clear that many Polish officers were cautious about what the Soviets wanted to know and the motivation behind the questioning. Berling also claims that the questionnaires appeared in early April 1940. The questions posed by the Soviets were extremely intrusive and seemed to be the basis of biographies which were often used by Stalin's security forces to look for weaknesses and inconsistencies in statements already made or to be made in later interrogations. Not only did the Soviets seek to discover each man's origins, career and beliefs, there was also a question which was a tripwire. The Soviets asked each man what he wanted to do or where he wanted to go to after being released and what were his motivations. It was a trick to get most of the Polish prisoners to reveal their hands. The most popular destinations were neutral countries which, in spring 1940, counted as Turkey, Romania, Hungary, Norway and Sweden as well as, possibly, Greece. Norway was on the verge of being invaded and conquered by the Germans at this point, with Denmark also suffering the same fate on the way.

There were alternatives which included returning to German-occupied Poland and to take up manual work or even enter into German captivity as prisoners of war. This rather spoke volumes about the state of Soviet captivity if many Poles would rather leave and voluntarily enter a German prisoner-of-war camp. This was no doubt a response to the continual harassment by the Soviet security forces, the notorious NKVD, and the continuous uncertainty of being held in the Soviet Union. A third choice was to remain in the Soviet Union and work with the Soviet authorities. The Poles were given two days to complete the forms and make their decisions. This was surely a Soviet trick in order to find which Poles they would be able to work with and those who would not do.

Berling saw through the Soviet ruse. He spent the two days going amongst his countrymen trying to convince them to remain in the Soviet Union. Berling could not be open in any persuasion. It would have been all too easy to tell them that, if they stated their desire to leave the Soviet Union, they were signing their own death warrants. Berling would have been aware that the NKVD were listening, watching and waiting. If Berling had tried to openly warn his compatriots, he would have condemned himself. Berling failed in his attempts to persuade Poles to remain where they were. Berling was shrewd enough to decide to stay in the Soviet Union. He had already been blackmailed into working with the NKVD.[9]

Clearly the Poles should have never been put into such a situation. But the Soviets had probably made up their minds to murder thousands of Polish officers as a method of reducing potential leaders and organisers. However, being cautious, the NKVD were also searching for potential leaders of a Stalinist Poland. They already had Berling but, as events turned out, he was not really trusted, nor was his army. The Polish Army which fought alongside the Red Army was a mere symbol of Soviet-Polish unity in the war against Germany and was shamefully used by the Red Army High Command. All Berling and the men who made up his army, the so-called 'Berling Army' or, correctly, First Polish Army, saw was a method to survive and return to Poland.[10]

Those who stated that they wanted to leave the Soviet Union had indeed signed their own death warrants. It had probably occurred to the NKVD that most Polish officers would react in this way. The Soviets wanted to rid themselves of Poles who might provide leadership against them. Equally, the questionnaires might have thrown up some names which suggested they might be willing to work with the Soviet authorities. Mass murder was already afoot even before the questionnaires were given out.

A report from Anders to Sikorski dated 24 April 1943 rather points to the efforts that the Soviet began to make from the end of 1939 which was to culminate in the Katyń massacres. The Soviets, according to Anders, had established about 100 prisoner-of-war camps, half of which were on Polish territory annexed by the Soviets after 17 September 1939. Very quickly, that is during September 1939, many prisoners of war were taken to the Soviet Union. In October 1939 most of the Polish rank-and-file prisoners were sent from Kozielsk, Starobielsk and other work camps on Polish territory. This change led to both Starobielsk and Kozielsk becoming, in essence, officer prison camps. At the beginning of 1940 most of the Polish rank-and-file military prisoners were sent by the Soviets to special camps in the Donetsk region.[11]

The isolation of the Polish officers was obviously deliberate and suggests that their mass murder was long planned. In theory, captured officers cannot be compelled to work for their captors in wartime but ordinary ranks can be. Without doubt those Polish troops sent to the Donetsk area were fated to be slave labourers along with hundreds of thousands of their compatriots. Stalin's Soviet Union was a huge concentration camp with slavery being the order of the day, especially for Soviet citizens. The fates of the Polish troops can only be imagined. As we know, even if it is true that officers captured in the field cannot be forced to work, equally they should not be murdered. But Stalin choose to slaughter Polish officers in 1940 anyway as he felt there were to be no consequences. Indeed, he was quite correct. The crimes committed in the Katyń forest have had no real settlement and certainly neither Stalin nor Molotov have had to answer for the bloodletting done in their names at Katyń.

Since 2010 the current Russian dictator, Vladimir Putin, has refuted the allegations relating to the 1940 Katyń massacre. The alleged air crash in 2010, which killed ninety-six leading Poles from politics, the military and the clergy, including the Polish president, Lech Kaczyński, and his First Lady, Maria Kaczyńska, all returning from ceremonies in Russia to commemorate Katyń has gone largely unremarked outside Poland. The world has accepted Putin's word that it was an accident, much as he didn't have troops in Ukraine in 2014 and afterwards, or that Russia hasn't wreaked havoc in Syria. The west is too often weak and indulgent towards Russia. The 2010 air crash was just too convenient.

Anders mentions the times and places of death for the Polish officers. He considered that the murders began with the liquidation of the Kozielsk camp on 3 April 1940 with the murders ceasing on 12 May 1940. Anders theorised that the Kozielsk camp was nothing short of a death camp, in as much as all the officers languishing there were under sentence of death. Anders then addressed the question of the camp at Starobielsk. In September 1939, it was a prisoner-of-war camp for ordinary ranks but from October it became an officer camp. Anders reported that mass murders began at Starobielsk on 5 April 1940 and continued until 12 May. There were 4,000 Polish officers, including 310 doctors. They were taken to Kharkov where they were divided with some going to Juchnov and afterwards to Griazov. Those officers managed to survive. However, Anders noted that, on 1 May 1940, in Kharkov there were several thousand Polish officers. He considered that their fates were that they were sent to slave labour camps in the Arctic or on the Ochocki and Berling Seas. All were missing.[12] They were missing alright – murdered during spring 1940! It would turn out that the Polish estimation of how many Polish officers had been murdered at Katyń was actually an underestimate.

The next day, 27 April 1943, in his fourth report to Sikorski on the matter of missing officers, Anders considerably alters his figures as it is clear that Katyń had focused the Polish authorities on where the missing Polish officers might be. It was quite clear that the Soviets were capable of anything. Anders began with a statement from Molotov, made on 1 December 1939, that the Soviets held over 300,000 Polish prisoners of war. There were a further 12,000 Polish soldiers interned in Lithuania and in Latvia. Anders reported that, since 1940, the Soviets had been seizing Poles in round-ups, regardless of their state of health, for service in the Soviet Union. Anders estimated that around 200,000 Poles had been taken in this manner, most destined for service in the Red Army. Anders observed that over 500,000 Poles had been taken by the Soviets since September 1939. Now, in April 1943, the Soviet authorities claimed they had only 20,000 Polish prisoners of war who were in remote parts of the Soviet Union. Anders was absolutely staggered that out of 500,000 Poles, most of them military personnel, only 30,000 could be accounted for. The rest were assumed to be missing. Anders considered that most of the missing Poles had been murdered one way or another in the Soviet Union or the 'east'. A few may have been sent to German-occupied Poland, but Anders considered them to be dead or that they would die soon. Anders was certain that Poles conscripted into the Red Army were mere cannon fodder and he did not fancy their chances of survival.

Anders then made the most startling and depressing of his assessments regarding the missing Polish officers. He bluntly told Sikorski that it was not a matter of a single case of mass murder at Smolensk but of a number of such atrocities. He made it very clear that it was not a case of 10,000 officers murdered but, indeed, it was that of around 500,000 murdered and missing men, murdered in a very short period of time. Anders then addressed the numbers of Poles imprisoned by the Soviet authorities from the beginning of 1940. In January, 50,000 had been arrested; February, 250,000, April, 300,000. In June 1941, 300,000 Poles were arrested with 250,000 already in prison. Altogether, Anders noted that 1,115,000 were in Soviet custody. He considered that this might well be the tip of the iceberg regarding Poles in Soviet captivity. Anders wrote that, of this figure, 40 per cent were already dead and the remainder were enduring the kind of conditions which had killed those who had already died.

Anders was well aware of the problems which lay before him and his countrymen and, despite the horrors committed by the Soviets on Poles as disinterred by the Germans, the Poles needed to distance themselves from what was perceived by many as German propaganda. It was a horrible situation. Nevertheless, Anders advised that the British and American governments should take on board the revelations of Katyń and consider further. The Allies should investigate further, and they would swiftly conclude that the Soviets were committing mass murder of all Poles who had had the misfortune of falling into Soviet captivity. Once the Allies realised this, Anders suggested that then there should be a commitment to evacuate those remaining Poles from Soviet territory.[13]

As hinted at, Anders was aware that if the Polish government-in-exile pursued the German revelations too closely it would appear that the Poles might be accepting the German version of events without question, or simply reacting to German propaganda in a positive light. Anders knew that this would be anathema to the Allies and the Soviets. He was probably aware that the Western Allies were already well versed of the horrors of the Soviet Union, especially under Stalin's dictatorship. It was also clear that Stalin was seeking an opportunity to disengage with the Polish government-in-exile as he already had a Polish puppet government ready to be installed at the earliest opportunity. He really did not need an excuse to commission his Stalinist collaborative alternative Polish government, but it is always nice to make somebody else take the blame for mistakes.

Sikorski's perceived pro-Soviet policy ensured that he had enemies amongst his compatriots. As Anders observed, hundreds of thousands had been murdered by the Soviets and it was very difficult to see how Poles could continue to work with Stalin and his government. It was as if Sikorski was trying to overlook the mass murder of his countrymen and women and, all too often, children. Perhaps sitting in the drawing rooms of Kensington, drinking tea, as perceived by his enemies, including Poles, had made him soft. However, Sikorski had been receiving Anders' reports and others regarding Soviet atrocities committed against Poles, but he did not know how to respond effectively to them. If he pushed too hard, the Soviet government would withdraw recognition of his government. This happened anyway.

It would have been all too easy for Sikorski to have broken with the Soviet government. This would have wrong-footed Anders and, without doubt, Sikorski's stock amongst Poles could well have risen, but at what cost? He certainly would have lost the backing of Churchill. Even Anders understood that such a situation was unacceptable since it would have provided evidence to the Germans of disunity amongst the Allies and would have certainly provided material for German propaganda. Sikorski was in the impossible position of being unable to please anybody: if he lost Churchill's support, he would have lost everything. Anders would have swept the board and then found that he was in the impossible position of not being able to appease people but getting all the blame as Sikorski was experiencing up to his death.

Stalin was not bothered at all. If Sikorski remained as head of the exiled Polish government, so be it. Stalin was already committed to establishing his own Polish government. Whether it was representative of the Polish people was irrelevant as it was to be imposed by the strength of the Red Army crossing Poland, moving ever westward towards Germany. The Red Army advance was determined by the main Allied aim: the destruction of Nazi Germany. The Red Army advance could not be faulted as a war aim but the follow-up by the NKVD was wrong, to put it mildly. Its actions against Poles, Balts and others was no different to the Nazi *Einsatzgruppen* units who were responsible for the brutalisation of local populations once an area was occupied by enemy forces. The sheer numbers of Poles being slaughtered by the Soviets pointed to genocide.

Once the Soviet crime was uncovered, literally by the German authorities, the magnitude of the murders was obvious, as were the victims. A Polish report on the mass graves detailed that it was quite clear that the victims were Polish. The uniforms were grey as typical of the Polish Army, regimental insignia was clear on the uniforms as were awards, identity papers, military paybooks and letters all found on the remains hidden in the mass graves. Even though the Germans had reported the crime to the world, the Polish report made it quite clear that attitudes towards the Germans should not be changed.[14]

There was no discussion on how one should react to a crime that was clearly a Soviet one, but it was very clear that Poland remained at war with Germany. The Polish government was not going to be distracted from who the enemy was. A further Polish report from the gravesites noted that evidence such as diary entries breaking off in March 1940.[15] This is clear chronological evidence as it is known that the shooting began on 5 April 1940. It is not surprising that diaries broke off at that point.

There is further evidence of the events of spring 1940 and the fate of Polish prisoners. After Katyń was revealed, Professor Wacław Kormanicki (Justice Minister) wrote a comprehensive paper on the Kozielsk camps which held the victims of Katyń prior to their murders at the hands of the Soviet authorities. Kormanicki reported that a common slogan from the Soviets was that 'Poland is no more and there never will again' (in Polish *Polski nie ma i nie będzie nigdy*). Nevertheless, clergymen on Christmas Eve 1939 managed to provide the traditional Polish celebration of that evening *Wigilia* (Christmas Eve supper). Kormanicki noted that plans to evacuate the camps began in March 1940 with the murders beginning around 6 April 1940 and continuing into May.[16] Kormanicki's paper makes it very clear that the Polish government-in-exile and others already knew what had possibly happened to their missing officers and other elite Poles but literally needed to know where the bodies were buried.

The Soviets, including Stalin, just assumed that the Poles were stupid whenever they demanded to know where the missing officers were. General Anders reminded Sikorski just how Stalin had treated them with contempt as once again the inconvenient question came up in talks between Anders, Sikorski and Stalin on 4 December 1941. As the Poles pressed for an answer, Stalin said that the men had probably escaped to Manchuria. At the time of the talks with the Soviets or 'Bolsheviks' as Anders and most Poles referred to them, the question of the three camps where the victims of Katyń were held was not pushed hard since the German offensive against the Soviet Union was the priority topic in the discussions. In April 1943, after the German revelations of Katyń, Anders noted that Stalin was maintaining the line that the missing officers had been murdered by the Germans while all the evidence pointed to it being a Soviet crime.[17]

Anders was able to follow up the above report with others which are ripe with detail and numbers which build the case for Katyń being a Soviet war crime. No matter, as at war's end Katyń was quietly forgotten and denied by the west and the Soviet Union but Anders' reports are overwhelming in detail. Reports coming from the graves illustrated just who was whom as the remains had been preserved along with their belongings. Ranks and IDs, along with personal effects, made it much easier to understand who was buried and when they had been murdered; the Soviets had never reckoned on the graves ever being discovered. In 1991, when the documentation for Katyń was released, the paper trail led all the way back to the top and it was clear that Stalin had signed off mass murder.

A Polish report of 17 April 1943 made it quite clear that Polish sources, possibly underground intelligence, was able to separate German atrocities against Poles from those committed by the Soviets. In both cases it is clear that a genocide of Poles was being carried out with the figures being in the thousands and at times hundreds of thousands. It was clearly stated that about 500,000 Poles had been murdered in German concentration camps; 80,000 men, Polish officers and Polish soldiers, had been murdered at Treblinka and Majdanek camps.[18] Those camps had yet to be designated 'death camps'. At the time they were considered to be concentration camps; the Holocaust was not recognised for what it was. But it is obvious how the Soviets, being one of the eventual victors, were able to conceal their own crimes as the world outside Poland did not really care.

Anders was also able to report of events at Kozielsk camp which were disturbing for other reasons. Despite those Poles who died for Poland and refused to betray their homeland, there were others who were determined to see another day who could reasonably be said to have betrayed everything that they had stood for or considered they had protected and preserved. Anders reported on the activities of Lieutenant Colonel Zygmunt Berling. A Major J.L. said that, on 14 June 1940, *after* the Katyń mass murders, he was travelling from the Starobielsk camp to another camp at Juchnov area when he read on the ceiling of the prison transport in which he was being conveyed a message which read 'We are travelling from Kozielsk. We are to disembark in the Smolensk area. After that we have to go further on foot'. Major J.L. also testified that, in either October or November 1940, the Soviets were trying to find Polish military personnel who were willing to work with them. It was at this time that

Berling was trying to drum up support for the Soviets from within the ranks of captive Poles at Kozielsk.[19]

Once again, this is clear evidence that the Polish government-in-exile knew that the Soviets had murdered the missing Polish officers as well as knowing of the activities of Berling. However, knowing is one thing; proving it is another. Decades later Berling was to write and publish his three-volume autobiography and was quite candid in his acknowledgement of his co-operation with the Soviet Union. Like many Polish officers, Berling had been detained by the Soviets and held as a prisoner of war. The Soviets also sought to find those who might co-operate with them. During the winter and spring of 1939–1940 they found few takers but one thing which was noted by many was just how subtle the Soviet authorities could be when it suited them.

Within days the Soviet government was accusing the Polish government-in-exile of deceit and being unfriendly as the Polish Embassy in Washington DC reported that the press in the USA were reporting both sides of the discussion around the Katyń discoveries. This left the impression that the Soviet version of events was somewhat hysterical and described by the embassy as being 'demented' while the Polish version of events was 'factual and calm'. The Soviets were trying to portray the Polish exiles as disloyal while the German claims about Katyń should be ignored as it was merely 'typical propaganda'.[20]

Attacks on the Polish government-in-exile by the Soviet government were reinforced by the Soviet Embassy in London. The Soviet government was determined to influence British public opinion against the Poles as well as getting other points of Soviet propaganda across to the British. This included the publication of the English-language *Soviet War News*, published daily and weekly. This publication frequently attacked Sikorski and his government. These attacks undermined Sikorski's policy of trying to maintain good relations with the Soviet Union. However, before the apparent discovery at Katyń by the Germans, information relating to mass murder of Polish officers by the Soviets was already beginning to filter through to the Allies.

In January 1943 a female Polish medical orderly, Katarzyna Gaszciecka, born in 1904, made a written statement concerning the fate of Polish officers who had had the misfortune of falling into Soviet captivity. Gaszciecka prefaced her statement by stating that, in June 1941 as a prisoner, she was about to be sent to a labour camp in Komi, in the Soviet Union. While sailing the White Sea she began to weep. A young Soviet soldier asked her why she was crying, and she told him that she was doing so as she reflected on her lot. Her husband, a Polish captain, had already been deported. The soldier somewhat callously informed her that the Polish officers were all dead. He jeered at Gaszcieka, telling her that the barges conveying the Polish officers had been deliberately sunk and that there had been no survivors. Once the young soldier withdrew, an older man who had been listening confirmed the story; he had been present. He also attested to the young soldier's words, but the older man sympathised with Gaszciecka: she claimed that he even wept.

Gaszciecka claimed that during her 'stay' in Starobielsk prison she saw in a bath house a 'note' signed by her husband on the wall. The note read that he was leaving for an 'unknown land'. Gaszciecka saw this in December 1940. She said that there were many such messages or 'notes'. There were also dates and other information written on the walls. The Soviet authorities had tried to whitewash them over, but it is clear that Gaszciecka could read them even if she had not been able to recall precisely what information they held. At the time she swore to herself to keep what she had seen and read a secret. This testimony collected in January 1943 was according to a pencilled note sent in translation to the American Ambassador to the Polish government-in-exile, Anthony Biddle Jr, on 25 March 1943.[21]

Gaszciecka's statement rings true. It was not the first time in the long litany of horrors by the Soviets in which prisoners were drowned by the deliberate sinking of the vessels conveying them. The Soviets, despite whitewashing the walls in the bathhouse, never really thinking that such crimes such as the mass murder of the Polish officers would ever trouble them, did the job in a somewhat slapdash manner while whitewash is not a perfect cover in any place. It has a tendency to allow the truth to show through or to eventually reveal itself. Gaszciecka was right to bury what she had seen deep inside herself. If the Soviets had realised that she had taken note of the messages in the bathhouse she would also have been killed.

The date, December 1940, is very relevant as it puts the ball back in the Soviet court since they occupied this territory in 1940 and not the Germans. All the evidence of course pointed to the Soviets as the murderers and, for once, not the Germans. What Biddle and his countrymen made of this testimony can only be guessed at, but they probably had an inkling. But direct evidence is always hard to swallow, especially if it shows one's confederates in a bad light. How much worse could it be? There can be no defence for genocide. It was inconvenient truth which did for Sikorski while the Soviets were given a field day to continue to peddle their shameless lies and propaganda which was always aimed at Sikorski and his government. What could the poor man do?

A leading critic of Sikorski and the Polish government-in-exile was Alexander, or to give his Ukrainian name, Oleksander, Korneichuk, who used the question of Ukraine vis-à-vis Poland. In this article Sikorski's integrity was attacked while the relevance of the Polish government-in-exile to Poles still living in Poland was questioned. Wanda Wasilewska, Korneichuk's wife, a Pole by birth, also wrote a similar article on 30 April 1943.[22] Many of the articles published in *Soviet War News* were re-published in *Soviet War News Weekly*. These were often reproductions of work previously published in Soviet newspapers. An example was Korneichuk's article of 22 February 1943 which was originally published in the Ukrainian newspaper, *Radianska Ukraina*, on 19 February. Wasilewska, a Polish Stalinist, had been a Soviet citizen and a member of the Supreme Soviet since 1940. She had collaborated with Stalin since then. Korneichuk was a member of the Ukrainian-Soviet hierarchy as well as being the Soviet Vice-Commissar for Foreign Affairs (Deputy Foreign Minister). From this it is quite clear that Wasilewska was able to use her connections to undermine Sikorski and wield her own influence.[23]

There were other Poles, not only in the Soviet Union, who published works which criticised Sikorski and his government. Most noticeably was Edward Puacz, a Polish socialist journalist, who during 1943 wrote a critique of all the exiled governments in London. While Puacz questioned the relevance of these governments to their compatriots living under German occupation, his real target was the Sikorski and the Polish government-in-exile.[24] The problem for all of the exiled governments marooned in London after 1940 was that, as time slipped by into years, as the sociologist, Alicja Iwańska, asserted decades later, they became symbolic.[25] Eventually they became irrelevant.

In releasing news of Katyń, the German government added to Sikorski's problems. The German timing, if it was deliberate, was immaculate as it completed the split in Polish-Soviet relations. There is evidence suggesting that the Germans knew of the existence of the graves at Katyń from the summer of 1942; Eden's minutes noted that, 'All the same it is puzzling that the Germans should have kept this information bottled up for so long.'[26] From German sources, it was known that a Polish work party, attached to the German army, had dug up Polish corpses at Katyń during 1942, apparently forearmed with the knowledge that they would be there.[27]

Hitler's propaganda chief, Joseph Goebbels, gleefully recorded in his diary, 'We are exploiting it with all the tricks of the trade'. He knew of the difficulties between the Polish government-in-exile and the Soviet government and, of course, meant to worsen those as this would help Germany's position in the war. He noted that part of the exploitation of the graves at Katyń included showing the bodies to 'Polish intellectuals' as a warning 'what awaits them if their cherished wish of the Germans being beaten by the Bolsheviks should ever come true'. As Rees notes, this was hypocrisy as the Germans had also targeted Polish elites.[28]

However, Sergo Beria, the son of the infamous NKVD leader, Lavrenti Beria, claimed that the German government knew of Katyń prior to April 1943 for two reasons: the first was that the Germans had used the area to shoot Poles. This made it easier for the Soviet government to later claim that the Germans had been responsible for the atrocities committed at Katyń. The second was that, following a decision taken after a conference between 'high officials' of the Gestapo and the NKVD in Kraków at the end of February 1940, the Soviets executed Polish officers at Katyń while, from 31 March 1940, the Germans carried out a parallel action, Operation AB, which was aimed at destroying the Polish elite. The Polish victims of the Germans numbered some 2,000.[29] There is further evidence of collusion between the Gestapo and the NKVD as Ślusarczyk asserts that there were at least four meetings between the two bodies – two in January 1940 and two more during March 1940 – one in Kraków, the others in the Polish resort of Zakopane. Historian Norman Davies also discusses co-operation between the Gestapo and the NKVD during March 1940 and confirms an SS action, AB-Aktion, in the German occupation zone of Poland.[30]

This would all seem to confirm Beria's version of events while even Bór-Komorowski, who later led the Warsaw Uprising, mentioned co-operation between the Gestapo and the NKVD during March 1940.[31] Thirty years later, Butler observed that the timing of the German announcement of Katyń turned out well for the Germans as it came at a time of 'tension between the Soviet government and the Polish government in London'.[32] By 1943 Germany was losing the war and therefore it was in the interests of the Germans to split the Allies as far as possible. Katyń was a clear opportunity to do so although it did not split the three major Allies but caused further distrust of the Soviets. A major split could wait until war's end but indeed from the very beginning of the war many Poles had been victims of Soviet mass murder.

The Polish reaction to the revelations of Katyń was swift and predictable. It was, however, not unified. Anders saw Katyń as evidence of the suffering that he and his compatriots had endured at the hands of the Soviets between 1939 and 1941. This was the period during which the Soviet Union and Poland were technically at war. Anders enraged both British and Soviet officials when, on 18 April 1943, his Order for the Day was for Requiem Masses to remember the dead whilst lambasting events at Katyń and the Soviet government. This order was published in the Polish language daily newspaper, *Dziennik Polski.*[33] Anders' order drew a sharp response from the Soviet ambassador, Ivan Maisky and from General Henry Pownall, C-in-C, Persia and Iraq Command. He was also Anders' commander.

Pownall issued precise orders to Anders, demanding suppression of all criticism of the Soviet Union by members of the APW.[34] Anders' reaction was priceless to German propaganda since it clearly exposed major differences between the Polish government-in-exile and the Soviet government. This was confirmed by the Soviets severing diplomatic relations with the Polish government-in-exile. Anders' reaction was also predictable as the Polish officer corps was already seething with discontent with Sikorski, his Soviet policy and the Soviet Union in general. Katyń stoked up their fury against their prime minister and C-in-C, General Sikorski.

However, the reaction of the Polish government-in-exile was foolish in the extreme as it played straight into the hands of the Soviet and German governments. Sikorski's Soviet policy was destroyed in a stroke. He was left politically naked as the Soviet government considered that it was thus able to remove itself from agreements made between itself and the Polish government-in-exile and begin to pursue its own policies. These were basically the annexation of east-central Europe and rebuilding the former Russian Empire. The German government was able to use the Polish-Soviet split in propaganda in Poland as Germany began its anti-Bolshevik crusade. It is not clear what the Polish government-in-exile could do, save protest. But the Polish request that the International Red Cross (IRC) should investigate the German findings at Katyń exasperated an already delicate situation.

On 15 April 1943 Polish representatives in Switzerland received instructions from their government in London to request the IRC to investigate the German allegations connected to Katyń. A day later the Polish Ministry of Defence issued a statement which implied that the Soviets were responsible for the massacre of Polish officers in 1940. Both actions took place with the complete knowledge of the full Polish cabinet and before the Polish government-in-exile had approached the Soviet Embassy in London for an explanation of the German allegations. This suggests two things – the Polish government-in-exile took the word of the enemy at face value and that the Poles believed without question that their ally, the Soviet Union, was capable of massacring thousands of Polish officers. It would seem that there was little, if any, point in discussing the matter with the Soviet government. This was quite telling. However, not all Poles in London were so reckless as Edward Raczyński, the Polish ambassador to London, did discuss the text hinting at Soviet involvement at Katyń, with Eden and Sir Alexander Cadogan, the permanent undersecretary at the FO. On their advice, the communication was amended.[35]

After Katyń political life for the Polish government-in-exile became very difficult with the British government vis-à-vis the Soviet government. A minute by Frank Roberts suggested that the Polish government-in-exile should have taken a different approach towards Katyń and the Soviet government. He suggested that approaching the IRC before speaking to the Soviet government was a mistake and that perhaps the Poles should not have approached the IRC at all. However, the British government recognised that, if the Polish government-in-exile had not taken a firm line in this matter, it would have lost all credibility throughout the exile Polish community, the Polish Army and wherever Poles were found outside the Soviet Union.[36]

Owing to the timing of the Katyń allegations the British government could not be seen to publicly support the Polish government-in-exile against the Soviets. It would have been foolish in 1943 to antagonise Stalin and his government since the Red Army was holding down the bulk of the German army on the Russian Front. At this time, the Allies were clearing North Africa and preparing to invade Sicily and the Italian mainland. The opening of a 'Second Front' remained a sore point between Stalin and the Western Allies and was still a year away. In a private letter to Churchill, Roosevelt observed that the Soviets were killing more Germans and destroying more equipment than the British and Americans in their operations. Roosevelt also feared a Soviet withdrawal from the war or even worse, Nazi-Soviet co-operation once more if Stalin failed to believe that the British and Americans would land in western Europe sooner rather than later. Overall, Roosevelt was more concerned than Churchill in keeping the Soviets in the war against Germany.[37]

As Conquest observes, the Western Allies did everything to sooth Soviet feelings but did nothing to consider the agony which Poles were suffering owing to the Katyń revelations. Indeed, American collusion was such that a true report on Katyń compiled by an American officer was filed in Washington DC where it 'simply disappeared'. By then Stalin had already formed his own group of Stalinist quisling Poles who were ready to serve him once they returned to Poland and hand it and their compatriots over to Stalin and his regime.[38] Quite simply annexation and treachery in equal measures!

By 1943 the Poles and their army was of little importance to the overall alliance against Germany. France was about to march up the ranks of important allies. French imperial territory in North Africa was already being used for the planned invasion of the European mainland from the south. For a main assault into Nazi-occupied Europe, France was needed – it had territory and large resources of manpower. Poland lacked such advantages. In a message to Churchill, South African prime minister, Field Marshal Jan Smuts, advised that the British and American governments should insist that the Poles cease in their accusations against the Soviet government in relation to Katyń and save it for 'better times' as the most important thing at the time was to preserve the Soviet Union as an important ally.[39]

Even if the British government could not admit publicly that the Soviets were guilty of the mass murder of Polish officers in 1940 and had to go through the motions of claiming that it was a German atrocity, in private British officials knew who was really guilty and were genuinely horrified.[40] Owen O'Malley,

British ambassador to the Polish government-in-exile, in a communication to Eden, observed that if the German army had captured the Polish officers who found themselves in Soviet captivity at Katyń they would have been put into prisoner-of-war camps and the civilians interned. He noted that the Germans rarely murdered their prisoners of war – not even Poles.[41] However, this might have been naïve if one considers Sergo Beria's testimony and, of course, this was before the Nuremberg Trials and others which proved the extent of the inhumanity of the Nazis towards anyone, including Poles. Nevertheless, O'Malley's opinion and comparison remains incredible with his damnation of Soviet ethics albeit only in private correspondence.

Cadogan observed that the Soviet government had been committing massacres for a long time and questioned how the Poles could be expected to live alongside them after Katyń. He was also critical of the moral dilemma faced by the British by refusing to condemn the Katyń massacres and, equally, could not discuss with the Soviet government the matter of discussing the execution of convicted German war criminals.[42] This meant that, to defeat Germany, the British had no option but to overlook Soviet war crimes to retain the Soviet Union as a major ally. On 28 April 1943, three days after the Soviet government had broken off diplomatic relations with the Polish government-in-exile, Churchill remarked to Eden that 'there is no use in prowling morbidly round the three-year-old graves at Smolensk'. Churchill urged the Poles to move on from Katyń. Churchill viewed Katyń and the statement from the Soviet government confirming its breaking of diplomatic relations with the Poles as 'a declaration of mortal war'[43] even if the British asked the Soviets about the events at Katyń and got the response that it was being dealt with and then not mentioned again.[44]

On the same day Churchill made his feelings clear to Stalin and expressed his disappointment with Soviet government breaking diplomatic relations with the Polish government-in-exile. Churchill informed Stalin that Sikorski understood the Soviet concerns and was willing to co-operate and asked Stalin to reconsider the matter with 'magnanimity'. Churchill considered that the relationship between the two governments should be restored. Stalin was told that both Churchill and Eden had pointed out to the Polish government that no working relationship with the Soviet Union was possible 'while they make charges of an insulting character against the Soviet Government, and this seems to countenance the atrocious Nazi propaganda'.

Churchill was desperate for diplomatic relations to be re-established between the Poles and the Soviets and called for Poles still in the Soviet Union to be allowed to join those already in Persia (Iran). He also tried to placate Stalin by saying that:

> The Cabinet here is determined to have a proper discipline in the Polish Press in Great Britain. Even miserable rags attacking Sikorski can say things which the German broadcast repeats open-mouthed to the world to our joint detriment and it will be stopped.

The next point in Churchill's communique to Stalin was:

> So far this business has been Goebbel's greatest triumph. He is now busy suggesting that the USSR will set up a Polish Government on Russian soil and deal only with them. We should not, of course, be able to recognise such a government and would continue our relations with Sikorski who is far the most useful man you or we are likely to find for the purpose of the common cause. I expect this will also be the American view.

Overall, Churchill's view was that the Poles had had a shock but would recover and re-establish the relationship as governed by the Polish-Soviet Treaty of July 1941. Churchill noted, 'No-one would hate this more than Hitler and what he hates most is wise for us to do'.[45]

This may well have been the case but for a few observations: Churchill and Eden knew that the Soviets had committed the atrocity. It was true that the German government was able to make great of the situation between the Poles and the Soviets which was clearly a breach within the Allies. However, it was also true that the Soviets had a puppet government ready and waiting to take control of Poland in the wake of the advance of the Red Army. The Poles were right in all of their assumptions and so were extremely frustrated when, at least publicly, there was little, if anything that they could do about the situation. It was clear that Sikorski was still willing to try to retrieve something out of the episode which without doubt would have confused and angered many of his countrymen and played straight into the hands of his enemies. This included Anders and his men who considered Sikorski to be a lightweight when it came to defending Polish interests in the face of Soviet aggression. Following Katyń, Sikorski's days were numbered.

A May 1943 Polish report regarding the establishment of the Polish eastern frontier, the so-called Curzon Line, in 1921, was published only a few weeks after the discoveries of the mass graves at Katyń and noted that the UK was not interested in east-central Europe. The only interest that the British historically had ever had in that part of Europe was that of Russia and so had only worked with Russian diplomats. This meant that any views which had circulated about Poland had been skewed towards a Russian view.[46]

This mentality continued into 1943. In 1938 it should be remembered that Churchill's predecessor, Neville Chamberlain, negotiated away Czechoslovakia to Germany as, bluntly, he had considered that Czechoslovakia, a far away and unheard of country, was not worth fighting for. This mindset continued even if the British had gone to war to defend Polish independence in 1939; it was not willing to fight for that country's integrity or borders. It certainly was not going to make a stance against the Soviet Union midway through the war with Germany.

The Curzon Line was first discussed as a bulwark against the Bolshevik threat after 1918. France and the UK merely saw Poland as a defensive line. The Polish report of May 1943 noted that the Allied attitude towards Poland after 1918 was vague, especially that of the British government. The overall stance was that Poland was there to prevent further Bolshevik expansion. It was against this background that, in 1943, Sikorski had to try to retrieve something from the mess that was his Soviet policy.

The Soviet reactions to the German allegations were those of fury and denial. This position was maintained by successive Soviet governments until 1991.[47] Stalin, in a missive to Roosevelt, denounced the entire German version of Katyń as 'anti-Soviet slander'. Stalin claimed that the Germans had committed the crime. He then continued denouncing Sikorski and the Polish government-in-exile for not 'countering the infamous fascist slander against the USSR' but had instead insisted on an inquiry by the IRC before asking for clarification from the Soviet government. Stalin considered that Sikorski's request to the IRC was evidence of collaboration between the Polish government-in-exile and the Nazis. Stalin opined that Sikorski, and his government should not have entertained the German allegations against the Soviet government but instead maintained a united front against German provocation.[48]

Churchill informed Roosevelt that the Poles were to issue a communique to the effect that they were about to alter their stance on Katyń and rein in the rhetoric. Churchill said to the American president that 'you will see that we have persuaded them to shift the argument from the dead to the living and from the past to the future'.[49]

This was sent on the same day as the telegram to Stalin arguing for a resumption of diplomacy between the Poles and the Soviet Union. Churchill and Eden had already discussed the question of Katyń and had agreed that there was no advantage in raking over the matter at that time. It was clear that the Soviets had indeed murdered thousands of Polish officers in April 1940, but April 1943 was not the time to allow the Germans to use this as a diplomatic coup and try to split the allies. Indeed, the Germans had their coup since a split had occurred and it was quite clear that the Soviets were unworthy allies of the Poles at least; the British and Americans were aware of Soviet atrocities before and during the war and, later, after the war.

The Allies remained focused on defeating Germany and so had to side with the Soviet Union and marginalise Poland, publicly at least. In a further telegram to Roosevelt, Churchill informed him of a communique he had received from the Poles who re-affirmed their wish to remain on friendly terms with the Soviet government and their abhorrence of the common enemy. Even so the Soviet attack of 17 September 1939 was mentioned as well as the fact that Poland had not produced any traitors or quislings.[50] The question of Poland not producing any traitors is a vexed one since it is obvious that every community will produce collaborators while living in the extremely dangerous conditions of wartime. Poland was guaranteed to produce such people willingly or otherwise.[51]

The common enemy of course was Germany but to say that there had been no traitors was not true unless it was meant that there had not been any puppet government established during the German occupation. That much is true, but it should be realised that a puppet government was established after 1943, the Soviet-backed government; its successors ensured Soviet rule until 1989. Clearly those Poles who collaborated with the Soviets between 1943 until 1956 should be seen as quislings since Soviet aggression at this point was overt and certainly not in the interests of Poland and its people. Later, this was toned down, but the communists never had Polish interests at heart. However, to query the wartime collaboration with the Soviet Union would be to overturn the nature of the alliance against Germany.

A side story to this horrific affair was that, at the beginning of April 1943, the Germans asked the comic novelist P.G. Wodehouse to join a press party to visit the Katyń site. Wodehouse had been captured by the Germans during summer 1940 and had been interned as an enemy civilian. During 1941 he had, at the behest of the German Ministry of Propaganda, given three talks on his experience of German internment. The talks were eventually proven to be harmless enough despite dark British mutterings of teachery. The entire episode marked Wodehouse down in the opinion of many British people and he was not really cleared of treachery until after his death in 1975. In the meanwhile, many, including himself, concluded that his conduct had been foolish rather than treacherous.

In April 1943, realising that he was in the doghouse in the UK and elsewhere, Wodehouse declined to see the site at Katyń or, as he put it, to 'look at the corpses of those unfortunate Polish soldiers who were murdered by the Bolsheviks in 1940'. Wodehouse knew that, from the point of view of a journalist and writer, the experience would have been something of importance, but he knew he had to refuse 'because of what had been said in England'.[52]

This of course related to his broadcasts from Germany. What is incredible after the failure of the 1941 Wodehouse broadcasts is that the German government still considered that he was appropriate to verify the horrors of the graves at Katyń. And so far removed from the stories of Jeeves, Bertie Wooster and so many other gentle souls, what Wodehouse would have made of Katyń can only be speculated. Given his statement of who the victims were and by whom and when the massacres were carried out, without doubt, had he gone public, Wodehouse would have become of interest to the Soviet government as it tried to kill off the German version of events at Katyń.

It might have been a better idea if the Soviets had also maintained this view and not broken off contact with the Polish government-in-exile. But this was not what Stalin wanted. By April 1943 he was sure that the Red Army would sweep all before it and that he did not need Sikorski or his government. Probably, the removal of Sikorski would have been a distraction to the Soviets as some would have tried to lay the blame at Stalin's doorstep.

The next stage of Soviet foreign policy was a return to the World Revolution and the establishment of Soviet rule as widely as possible. The revolution was pushed westwards from Russia to Germany in the guise of liberating Europe from Nazi occupation. Nevertheless, Churchill maintained his defence of Sikorski against Stalin, observing that Sikorski was far from being in league with the Germans and was condemned by many Poles for being too pro-Soviet.[53] While, despite his bluster to Roosevelt and Churchill, Stalin was well aware that he was personally responsible for the massacre of Polish officers at Katyń and elsewhere since he had authorised the killings.[54]

Following the break in diplomatic relations between the Soviet government and the Polish government-in-exile, the Soviets heaped scorn on the Polish government-in-exile, especially Sikorski. The Soviet government questioned Sikorski's right to represent all Poles to such an extent that Ivan Maisky was called in by Churchill on 30 April 1943 to receive an official reprimand from the British government. Maisky stated that the Soviet government had no intention of seeking to replace Sikorski or the Polish resident, Władysław Raczkiewicz. However, Maisky insisted that the Polish government-in-exile should be 'reconstructed'. What he meant was that it should be reshuffled in such a way that would be acceptable to the Soviet government before normal diplomatic relations between the Polish government-in-exile and the Soviet government could be restored. Churchill maintained his displeasure of an ally attacking another ally.[55] There were already hints that Stalin wanted to 'communise' Europe after war as Wasilewska attacked Sikorski's government in *Izvestiya* on 28 April 1940 while Sergo Beria considered that the decision to murder Polish officers during April 1940 had everything to do with the plans to spread communism across Europe.[56]

Stalin, however, was not for turning as he continued relentlessly to undermine Sikorski, depicting Sikorski as being 'helpless and browbeaten by his vast pro-Hitler following'.[57] Both Churchill and Roosevelt defended Sikorski against Stalin, arguing that he was the most useful Polish leader that they or Stalin was likely to find. It was also pointed out by the two western leaders that Sikorski was in grave danger of being overthrown by his own people for not being sufficiently anti-Soviet.[58] Unmoved, Stalin continued to exploit domestic Polish opposition to Sikorski's Soviet policy to further weaken Sikorski and his government. Stalin's tactics were extremely effective and caused Churchill, who continued to see Sikorski retained as Polish prime minister, to express privately the view that perhaps the Polish government-in-exile should be reconstructed owing to its 'foolish and improper blunder over Katyń'.[59]

Churchill had plenty of sympathy for the Poles as he remarked to Roosevelt that the Poles were not reasonable, but the Soviets were impossible.[60] This was the situation in a nutshell and simply even had the Poles been co-operative, it would have made no difference to Stalin or his government. The Soviet Union and the Allies were committed to the defeat of Germany, but the Soviet government, under Stalin, was also committed to the further spread of communism. Poland was to be conform with this or be destroyed as far as Stalin was concerned.

During May 1943 Stalin continued to urge Churchill to do something about Sikorski. He continued to blame the Polish government in London for the break between them and the Soviet government. Stalin maintained that the Soviet, American and British governments should work together to improve the current Polish government.[61] Churchill was robust in his defence of Sikorski and would not countenance his removal. He told Stalin that he believed that Sikorski should be retained and that there was no better Polish leader than he. Churchill also informed Stalin that it would be difficult to find a better Polish government than the one in London.[62]

Churchill was well aware that Sikorski had many difficulties trying to maintain order within the exiled Polish camp. He knew that the July 1941 agreement with the Soviet government had been controversial and had cost Sikorski prestige with many Poles questioning his Soviet policy. Exiled Poles did not like any co-operation with the Soviet government, and this led to a fatal weakening of Sikorski's leadership. Once Anders was able to rival him, Sikorski's star began to wane. Churchill was also aware that Anders was often briefing against Sikorski and was totally anti-Soviet. Given the inhumane treatment that Anders and his followers had received at the hands of the Soviets, this was not surprising but to conspire against Sikorski given his office and status was nothing but treason.

Churchill, the FO and the WO were aware of what was going on regarding Anders and Sikorski. However, if they had realised the depth of the conspiracy against Sikorski, the British would have been mortified.

The British government attempts to persuade Sikorski to reform his government were almost impossible to realise because, as Maisky admitted to Eden, the only important Polish politicians outside the Polish government-in-exile were even more hostile to the Soviet Union than those already in it.[63] Stalin had already told Clark Kerr, the British ambassador to the Soviet Union, that he would not resume relations with the Polish government-in-exile until that government had been reformed.[64] This, of course, meant that Stalin was demanding a pro-Soviet Polish government-in-exile. He was fully aware that there was little chance of this happening, and he did not really want it to happen as he already had a pro-Soviet Polish government in waiting; a second such creation would only muddy the Soviet waters. Eventually, reports were received of fighting between Soviet and Polish units in Iran. The reports were swiftly denied by all sides, but they were symptomatic of the hostile atmosphere between the Poles and Soviets.[65] Katyń failed to reconcile Sikorski and Anders. The main reason was that Sikorski's attempts at rapprochement with the Soviet Union were considered by most Poles, especially Anders, to have been misguided and Katyń was the proof of this.

As could be expected, there was an extreme reaction to Katyń from members of the Polish Army. On 17 April 1943 Anders reported that morale within the ranks of the APW was suffering and that there was a complete lack of confidence in the Polish government-in-exile. Three days later, Anders, in talks with General Tadeusz Klimecki, Chief of the Polish General Staff, called for changes in the Polish government.[66] This was at the same time that the Soviet government was also making that demand but, of course, coming from a different direction politically – simply left versus right. Anders' insubordination should have been dealt with promptly: arrested certainly; tried as a traitor, probably. If he had been found guilty, he would have suffered the consequences of treachery during wartime. However, it would seem that Sikorski's power was already on the wane and that Anders was in the ascendant. As we have seen, Anders was more useful politically and militarily to the Allies than Sikorski. Yet, as a Pole, Anders, like Sikorski, could be isolated very easily if necessary. Nevertheless, the exiled Poles continued in their infantile political games rather than concentrating on how best Poland might be able to regain independence post-war.

On 1 May 1943 General Tadeusz Klimecki, Chief of the Polish General Staff, warned the government-in-exile that the situation in the APW was worse than he had expected. Most of the APW was opposed to the government-in-exile with Anders openly supporting activities directed at Sikorski.[67] It was all too reminiscent of inter-war Polish politics where the Polish Army demanded a role in Polish society and political life that was incompatible with its duty, the defence of the Polish state and nation. Klimecki feared that if Anders resigned this would lead to further political divisions within APW and that Anders would pit his forces against the Polish government-in-exile. A high-profile resignation such as that of Anders would have been evidence of a split between APW and the government-in-exile. The British government feared this and instructed British officials in the Middle East to prevent Anders from taking any 'irrevocable step' such as a very public and damaging resignation. Furthermore, Churchill had already made it quite clear that if the APW failed to continue in its support for the war against Germany, the UK government would withdraw its support for Poland.[68]

Earlier, on 3 April 1943, Churchill had told Cadogan that:

> General Anders should be given no encouragement and should be warned that he was answerable for the good discipline and loyalty to the Polish Government of the troops entrusted to him. The troops should be made aware that any failure on their part of discipline or of readiness to act against a common foe in a coherent manner will relieve the Allies, and particularly Great Britain, of the obligations that they have to secure the existence of a strong Poland after the war.[69]

This is clear evidence that the British government was fully aware of problems within APW and that Anders was clearly the leader of this dissent and could have been held responsible for any acts against Sikorski and certainly anything which harmed the Allied war effort against Germany and its allies.

Katyń, as already discussed, compounded Sikorski's problems and raised British anxiety regarding the morale and potential for mutiny within the Polish Army by 1943. This was the year when the Allies had reached a critical point in their pursuit of the war in the Mediterranean area and had already planned to invade Sicily from North Africa. Such operations called for well-disciplined forces, including the Poles. A dysfunctional APW would have been unwelcome and if it did not conform then it would be left out of active operations. To have been excluded from Allied operations in the Mediterranean theatre would have been disastrous for the Poles since fighting the Germans was the only thing to unite Polish forces at the time. Without doubt Stalin would have used it as anti-Polish propaganda.

It was clear that anything which threatened Allied operations in the Mediterranean area or elsewhere was to be discouraged or removed. It was to this end that Sikorski was encouraged by the UK government to go to the

Middle East and restore order. Klimecki had already concluded that such a visit was essential as he had already established that the rank and file were politically sound and that only the Polish command was addicted to politics, with a small number of officers taking advantage of the situation.[70] In 1965, Jerzy Klimkowski, the leader of the dissident officers, denied that Sikorski's trip to the Middle East was necessary while claiming that there was no question of mutiny in APW.[71]

However, a British security report noted that, according to a supposed Polish intelligence source, Sikorski's position was worsening as thirty to forty Polish generals, who represented most of the Polish general officers in the UK, were growing more emphatic in their demands that Sikorski should cease meddling in politics and confine himself to military affairs.[72] This suggests that, once again, senior Polish officers did not understand the true state of inter-Allied military-politics and Poland's position in that alliance. Basically, Poland was a tiny cog in the alliance, and it was only Sikorski's advocacy of trying to reach a working relationship with the Soviet government which kept Poland within it, no matter how miniscule the Polish role. Sikorski, despite his perceived failings, was the only Polish leader acceptable to the Allies in 1943.

Indeed, before he left for the Middle East, Sikorski asserted that he would 'do all in his power' to make Polish troops understand the need to co-operate with the Soviet Union.[73] This was on the back of the FO noting that a visit by Sikorski to the Middle East was a matter of the highest political importance owing to the poor state of Polish-Soviet relations, especially as German propaganda was emphasising the dire relationship between the Soviet government and the Polish government-in-exile.[74] The government-in-exile were not unaware of what the Soviet government was doing. In a report from the Polish Embassy in Washington DC Sikorski was informed, as if he needed educating on this matter, that the Soviet government was heading up a 'disgusting campaign' against the Poles against the background of the murders of Wiktor Atler and Henryk Erlich, the missing Polish officers and the breakdown in Polish-Soviet diplomatic relations.[75] Some of this needs unpacking before we move on.

The missing Polish officers have already been encountered in this narrative as has the severance of diplomatic relations between the exiled Poles in London and the Soviet government. The reference to Alter and Ehrlich concerns the murders by the NKVD of two prominent Polish Jewish Socialist activists. In 1943 their deaths were still somewhat unclear while the reasons for them were very clear to the Polish government-in-exile; both men had been pushing for Polish Jews to be allowed to join the Polish Army in the Soviet Union. The Soviet government had forbidden this, claiming that such men were Soviet citizens and therefore should be in the Red Army. Overall, it was part of a campaign to intimidate Sikorski and his supporters as well as causing division between Sikorski and Anders. Sikorski desperately needed to prove that he, and not Anders, was still in control of exiled Polish affairs in the west. The Soviets, having a puppet government in-waiting, could afford to sit back and allow the western Poles to devour one another.

This meant that, owing to the collapse of the diplomatic relations between the Soviet government and the Polish government-in-exile following the revelations of Katyń, Sikorski was forced to go to the Middle East to demand obedience from APW and its commander, General Anders. This was something that he should have never had to do, but Sikorski was a victim of the lack of professionalism of the Polish officer corps and the lack of Polish democratic credentials. Nevertheless, he set out on his final trip to the Middle East to beard Anders in his lair and try to salvage something from the wreck of exiled Polish politics outside London, the correct seat of Polish political legitimacy. Anders was queering the pitch by his actions and needed to be bought to heel.

Chapter Twelve

The Final Trip East

Tendyra suggests that Sikorski's approach to Anders during his visit to the Middle East was wrong from the beginning. It was clear that he needed to confront Anders and his disloyal army. Sikorski also still needed to promote accommodation with the Soviet Union to try to get anything like a place at the table when peace talks and conferences about post-war Europe might be held. To remain at odds with the Soviet government or simply with Stalin was to doom the Polish government in London to irrelevance. Amazingly, despite the events of April 1943 and being exhausted, and who would not be so in his position, Sikorski was still determined to reach accommodation with the Soviets.

Meiklejohn Terry considers that Sikorski was possibly becoming more emboldened in his attitude post-Katyń, was less dependent on domestic support and saw the way forward as being to fall in line with the Western Allies in his approaches towards the Soviet government. On 1 May 1943 he admitted to American diplomat Averell Harriman that the Polish statement on Katyń had been a serious error. He told the American that he would go as far as dignity and taking the views of his colleagues and people allowed him and do his utmost to restore relations with the Soviet government and asked for American help in this endeavour.

Three days later, in a broadcast to Poland, Sikorski pronounced this as an official policy. It was not long after this that rumours of assassination threats against Sikorski began to surface while his friends pleaded with him not to go out to see Anders and his army. But it was a trip that Sikorski needed to make.[1] Sikorski was no coward and he had to face Anders and his army, or, without doubt, he would have been deposed as leader of the Poles in the west. He also needed to reduce Anders' authority by altering the structure of the Polish Army in the Middle East.

On 10 June 1943, in a meeting with senior Polish officers in Iraq, Sikorski raised the question of structural alterations of APW to try to meet a serious manpower shortage in addition to meet operational and training requirements. Anders was offered a choice by Sikorski: he could be either commander of the army or of Polish II Corps. It was not much of a choice: had Anders taken the role of commander of the army, he would have remained the highest-ranking

Polish officer in the Middle East but without a field command. If he chose the post of commander of II Corps, another officer would be his superior.[2]

Earlier British reports speculated that there had been a rift between the APW and the Polish government-in-exile. The FO considered that if this was the case the situation should not be allowed to fester. The suggestion was that the majority of the APW believed that the Polish government-in-exile was composed of Sikorski 'yes men' and were subordinate to his personal ambitions rather than what was good for Poland. It was further believed that Sikorski wished to remove Anders. This led to mistrust of Sikorski by APW, and it was reported darkly that, in the event of a 'showdown', the APW, to a man, would support Anders.[3] However, the FO was unable to find any evidence to support its claim that Sikorski sought to sack Anders.[4]

This was not a good image and was all too reminiscent of Polish armies supporting a favoured officer rather than their C-in-C. At the same time Frank Roberts at the FO noted that there remained no alternative to Sikorski as prime minister of Poland.[5] Some Polish politicians complained that the Polish Army was medieval and feudal in its attitude. One, the influential journalist and politician Adam Ciołkosz, pleaded for a Polish army which was national and not Sikorski's Army or Anders' Army but just the Polish Army.[6] Ciołkosz, in his appeal for a true national Polish Army rather than armed factions, hit the nail on the head regarding the attitudes of Polish officers even during the dire days of the Second World War. For some the Polish Army had been a springboard for rapid social advancement, and nothing had changed. Some senior Polish officers continued to seek personal political gain which was frequently at odds with the policies of the Allies and certainly did not help in the so-called return to Poland.

After two years of unrivalled authority over his divisions Anders did not welcome the threat of any diminution of his power and influence. Sikorski's aim was to separate combat and support units within APW. Any reduction of Anders' potency would have been a bonus for Sikorski. Anders was pressed further by Sikorski to improve his attitude towards the Soviet Union. Sikorski claimed that progress was being made in that direction 'helped by the friendly attitude towards us by the British and American governments'.[7] Anders, in turn, had been persuaded by British officials in the Middle East to take a less confrontational stance towards Sikorski. Anders told British officials that he intended to speak 'very freely' to Sikorski, citing his various perceived grievances. Hopkins advised Casey to 'urge him (Sikorski) to maintain a moderate and calm attitude' during his meeting with Anders on 26 May 1943.[8]In turn, Anders was rehearsed by British officials in how he was to receive Sikorski.[9]

Without doubt, Sikorski failed to understand the justified fears that the APW harboured regarding Soviet policies towards Poland and the Poles. Instead, Sikorski continued to harp on about the continuation of political interests in the APW, especially at senior levels.[10] It might have been useful to have met them halfway, accepting that there was a lot of politics in the Polish Army and trying to work with senior figures to present a unified front to the Soviet government and to the Allies and not allow them to divide the Poles and take advantage where they could.

The Allies, especially the British and Americans, would not accept political interference in Allied armies while the Soviet government ideologically could not allow military officers to interfere with politics. The fear of the army hijacking the revolution haunted the Bolsheviks, especially Stalin. The French Revolution had been stolen by Napoléon and his army; Russian revolutionaries were not going to lose their revolution the same way. During the 1930s Stalin had purged the Red Army of many senior officers which had caused him dearly in 1941 while political officers had been a fact of life in the Red Army for over twenty years. Therefore, none of the Allies was going to easily understand if Sikorski had decided to entertain politics in the Polish Army, especially if it held no advantage to the Allied war programme. Anders, however, was able to evade any attempt by Sikorski to reduce his authority and managed to retain command of both APW and Polish II Corps. Once APW was combat-ready, Anders proposed to relinquish command of APW.[11]

It should be realised that Sikorski's trip to the Middle East during the summer of 1943 was fraught with danger. Air travel was dangerous at this time, let alone flying during wartime. Aircraft were still relatively primitive and prone to accidents, but Sikorski had been particularly unfortunate (or fortunate) with two air incidents in 1942 which seem to point to sabotage, if not attempted murder. The 1942 incidents relate to Sikorski's trips to North America and should not be ignored, given that he died in an unexplained accident in which he and his entourage lost their lives on an overseas visit.

The first attempt on Sikorski's life concerned Wing Commander Kleczynski (PAF) who somehow had managed to smuggle an incendiary bomb onto Sikorski's aircraft bound for the USA from the UK. Kleczynski claimed that he had brought the bomb aboard as he considered that, if the aeroplane was forced down over enemy territory, the bomb could be used to destroy it and the nature of its journey. Later Kleczynski claimed, when interrogated by British security officials, that he had forgotten that he had brought the bomb onto the plane and had only remembered it when he smelled burning. Kleczynski then panicked, thinking that the bomb was about to explode. The British claimed that they were convinced by Kleczynski's account of the events and considered that in view of his 'distinguished career' that he should not be punished as he was consumed with 'mental anguish'.[12] Two days later Kleczynski was recalled from his post as Polish Air Attaché to the USA on a long leave to 'recover his health'.[13]

This was all rather convenient but the thesis of Kleczynski suffering some form of mental breakdown was extremely convenient to both British and Polish governments as it overlooked the conspiratorial nature of his actions. Kleczynski had obtained his bomb as early as December 1941 from Second Lieutenant Eugeniusz Jarewicz. This officer was involved in the experimentation and construction of sabotage equipment, as well as training officers in the used of British sabotage equipment.[14]

Jarewicz, also interrogated by British security services, confirmed that Kleczynski wanted the bomb to destroy an aircraft forced down over enemy territory.[15] The fact that at least two men were involved in this episode is evidence of a conspiracy. As the events in question took place between 21 and 22 March 1942, a question is raised: how and where did Kleczynski keep his bomb after obtaining it in December 1941? It is unlikely that he 'forgot' the bomb which he had placed on Sikorski's aircraft. To muddy the waters further over this incident, the British refer to a time bomb rather than an incendiary bomb, discovered prior to Sikorski's departure to the USA.[16] Was this another device? The record is not clear.

The muddling of accounts is once again convenient since it allowed Kleczynski to escape censure or punishment. Jarewicz seems to have escaped any retribution from the Polish authorities while the British did not appear to be interested in him at all. Kleczynski was placed under observation in an Edinburgh mental health unit but was subsequently released. Later, very conveniently, he was struck by a tram in Edinburgh and killed.[17]

It should be considered that, in the conditions of 1942, Kleczynski might have been treated more harshly within the penal system as it was clear that he had conspired to murder Sikorski. If he had succeeded, he would have attracted the death penalty, the punishment for murder in the UK at that time. However, such was the delicate political situation between the Poles and the Soviet government, that all dissent concerning Sikorski's Soviet policy was closed down. It would have been embarrassing for the Western Allies to have German claims of disunity amongst Poles regarding co-operation with the Soviet Union proven. Therefore, it became necessary for the Kleczynski incident to retreat into obscurity as the actions of a madman.

If treated in isolation, the British and Polish governments' wish to allow the Kleczynski episode to be treated as a mental health problem may have seemed plausible save for a second incident, once more in North America. During

December 1942 Sikorski made a further visit to the USA. On 1 December, whilst in Montreal, Canada, all four engines of his aircraft failed. Investigators swiftly detected sabotage but not the perpetrators.[18] Again, there appears to be a discrepancy in the narrative as Major Victor Cazalet, British Liaison Officer to General Sikorski, recorded the flight from Montreal to New York as being at the end of November 1942 in a twin-engine Hudson. Both engines (rather than four engines) failed on take-off.[19] Once more there was little, or no, interest by the Western Allies to discover who was responsible for this attempt on Sikorski's life. If they had, it would again have broadcast the splits in Polish Army and the exiled Polish communities. Historian David Irving asserts that the British authorities were so anxious to play down the incident that they tried to persuade Sikorski that there had been no incident at all.[20]

Despite the clear attempts, all of which appear to point directly to the Poles as perpetrators, which Sikorski would have known, he kept faith with his Army and remained convinced of the worth of the APW.[21] In Qizil Ribat, near Baghdad, he played up to his pre-war and contemporary enemies, the Piłsudski-ites, by ordering soldiers to sing *Pierszwą Brygadę* (The First Brigade), an anthem synonymous with Marshal Piłsudski and virtually banned from the army. Sikorski's gesture to the APW may have angered Polish politicians but it was popular amongst the Piłsudski loyalists.[22]

Sikorski continued to remain optimistic about Poland's international situation. Yet, he was critical of both London and Washington for their ambiguous approaches towards post-war Poland especially the question of the eastern frontiers with the Soviet Union. Overall, Sikorski preferred the British as they were fellow Europeans, but it seemed that he was no longer confident of American support in his struggles with the Stalin and the Soviet government.[23] However, regarding Poland and its military-politics, Sikorski needed Anders and the APW far more than they needed him. It was a dreadful position for Sikorski to find himself in. And so, to that end, Sikorski had set out on his trip to the Middle East.

It might be said that, once Sikorski was in the Middle East, he was able to assert his authority over Anders but he never really dominated his erring general. Sikorski told Eden that once Anders was presented with his wrongdoing he was like 'a small boy who had done wrong but was now contrite and has been forgiven but would have to watch his step in future'.[24]

This was hardly true as events will show. Sikorski was a proven liar and said anything to look as if he was in control of his own people. The problem was that Anders was hardly one of his people and needed nothing from Sikorski save his removal. Anders, on the other hand, had everything including an 'army' which the British wanted owing to its location fitting into the British scheme of military operations in the Mediterranean area. Sikorski had gone to the Middle East not only try to confront Anders but also to make another attempt to rein in the APW and Anders by attempting to split command of that force.[25] Clearly, Sikorski failed to do this. Nevertheless, on the eve of Sikorski's death, the FO considered that the difficulties between Sikorski and Anders had largely been sorted.[26]

This was wishful thinking by the FO. It was more than likely that Anders allowed Sikorski and the British to believe that he had agreed with Sikorski. However, once Sikorski began his return trip to the UK, Anders reverted to type and carried on as before. There was little that Sikorski could do about it as Anders ruled the Polish roost in the Middle East. With the death of Sikorski and his entourage on 4 July 1943 when his aircraft crashed into the sea as it took off from Gibraltar, it no longer mattered, and Anders was left the most dominant Pole in exile and the most useful as far as the British government was concerned. Sikorski's death was very convenient for Anders. Even more conveniently, Anders was laid up with malaria from 5 to 11 July 1943.[27]

On 17 July 1943 Anders received confirmation that II Polish Corps was to be transferred to the Middle East. This operation was to begin in mid-August 1943. Anders had made himself very useful to the British. He had created an 'army' out of Polish prisoners in the Soviet Union. He had managed to get his army out of the Soviet Union into Iran and then Iraq. The August move to the Middle East was confirmation that Anders' troops were to be used in the Italian campaign which had opened in July 1943 with the invasion of Scilly. In contrast, Sikorski's force, I Polish Corps, remained marooned in Scotland for another year before they too returned to the battlefield for the first time since 1940. The problem of the death of Sikorski remains with his legacy of that of the wartime Poles. His death should be examined in the next chapter.

Chapter Thirteen

Gibraltar, July 1943

Sikorski's death off Gibraltar on 4 July 1943 has yet to be resolved satisfactorily. Many Poles struggle to believe two things: one, it was an accident, probably due to mechanical failure, and certainly more likely than Churchill and the British security services being involved in a targeted assassination. The most outrageous thought for Poles is that perhaps the Polish Army was involved in the death of Sikorski. Sikorski's death remains complicated and is an early example of the modern conspiracy theory.

The British historian Michael Burleigh reminds us of the perils of air travel as he notes the death of Sir Edward Gent, first governor of the Malayan Union, who also met his death on 4 July, but four years later in 1948, when his aircraft, an RAF Avro York, collided with a Douglas DC-6 operated by the civilian Scandinavian Airlines Service in the approach to landing at Northolt airport just outside London.[1] Regarding conspiracy theories, Burleigh notes the death of the then United Nations Secretary General Dag Hammarskjöld who died in an aircraft crash over Ndola, Northern Rhodesia (modern Zambia) on 18 September 1961. Some continue to insist that he was assassinated, but it would seem that the accident was probably due to pilot error during a night flight.[2] It is just a fact that some people will not except evidence. Instead, they prefer to believe their own version of a situation – alternative facts if you will or, quite simply, nonsense and, of course, much of the time, lies. This can happen in any society as has been witnessed in recent years in the USA and the UK. In 1943 truth was in short supply as it was in later years, as we shall see below.

Stalin did not help matters because, as Yugoslav communist Milovan Djilas reported, Stalin told him to beware of the British, especially Churchill. Stalin informed Djilas that just because the British are allies with the Yugoslav communists and with the Soviets, there was still no reason to trust them. Stalin was speaking of possible attempts on the life of Tito, the Yugoslav communist leader and head of the Yugoslav partisan army. Stalin maintained his line that the Yugoslavs should be vigilant against the British intelligence services and the British in general, saying 'They were the ones who killed General Sikorski in a plane and then neatly shot down the plane – no proof, no witnesses'.[3]

Of course, this is quite frankly arrant nonsense. Sikorski was not shot, and his body was recovered, as was the aircraft. The one thing which was established was that Sikorski's aircraft was not shot down at all. This was Stalin shooting a line and says more about him and the system which he represented. It was the sort of thing that perhaps the Soviets might have done. Earlier in 1943, Churchill had said that there was no point in prowling around three-year-old graves. Stalin's attitude towards opposition was that they had to be at least alive to oppose anything or anybody. Those positions did not help in the matter of Sikorski's death.

Returning to Djilas, by 1948 when he recorded his final trip to Moscow shortly before the Yugoslavs split with the Soviet Union, he seems to have had an epiphany. True, the Yugoslavs, owing Stalin and the Soviet Union very little, were on the verge of falling out, but Djilas still dwelt on Stalin's version of the death of Sikorski. However, once his aircraft was finally leaving Moscow, safely even if it left disregarded as the Soviets put the Yugoslav contingent onto their aircraft without any honours, Djilas began to reflect. He remembered Stalin's story but put it behind him.[4] It would seem that if anybody was capable of doing harm to Djilas and his party, it was not the British, even in 1948, but more than likely Stalin and the Soviet intelligence services.

As already noted, Sikorski primarily went out to the Middle East to challenge General Anders and the possible treasonous attitude that he was taking towards Sikorski and the Polish government-in-exile. Anders was and remained under Sikorski's command and was subject to loyally serving him and his government. Anders certainly had room to dispute Sikorski's Soviet policies which indeed appeared to have been pro-Soviet and it was natural that Poles, such as Anders and his army, having suffered horrifically in Soviet captivity, were furious with Sikorski. But, as is quite obvious, Anders, by dint of duty and respect, should have afforded both and saved his questions and observations for private sessions while maintaining a united public front.

There was another aspect to the trip to the Middle East or more accurately the Mediterranean area as it was to encompass relations with the Spanish government. After the Fall of France in 1940, the Spanish government had believed that Germany and its Allies would win the war. Even so, Spain, after three years of civil war between 1936 and 1939, was completely wrecked as a nation and did not ally itself with Germany. However, by 1943, the war had altered; the Allies were beginning to win. The Polish and, ultimately, British interest in Spain was that there were relatively large numbers of Polish troops interned there who had been intercepted by the Spanish authorities en route from France to Gibraltar off the southern Spanish coast. One of those camps, described as being a virtual concentration camp, was the Miranda del Ebro camp.

Since 1940 the Polish government-in-exile had been increasingly aware of the importance of Gibraltar, not only as a point for operations against North Africa but also whence more Polish troops might be obtained for the Polish Army. Therefore, the Polish government-in-exile established a military mission at Gibraltar. In March 1943 Lieutenant Ludwik Łubieński was appointed Chief of the Mission, attached to the Governor of Gibraltar, Lieutenant General Sir Noel Mason-MacFarlane. Łubieński was to be a witness to events in Gibraltar during July 1943.

By 1943 the Spanish government, realising that the Allies would more than likely win the war against Germany, began to take a friendlier attitude towards them. They began to relax the harsh regulations imposed on Polish and other Allied soldiers still held captive in Spain. During this time, the British government and the Polish legation in Madrid had begun to pressurise the Spanish authorities into releasing those captives. Arrangements were made for Polish soldiers to be released with the necessary documents, including transit visas for Portugal, to allow them to cross into Portugal and then travel to Villa Reale, a small port, for onward movement to Gibraltar.

Polish troops released from Spanish captivity, who afforded a great more co-operation than the Soviet government had provided for Poles held in the Soviet Union, were released in groups and then escorted by representatives appointed by the Polish Legation to Madrid. The departures of each Polish convoy from Madrid and arrival in Villa Reale were of course signalled to Łubieński in Gibraltar. This ensured that arrangements were made to ship the men involved from Portugal to Gibraltar. Once there, they were registered, put into uniform and began training ready for future deployment, normally in the UK. It usually took a month before they were shipped to the UK in convoys. During Łubieński's eight months of office in Gibraltar, 2,782 Polish soldiers were taken to the UK by ship and became part of the Polish Army there.

Regarding Sikorski and Gibraltar, Łubieński recorded that by the last week of June 1943 Sikorski's trip to the Middle East was almost over but, despite a week's rest in Beirut, he was exhausted. This is attributed to the heat of the Middle East, physical strain and political pressure, which were all too much for Sikorski. It was concluded that a few days of total rest was necessary, and this was arranged for Sikorski in Egypt. However, a cable from Churchill, which Łubieński considered rightly or wrongly interpreted as an 'impatient recall', caused Sikorski to change his plans and fly back to the UK immediately.

Sikorski requested that the same pilot, the Czech Flight Lieutenant Eduard Prchal, and the same aircraft, Liberator AL523, should be provided for his return flight. Sikorski was impressed by Prchal's skill and experience and, as a mark of his esteem, had presented him with a silver cigarette case which he had had inscribed. Given that Sikorski had requested Prchal to fly him on the return leg of his trip rather dismisses some of the more lurid conspiracy theories often peddled by Poles at all levels.

Sikorski's party departed from Cairo early on 3 July. His party consisted of Sikorski, his daughter, Madame Zofia Leśniowska, a member of the Polish Women's Auxiliary Forces, General Klimecki, Colonel Marecki, Chief of Operational Staff, Sikorski's naval ADC Lieutenant Ponikiewski, his Personal Secretary, Mr Kułakowski and Colonel Victor Cazalet, his British Liaison Officer. There were three last-minute additions to this party: Brigadier J.P. Whitely, like Cazalet, an MP in addition to his military work, and two civilians, Walter H. Lock and Mr Pinder, both believed to have been senior figures in the British secret services.

While this was happening there was a particular diplomatic foul-up as Łubieński explains. In Gibraltar he was phoned by the Governor's Military Assistant, Major Anthony Quayle, later the famous actor Sir Anthony Quayle who, in 1943 was serving his country like everyone else. Quayle requested that Łubieński call at the Governor's office at once. Once there he learned that the Governor was 'in a spot'. He had just learned of Sikorski's plans and the request whether he could stay at Government House. The problem was that Whitehall had messed up. As will be recalled, the Soviet government had already broken off diplomatic relations with the Polish government-in-exile, but it transpired that the FO had cabled that the Soviet ambassador, Maisky, would be arriving in Gibraltar on his way to Moscow. He would be flying in a Soviet aeroplane and arriving in Gibraltar the same afternoon as Sikorski and he and his party wanted to spend the night at Government House.

Mason-MacFarlane could hardly host both parties at the same time. If they met it would without doubt cause an embarrassing scene. Mason-MacFarlane knew who he preferred to host: Sikorski, whom he genuinely liked, but he totally disliked the Soviet Union after heading the British military mission in Moscow and had a particular antipathy towards Maisky.

Mason-MacFarlane told Łubieński that he intended to cable the FO and say that he could not accommodate the Soviets as Government House was full. He suggested that Maisky's arrival might be postponed until the following morning, 4 July. From there, Maisky could fly on a few hours later to Moscow. Some strict scheduling had to be improvised to dupe the Soviets and so arrangements were made with the Air Officer Commanding that Maisky's aircraft should leave for Cairo at 11:00 hours on the grounds that bad weather was anticipated later that day. This led to Maisky arriving in Gibraltar at 07:00 hours on Sunday morning (4 July) to be met at the airfield and installed in the Governor's private rooms to have some rest. Mason-MacFarlane breakfasted with him and Maisky left Gibraltar at 11:00 hours.

On the same evening, at 18:30 hours, Mason-MacFarlane, his Air Officer Commanding (AOC) Air Commodore Simpson, Admiral Collins and Łubieński, with various other officers assembled at the airstrip at Gibraltar to meet Sikorski. Seven minutes later, Sikorski's Liberator made a perfect landing. Simpson commented on the skill of the pilot landing on the short runway in such a heavy aircraft. Within a short period, Sikorski and his party had disembarked, greeting his old friend Mason-MacFarlane and the rest of the Gibraltar entourage before Mason-MacFarlane informed Sikorski that everything was in order and said, 'My house is at your disposal'. This should be contrasted with the attitude towards Maisky and the Soviets, an attitude which was kept private owing to diplomatic decencies but incredible still.

Łubieński narrates that, as the Sikorski party drove away from the airfield, nobody took any notice of the two British civilians who had travelled in Sikorski's aircraft. They had travelled with Brigadier Whiteley with the permission of Sikorski but had nothing to do with the Polish party. On arrival, the two British civilians were taken into the care of a representative of a military intelligence unit in Gibraltar. They remained in that care until the plane left the next night.

Łubieński relates how some things were quite different regarding the overnight stay of Sikorski's aircraft. He described that normal Transport Command aircraft ferrying passengers from the Middle East to the UK would have RAF officers board the aircraft to check off its passenger list and cargo against the aircraft manifest and then search for contraband or unauthorised passengers. Such measures were not so rigorous on VIP planes. A maintenance crew headed by Sergeant Moore, an expert on Liberators who had attended a Liberator maintenance course in California provided by the manufacturers, waited to service Sikorski's Liberator once it landed. Moore spoke to the aircraft's flight engineer and asked if the plane was serviceable. Both the flight engineer and Prchal told him that the Liberator was in perfect order. Moore called over Corporal William Davis and ordered him to put a continuous guard on the aircraft immediately. Furthermore, in what Łubieński considered to be unusual, he ordered Davis to have an airman remain on the aircraft throughout the night and to keep close to the rear hatch.

While this exchange was happening, Sikorski and Mason-MacFarlane's party were driving thorough Gibraltar. It was during this ride that Mason-MacFarlane told Sikorski of his difficulty of having to host him and Maisky at the same time and that he hoped that, during the small window of the Soviet visit on the morning, he could keep the Poles and Soviets from meeting. Sikorski took it well. After all, he and Mason-MacFarlane were friends and shared antipathy towards the Soviet Union. After a brief talk with Mason-MacFarlane over tea, Sikorski made his excuses and retired to his room to rest.

After a short break, Łubieński was summoned by Sikorski to report on progress on the evacuation of Polish troops from Miranda del Ebro and other matters relating to the war. As Łubieński had virtually finished his work, Sikorski suggested that he should return to London with him to receive fresh orders. Łubieński was told to speak with Prchal and find out if there was room for him on the journey to London. He was told that if he had no luggage there was indeed a space for him. There was other work for Łubieński which included shopping with some of the Polish party before dining *en famille* with the Governor. Then, before retiring, Sikorski dictated a draft telegram for Roosevelt, wishing him all the best for the American National Holiday of 4 July. Towards midnight Sikorski also decided to award Polish decorations to some of the Gibraltar officers. Such decorations and ribbons were stowed on the Liberator which necessitated a trip out to the aircraft.

Once at the airfield, Łubieński was confronted by two sentries. Łubieński explained what he needed from the aircraft and, with Sikorski's private secretary, Kułakowski, was accompanied by the two sentries to the aircraft door which was opened from within by an RAF NCO. As Łubieński wrote, 'Clearly the station commander was taking no chances of the plane being sabotaged'. Obviously, this was uppermost on people's minds owing to the previous incidents already related. The suitcase containing the awards needed by Sikorski was passed out to Kułakowski and he and Łubieński returned to Government House. This appeared to have been a relatively normal and human situation that had just passed. Nothing really had really happened.

At around 07:00 hours on Sunday, 4 July, Maisky arrived at the Gibraltar airfield. He was, as expected, in a Soviet plane with a Soviet crew. The aircraft was parked close to Sikorski's aeroplane and an RAF maintenance party was detailed to service it. Maisky's party was taken up to the 'Convent' where Maisky was afforded the governor's personal suite of rooms in a distant part of Government House. Mason-MacFarlane told Łubieński that the Soviets had arrived and that, at 11:00 hours, he personally would conduct them back to their aircraft as they continued their flight to Moscow. The entire episode was a conspiracy on the parts of the British and Poles and Mason-MacFarlane said to Łubieński 'with a smile, "I will show a white handkerchief as a signal that the coast is clear, and then you can let your Prime Minister's party out of their rooms".' It was worthy of the best of British theatrical farce!

Łubieński noted that, on his last day alive, Sikorski had been in an excellent mood. He had slept well and was refreshed. He was also amongst friends which was important. The weather was fine. During the night, a Polish courier,

Gralewski, codenamed Pankowski, from Warsaw had arrived in Gibraltar. Gralewski had undertaken a long and difficult journey and had been travelling since the end of February across occupied Europe and Spain to finally stand on British soil in Gibraltar. Łubieński took Gralewski straight to Government House where he was introduced to General Klimecki and Colonel Marecki, who presumably interrogated him. An hour later, Gralewski was taken to Sikorski. Gralewski made his report which so convinced Sikorski of the urgency of the secret information carried by Gralewski that he decided that Łubieński should give up his seat on the Liberator to Gralewski who should fly to London with Sikorski that night. The rest of the day was spent by Sikorski doing the usual things that a visiting dignitary did, inspecting guards of honour, awarding decorations and attending an official luncheon. This he did until late afternoon when he returned to the Convent.

At 18:00 hours he attended a cocktail party in the Gibraltar Library Garden to commemorate the 167th Anniversary of American Independence. Łubieński noted the comprehensive mixture of those attending which included many local dignitaries and chiefs of Allied military missions and was the first that Gibraltarians knew of Sikorski's presence on the Rock. The cocktail party lasted until 20:00 hours when the party retired to the Convent for dinner. Prchal had already phoned to say that he wanted to take-off at 23:00 hours.

The Sikorski party was driven out to the airfield in several cars, accompanied by Mason-MacFarlane and all the Gibraltar Command senior officers. The two mysterious British intelligence officers from Cairo drove up and climbed aboard. Prchal announced that the aeroplane was ready, and leave-taking and boarding began. Sikorski took his farewell of Łubieński, saying that they would meet in London soon and not to delay his departure from Gibraltar. The aircraft door was closed, and it began to taxi and prepare for take-off. The Governor, his party and Łubieński watched the take-off. Nothing seemed amiss until the aircraft crashed into the sea. And pandemonium broke out.[5]

Chapter Fourteen

Investigation

What was to follow was yet another unpleasant investigation by the Polish government-in-exile. Certain senior Polish officials would have known of the previous attempts on Sikorski's life as he had flown seeking support for the Polish cause. Following hard on the heels of the horrific Katyń revelations, for which the Polish government-in-exile was denied a genuine and true investigation in public, at least it now seemed that the London Poles had an urgent inquiry into the death of their leader.

The Polish government-in-exile could not be certain who might prove to be the culprit. Even if it the Soviets had been responsible for the downing of Sikorski's aeroplane, it would have been difficult to make that public: Katyń had proved this. Since there has been nonsense bandied about by exiled Poles and others that the British were responsible, again this would have been impossible to make public since it would have played directly into German hands as a gold nugget of propaganda. What probably worried the Polish government-in-exile was that there might have been clear evidence that renegade Polish officers from II Polish Corps or, in other words, Anders' Army had been responsible for the death of Sikorski. Therefore, it was not only a tragic time, but it was also one that, had it been proven, would have displayed an open rift within the exiled Polish camp allegedly loyal to Sikorski. What seems to have happened over the years is that an accident is more or less ruled out by successive generations of Poles.

By the next day the blame game had begun, and it suited the Germans to begin. By the evening of 5 July, German propaganda broadcast across Europe that the British secret service, MI6, had been responsible for the death of Sikorski. The Germans claimed that Sikorski's policies were proving to be difficult for the British government. This can be dismissed as mischief-making.[1] Nevertheless, the intrigue had been started and has never stopped. Many Poles consider two things: the leader could not have died in something as mundane as an accident, even though several senior Allied officers did suffer such misfortune; or the British, especially Churchill, were to blame as only they were responsible for the betrayal of Poland at war's end. Indeed, this was more of a joint effort with Roosevelt cutting his own deals with Stalin which adversely served Poland. However, what most Poles seem to forget is that it was the Red Army and Polish quislings who were responsible for the annexation and occupation of Poland by the Soviet Union between 1944 and 1989, and not the Western Allies.

Ludwik Łubieński, a creditable Polish eyewitness, considered that the entire incident was an accident. At the time of the crash everything was done to retrieve survivors but only the pilot, Flight Lieutenant Prchal, lived. Otherwise, the rescuers were pulling in bodies including that of Sikorski. Brigadier John Whiteley MP was picked up at the same time as Sikorski's corpse was taken from the water. On the brink of death at the time, Whiteley died a little afterwards. General Klimecki, Sikorski's Chief of Staff, was also found at the same time. He looked uninjured but was indeed dead. Four bodies, including that of Sikorski's daughter, were never found.[2] The tragedy at Gibraltar could not be understated which makes the unnecessary allegations around the crash all the worse.

British officials on Gibraltar and afterwards ensured that Sikorski's remains were accorded the dignity that should be afforded to those of a Head of State. Sikorski's body, with that of General Klimecki, after a funeral Mass in the Roman Catholic Church in Gibraltar, was taken by the Polish destroyer *Orkan* for burial in the UK.[3] This was the easy part of proceedings. The tragedy was about to begin and is yet to conclude so long as there are Poles who love to have a conspiracy. It should be noted that not many British are that interested in the conspiracy theories surrounding the death of Sikorski. Perhaps because they are just not interested but more to the point Sikorski is not a widely known figure outside Poland.

A court of inquiry opened on 7 July 1943. Held at Air Headquarters Gibraltar, it was tasked to establish the cause of the crash. Twenty-eight witnesses were called, included Prchal, who had recovered quickly from his injuries. A Liberator Mark II identical to Liberator AL523 was flown to Gibraltar for the inquiry. Secret tests were performed on it to try to establish what might have happened at the time of the accident.

In his testimony, Prchal stated that the controls had locked. However, the court officers could not find any evidence of this or an explanation why it might have happened. The Air Ministry eventually wrote a draft communiqué which was transmitted by the FO to Raczyński, the Polish Ambassador to the UK on 1 September 1943. The message within was quite bland. Part of it read that 'after most careful examination of all the available evidence, including that of the pilot, it is not been possible to determine how the jamming occurred, but it has been established that there was *no* sabotage'.[4]

The Polish government-in-exile was not convinced and, on 3 September 1943, rejected the finding of the inquiry. It seemed that the government-in-exile was willing to run with the German propaganda story of sabotage, claiming that the British inquiry had not illustrated just how sabotage could be ruled out. The

Poles tried to redraft the official British communication but were rebuffed. On 21 September the British 1943 restated their original position that there had been an absence of sabotage and that Prchal was an outstanding pilot. The Poles continued to dispute the evidence put forward until early 1944. As Łubieński notes, the mystery continues to this day.[5]

Just why the British authorities were unwilling to make any further inquiry is curious, but one only has to look at the date of proceedings. Sikorski died on 4 July 1943. The Germans were on the back foot in Europe and elsewhere. They had already been driven from North Africa and the Allies landed in Sicily during the second week of July 1943. On the Eastern Front the Germans were also losing to the Soviet Union following the Axis defeat at Stalingrad. The Allies sensed that the war was coming to an end. It was not an occasion to spend too much time speculating endlessly why Sikorski's aeroplane crashed off Gibraltar. Simply, the British ruled out sabotage as far as they could see and that was enough. A criminal act had not been carried out and aeroplanes crash. They still do.

My best man, Derek Holmes, a pilot, once told me once as he handed me the controls of the light aircraft we were flying that, basically, it was landing and take-offs that are dangerous. The British writer Simon Courtauld notes that Gibraltar airport is still potentially dangerous in the twenty-first century as it is often surrounded in fog.[6] Even Molotov, Stalin's Foreign Minister, recognised that aircraft crashed. When Churchill tried to commiserate when Soviet personnel had died in an air crash involving a British aircraft, Molotov shrugged him off saying that it 'was a very sad fact, but accidents in aviation were always possible'.[7] And this was from a man with a very strong sense of suspicion operating on behalf of one of the most paranoid men in twentieth-century history, Stalin.

Sikorski's aircraft was taking off from a particularly dangerous place, the Rock of Gibraltar, straight out into the sea. There was no lengthy runway. Enough to take-off from but only by a skilled pilot. Prchal was such a pilot. There should be no mystery or conspiracy theories. Planes crash and people die – it's tragic but that's all. Therefore, if in this century with all the technical aids used for navigation and no suspicion of an enemy aerial attack, as was the case in 1943, landing or taking off at Gibraltar is still a dangerous venture. How much more hazardous was it when Sikorski died? It is obvious: the technology and aircraft were not advanced compared with those of today; the entire venture was riddled with danger and Sikorski and his entourage were just unlucky. As with all conspiracy theories there is nothing to discuss. Sikorski died in an air crash – end of story. Regrettable and the end of Poland for nearly two generations.

David Irving is one of the few British writers to have tried to tackle the question of the death of Sikorski. This he did in 1967 when memories were still relatively fresh and before he became the controversial figure that he is today. Irving addresses the Polish concerns but noted that the Polish inquiry was conducted 'in a vacuum'. Following the official British inquiry, the Polish investigation was hampered by the fact that it was not able to cross-examine witnesses from the original inquiry. It was not even possible to take fresh evidence from the original witnesses. The fresh evidence was taken from Poles who had been in Gibraltar at the time of the Sikorski crash. As Irving noted, there was precious little evidence anyway and nothing which could have led to a fresh investigation.

For Irving, it was tragic that the Poles should have been so suspicious and he had felt that there was little that they could do about the matter. They could not prove their case in any way.[8] Quite simply there was nothing to prove. However, the Poles remained suspicious. Tadeusz Ullmann, a quiet Polish civil servant from the Polish Ministry of the Interior (Home Office), checked through the British findings and queried them. He raised several points: how many people were on the aircraft and who were they really? The question of a mailbag poorly stowed and jamming the aircraft's rudder was raised. It had been considered a matter for an internal British inquiry since it was ruled not to have been sabotage but a minor matter of military indiscipline. Ullmann was not convinced that the inquiry had really checked to see if the Liberator's elevator controls could be locked in flight. He was interested as to why there had been no explanation of why only the pilot and Cazalet had been wearing Mae West life preservers. And why had Prchal later denied that he had been wearing one?

All these questions were raised by Ullmann who had been in Gibraltar throughout the inquiry. He also observed that the investigation into the crash had lasted nearly a month, but its findings had been reduced to twenty-three pages of typescript. He was suspicious that the copy supplied by the British government had not been altered or cut. Ullmann and Major Dudzinski had complied a three-page report on his stay on Gibraltar. He had noted that Prchal had been picked up wearing a fully inflated life-jacket while the dead did not (later it seemed that Cazalet did). Dudzinski somehow did not pick up on Prchal's denial that he had been found wearing his Mae West or had not attached any importance to it. Both Ullmann's and Dudzinski's observations and commentaries were forwarded to the Polish attorney general for further comment.

The Poles immediately held their own commission of inquiry which sat to consider what they considered to have been inconsistencies in the British findings. This commission was being pressured to get a move on as the British Air Ministry wanted to release their own communiqué. The Polish commission held its one and only session in the morning of 11 September 1943 at the Polish General Staff's Headquarters in the Rubens Hotel in Buckingham Palace Road. The Polish report was sent to the Polish Council of Ministers (the exiled Cabinet) three days later. The report was not damning. It was stressed that Prchal's assertion that the aircraft's control had been jammed could not be proven. The Polish made the allegation that some parts of the aircraft could not be found. It seemed that this was based on information from British officials on Gibraltar. Irving seems to suggest that this should not be taken as evidence.

The problem with the Polish commission was that it was trying to make their version of events fit the facts from which they could not get away from. It is quite clear that the Poles were prejudiced against Prchal and got worked up by him wearing a life-jacket while nobody else was. The suggestion was that Prchal had been charged to stage an accident and therefore knew that the aircraft was to hit the water and so he was prepared by wearing a life-jacket. Irving argues that this is nonsense.[9] Prchal was probably the only person wearing a life-jacket owing to his sense of discipline and military routine. The Poles were notoriously slack in such matters.

We had seen this in 1940 when Sikorski was removed from the frontline in order to be evacuated to the UK. The Polish military leadership had fled to Romania in 1939 whilst their army was still fighting. The Polish Army in Scotland after Dunkirk was a rabble until General Maczek arrived and installed discipline, order and pride into the men. Discipline within Maczek's ranks broke down by late 1944 when reports of his troops were received in relation to uncoded messages being sent from the front and panicking rather than engaging enemy patrols.[10] The criticism of Prchal's wearing of a regulation life-jacket says more about the, at times, poor discipline of Polish troops and the arrogance of the Polish elites.

In relation to the British communiqué, the Poles considered that it should be short and more cautious about the reasons for the accidents. The British opinion of Prchal certainly annoyed the Poles since they considered that such high praise was 'quite unnecessary'. The Polish commission wanted the evidence concerning the jamming of the elevator controls altered to that being view of the pilot and written as 'according to the pilot's statements'. The British Air Ministry was also prepared to state that 'it had been established that there was no sabotage'. The Poles wanted the wording to read, 'it has not been established that there was sabotage'. Irving seems to support this stance as there was no clear evidence of what might have caused the accident in the first place.

The Polish suggestions were forwarded to the Air Ministry and ignored. The British official communication was published on 21 September 1943. It still contained the same assurances concerning the absence of sabotage and its praise for Prchal. The report was published in *The Times*, London and read 'The report of the Court of Inquiry has now been received. It is apparent that the accident was due to the jamming of the elevator controls shortly after take-off, with the result that the plane became uncontrollable. After most careful consideration of all the available evidence, including that of the pilot, it has been established that there was no sabotage. It is also clear that the captain of the aircraft who is a pilot of great experience and exceptional abilities was in no way to blame. An officer of the Polish Air Force attended throughout the proceedings'.[11]

The Poles continued to challenge the findings regarding Sikorski's death until early 1944. The British considered that case closed by the end of September 1943 and would not be investigating the case any further. The problem with the Poles was that they could not move on from the somewhat bland statement that there had been no sabotage. The Poles were hung up on this statement; it seemed too off the cuff. The British did not feel that it was necessary to go further with this statement as they probably hadn't thought about it too much.

Gibraltar was tightly guarded and strict security was followed, especially with such a high profile personality as Sikorski. There was a lapse of discipline concerning the loose mailbag which possibly jammed the aircraft controls, but deliberate sabotage was ruled out as there was no evidence, while they had no warnings that Sikorski might be the target of assassination. That was the Polish guilty little secret which was nesting and poisoning the breasts of the Polish military and civil leadership. Few in British circles knew that Sikorski had been the victim of previous assassination attempts. Perhaps if the British Court of Inquiry been made privy to this they might have looked more deeply into events at Gibraltar on 4 July 1943.

As we have already seen, there had indeed been attempts on Sikorski's life, all of them made by serving Polish officers. Three lawyers from the Polish Ministry of Justice were charged with secretly reviewing all the evidence of both British and Polish inquiries. In early October 1943 the lawyers reported back to the Polish Minister of Justice that, based on the evidence, sabotage could not be ruled out, but the earlier British statement had been too clear that there had been no such activity.[12] The problem here was, that as stated earlier in this narrative, the British inquiry was not really looking for sabotage as they were not expecting to encounter any.

The trio of Polish lawyers recommended that the American manufacturers of Liberator bomber aircraft should be asked if there had been any other instances of elevator controls jamming. It was also recommended that earlier incidents involving Sikorski and aircraft should be re-examined in the light of this fatal accident. It was admitted that even investigations into the earlier incidents might not establish the cause of the Gibraltar crash but, if it could be proven that the earlier incidents had involved sabotage, then it was more than likely that the Gibraltar accident could have been an act of sabotage. On 18 October 1943 the Minister of Justice wrote to the new Polish Prime Minister Stanisław Mikołajczyk, recommending an investigation of the defects in the other aircraft in which Sikorski had travelled, especially the case in Montreal.

In the USA the previous incidents were now talked about amongst a few diplomats including Sumner Welles, the American Undersecretary of State, who also believed that Sikorski was assassinated in Gibraltar. In Congressional Hearings after the war, Welles was asked to explain an earlier reference to the 'assassination of General Sikorski'.

Welles reply was interesting:

> I have always believed that there was sabotage. You will remember, Mr Chairman, that he was brought down in the plane just as he was taking off from Gibraltar. The plane crashed. I remember that when General Sikorski came to the United States the year before, his plane, in taking off from Montreal, had crashed when it was about 100 feet above the ground.

Welles considered that it all seemed to be unlikely to be 'coincidence'. However, he considered that the Soviets lay behind every plot.[13]

Post-war America was rife with 'reds under the beds' and the Joseph McCarthy enquiries which became witch hunts and finally discredited, but not before ruining a lot of innocent lives. However, it was not unreasonable that Welles believed that perhaps the Soviets were responsible for Sikorski's death since Soviet assassination squads were active during, before and after the Second World War. Even today, Russia still sends assassins overseas to murder those who criticise President Putin and Russia. What is interesting is that Welles makes no mention of German assassins. Security was probably too tight in Gibraltar while there was a Soviet presence on the rock at the same time that Sikorski was there. Much talk had also been made of the presence of the British traitor, Kim Philby, who was working for MI6 but was indeed betraying his country to the Soviets.

However, what the Poles could not get away from was that the first attempt, as already discussed in this work, were the actions of a Polish officer who had brought an incendiary bomb aboard Sikorski's aircraft. This was not sabotage; it was an attempt at cold-blooded mass murder as not only would have Sikorski died but also his entourage, including the bomber if he had been successful. As already narrated, the culprit was not willing to die and so panicked and revealed what was going on. The cover-up by both the British and Polish intelligence services was breathtaking while the would-be bomber died anyway. He was run over by an Edinburgh tram. It is not only the Soviets who can stage accidents!

The Montreal incident might well have been sabotage or just the primitive state of aircraft at the time. Sabotage was detected, however, but no blame apportioned. Once more, there was an attempt to cover up the entire incident, including confusion of the type of aircraft involved which ranged from a twin-engine aircraft to that of a four-engine plane. Furthermore, high Allied officials tried to convince Sikorski that nothing had happened. Sikorski was many things, including vain and foolish, but even he was not chump enough not to believe that someone had just tried to kill him. Nevertheless, Sikorski played down the entire incident and there appeared to have been a worldwide blackout regarding it. Nothing appeared in the press anywhere, not even in the local Montreal press.[14]

The problem was, and the Polish government-in-exile was well aware of it, that every time there had been a potentially life-ending air crash involving Sikorski, the Polish military had been involved or been perceived to have been involved. At first it might seem that it was the work of individual officers who opposed the politics of Sikorski but, by 1943, the Poles in the west had another champion, General Anders.

Without doubt Anders loathed Sikorski and his Soviet policy. Since 1936 Anders had been a man of the extreme right politically and 'had flirted after 1936 between the rightist wing of the *Sanacja* regime and the near fascists of the Polish Right'.[15] His experience of Soviet captivity had only hardened his views and here was Sikorski willing to compromise Polish territory in order to reach an understanding with the Soviet government. The exposure of Soviet atrocities at Katyń followed by the severing of diplomatic ties with the Polish government-in-exile by the Soviet government exasperated the problem. The fact that the Allies would not publicly support the Poles against the Soviets only furthered Polish anger.

In view of Sikorski's perceived failures, Anders indeed appeared to be an alternative leader. However, it should be remembered, as already narrated, that the former regime and its supporters had always plotted against Sikorski. This included the Polish underground army as well as Anders' Army after 1942. It is quite understandable why Anders and his veterans of the Soviet Gulags hated the Soviets, but it was quite another thing to work against one's commander-in-chief and prime minister. Simply, it is treason and should be held as such. This is not a light-hearted suggestion because, as late as the early 1960s, Anders was branded as an enemy of Sikorski in the British courts. This was the result of Anders going to law against a small Polish émigré publication which defined him as an enemy of Sikorski amongst other things. Anders won most of his case but the charge of being an enemy of Sikorski remained.[16]

Therefore, this brings the case of what happened in Gibraltar and how it shapes the legacy of Sikorski. Sikorski was braver than many might have understood. He was a so-so Polish politician and might well have disappeared into the obscurity of Polish history. He certainly has retreated into the mists of history as few, outside Poland, unless they have an interest in Polish history, will have heard of Sikorski. Some might be familiar with his current namesake, Radek Sikorski, but again that is unlikely.

Sikorski's bravery is found not in the fact that he accepted the post of Polish prime minister in exile or that he led troops at the front. His bravery lies with his Soviet policy. He did what is the hardest thing to do: attempt to ameliorate the situation of one's country by engaging with a sworn enemy and in the teeth of contempt from one's contemporaries. Sikorski knew from the very beginning of his relationship with the Soviet Union that he was treading a difficult path. The first treaty or understanding made, the Maisky-Sikorski Treaty, saw the resignation of four of his ministers. At the time Sikorski was trying to negotiate the release of hundreds of thousands of Poles, most of whom were being used as slave labour in Soviet prison camps. At this time, he had the support of General Anders but, as negotiations with Stalin and Molotov ran into the sand and the Soviet government realised that even though Churchill personally supported Sikorski, the overall message was that the Poles were not sacred cows.

Once it was realised by Anders that Sikorski was willing to negotiate territories in eastern Poland for lands to be acquired from Germany at war's end, he became exasperated. But, as already discussed, pre-war Anders was a man of the extreme right; the Soviet Union was anathema to him and his brutal treatment at the hands of the Soviets confirmed his views. Once Anders was appointed commander of the APW he was given a powerful weapon: an army, or at least a military force of his own. The location of APW allowed him to defy his commander-in-chief and plot against him. Within APW was a hardcore group of far-right militant officers, led by his own ADC, who actively conspired against Sikorski. Anders, if he had not been complicit in their activity, should have squashed them before they got going. However, he at least tacitly supported the activities against Sikorski even if he dressed it up as anti-Soviet rhetoric. The anti-Soviet speeches by Anders did not help Sikorski and were a hindrance to him.

The British government, the FO and the WO, were all aware of Anders' disloyalty as at times they worked with him, especially concerning the conduct of the war. Anders and his army were conveniently placed in the Middle East and ready to reinforce Allied troops in the Mediterranean theatre of operations.

Eventually, APW did land in Italy and took part in the Italian campaign, serving with great distinction. However, before that came to pass, the British government was becoming alarmed as reports were beginning to emerge that Anders and his men were becoming so antagonistic towards the Soviet Union that it could not be supported. That was the very reason why Sikorski was sent to face down Anders in the first place during June 1943. Sikorski was no coward and set out to beard Anders in his den. Without doubt, if Sikorski had tried to recall Anders to London, Anders would have made excuse after excuse as to why he could not attend his C-in-C and prime minister. Therefore, it became a case of Mohammed going to the proverbial mountain. But Anders just played Sikorski. He pretended that he would behave but it was Sikorski who was dead within days. Anders lived on in frustrated exile until May 1970.

Without Władysław Sikorski there would not have been a workable Polish government-in-exile after September 1939. Most of the post-1926 Polish administration was tainted with militarism and membership of the inter-war Polish military junta. Sikorski, being in a form of internal political exile, was also not guilty of presiding over the military defeat of Poland. However, he also held a senior military rank in the Polish Army and could compel Polish service personnel to obey him and his commands. French and, later, support from the British, namely Churchill, ensured that he was respected, but only up to a point. As a minor ally, the Poles were always on a need-to-know basis with the major Allied governments, something which dismayed Sikorski. The fact that in July 1940 the British looked the other way when Polish officers restored Sikorski to office at gunpoint made the relationship between the Polish government-in-exile and the British quite clear: Sikorski was the anointed one.

The fact that armed Polish officers successfully mounted what was quite clearly a coup in central London and got away with it illustrated totally the importance of Sikorski to the British authorities. At the time, it will be recalled, the British Isles faced invasion from Germany and the Poles, after the British, with Commonwealth and Imperial troops, had the second-largest contingent of men under arms. They were important to that extent. Polish pilots in the Battle of Britain were feted for their bravery and gallantry. Without Sikorski those things might not have happened or certainly not as easily.

As Sikorski was establishing himself in western Europe during 1939 and 1940, the situation in Poland was not so smooth. The underground army was nominally loyal to Sikorski and the government-in-exile, but it was also led by senior officers who had been loyal to the pre-war junta. Sikorski was to learn that the fledgling underground army was not necessarily loyal to him. It was not until 1942 that the Home Army, or *Armia Krajowa*, was established. This was indeed loyal to Sikorski and to his government. What can be gleaned is that Sikorski was not necessarily loved by Poles. He was a symbol of Polish resistance to its enemies which, until summer 1941, were both Germany and the Soviet Union.

While the Soviet Union was not an ally of the British, Sikorski was able to manage, albeit at a distance, a relationship with the Soviet Union as he sought to try to free imprisoned Poles from Soviet captivity even before the German invasion of the Soviet Union during June 1941. That ultimately facilitated the release of Polish prisoners held in the Soviet Union, but it was a reluctant and very slow release since the Soviets considered that they needed slaves while cannon fodder for the Red Army was needed. The question of Polish releases and recruitment was always a vexed question in negotiations between Sikorski and the Soviet government, normally represented by Stalin and Molotov. The questions of frontiers and population exchanges were always areas of contention. The Allies were also to realise that dealing with the Soviets was pretty much impossible since pledges were broken easily or were not there to be kept but just a method of moving a subject along to where Stalin wanted to be irrespective of what his interlocutors wanted. He didn't care.

Sikorski's greatest legacy was his desire to return Polish independence. He didn't live to see it. Neither did Anders. Few senior Poles of the wartime generation did. Maczek and Edward Raczyński, by living to be over 100 years of age, did live to see Polish independence being returned in 1989. Both also lived to see the first democratically-elected Polish president, Lech Wałęsa, elected to that office in 1990. It is not clear what sort of Poland Sikorski really wanted to head post-war. He was determined to return at the head of the Polish Army but was he willing to see it as a democracy?

It might have been that, like his French contemporary, General Charles de Gaulle, he might have returned with an armed force liberating native soil with Polish troops just as de Gaulle had sent Leclerc's armoured division to liberate Paris in August 1944 following an uprising there; the French armour was supported by 4th American Infantry Division. The Poles did indeed rise in Warsaw during the time of the Paris uprising, but the nearest ally was the Red Army which had no interest in allowing the Polish uprising to succeed and so the AK was destroyed. It is a matter of debate if Sikorski would have allowed such a poorly prepared operation to have gone ahead in the first place. Anders certainly condemned it.

Sikorski was constantly embattled somewhere in his final years. He wanted to establish a cadre force to provide a basis for a post-war Polish Army as he was convinced that eventually Poland would have to wrestle control of that country from the Soviets or go to war against the Soviets sometime in the near future. One only has to consider the war between Russia and Ukraine to understand what Sikorski was talking about. It should also be remembered that Sikorski was farsighted in his writings about the future of war and his expectations for the post-war future of Poland.

An army to defend itself from Soviet aggression was perfectly sensible from a Polish perspective but it got in the way of the overall campaign against Germany. The Allies and the Soviet Union were determined to destroy Nazi Germany. The British and Americans desired to liberate occupied countries. The Soviets merely wanted to oust the Germans and replace them with a Soviet system of rule. The fate of Poland was no different: liberated and annexed at the same time between 1944 and 1945. Sikorski foresaw all of this but thought that he could deal with it at the end of the war as he was determined that no important decisions could be made about Poland until peace was made. Anders certainly understood this but knew that there was little that could be done unless the USA became involved. The USA was certainly not going to stay in Europe any longer than was necessary. Churchill also understood that the Soviets needed to be dealt with and tried to put into action Operation Unthinkable. His chiefs of staff briefed against this plan for an attack against the Soviet Union after the defeat of Germany.[17] Churchill lost office in July 1945 following a general election during that month. It is interesting to note that the enemy was clearly becoming the Soviet Union as many Poles had feared.

And that is the very reason why Sikorski died if we want to consider sabotage on his final journey. Polish officers, especially those in the Middle East, despised his Soviet policy as he tried to placate both Soviets and Allies while attempting to preserve Polish interests. He could not please everyone or, indeed, anyone. Churchill still championed him in negotiations with Stalin. The Soviet dictator didn't care about Sikorski as he was aware that eventually the Red Army would advance westwards and annex Poland on the way to Germany. But Polish officers were totally vexed with Sikorski and probably had the motive to assassinate him. Even so, they lacked the opportunity to do so in Gibraltar as far as one knows.

The life and death of Sikorski remains obscure. His death is still a mystery, and it was probably just an aircraft malfunction, but people don't like their heroes dying mundane deaths. It's undignified! His legacy is hard to judge. I recall that when his remains were flown from his grave in the UK to a final resting place in Poland, Poles of my acquaintance wanted to know just who was paying for this. Not the most fitting tribute to a Polish hero. Especially to one who paid the butcher's bill of war with his life as did millions of other Poles during the Second World War. The slaughter of Poles between 1939 and 1948 as they tried to defend their homelands, their families and culture often goes unnoticed. It is yet another forgotten holocaust. There will be others.

Notes

Introduction

1. Meiklejohn Terry, *Poland's Place in Europe. General Sikorski and the Origin of the Oder-Neisse Line, 1939–1943*, Princeton, Princeton University Press, 1983, pp.xi-xii.

Chapter 1

1. Terlecki, *General Sikorski*, Kraków, Wydawnictwo Kraków, 1981, p.16.
2. Garlicki, 'Relations between Sikorski and Piłsudski 1907–28' in *Sikorski: Soldier and Statesman. A Collection of Essays*, (ed.) Keith Sword, London, Orbis, 1990, pp.29–42.
3. Ibid, p.29.
4. Ibid. pp.29–30.
5. Rzepecki, 'O. Władysławie Sikorskim w Legionach' *Wojskowy Przegląd Historyczny*, 1965, p.260.
6. Wapiński, 'Sikorski's military and political career 1908–18, p.22. In *Sikorski: Soldier and Statesman. A Collection of Essays*, (ed.) Keith Sword, London, Orbis, 1990, pp.15–28.
7. Ibid, p.24.
8. *Wiadomości Polskie*, No. 97, 8 October 1916, quoted in Wapiński, p.25.
9. Rzepecki, 'O. Władysławie Sikorskim w Legionach' *Wojskowy Przegląd Historyczny*, 1966, p.59, quoted in Wapiński, p.26.
10. Wapiński, pp.26–7.
11. Garlicki, p.39.

Chapter 2

1. Garlicki, p.39.
2. Peplonski, *Wywiad w Wojnie Polsko-Bolszewickiej, 1919–1920,* Warsaw, Bellona, 1999, p.222. Stanisław Maczek, *Od Podwody do Czołga: Wspomnienia Wojenne, 1918–1945*, Edinburgh, Tomar, 1961, p.37.
3. *General Władysław Anders: Soldier and Leader of the Free Poles in Exile*, (eds) Joanna Pylatt, Jan Ciechanowski and Andrzej Suchcitz, Polish University Abroad, 2008, Papers from the Conference Organised by the University Abroad, 15–16 June 2007, pp.11–12.
4. UK National Archives, Kew, London (NA Kew), WO 106/6238, Report on the Franco-British Military Mission to Poland, July–August 1920, Major General Sir Percy Radcliffe KCMG CB DSO, Director of Military Operations, 1 September 1920.
5. Suchcitz, *General Władysław Anders*, pp.11–12.
6. NA Kew, WO 106/6238, 1 September 1920.
7. Ibid.
8. Beevor, *Russia. Revolution and Civil War 1917–1921*, London, Weidenfeld & Nicolson, 2022, p.447.
9. NA Kew, CAB 1/29/18, Mission to Poland, July 1920. Copies of Letters from Sir M.P.A. Hankey to the Prime Minister and Others, Hankey to Lloyd George, 28 July 1920.

10. Ibid., 26 July 1920.
11. Ibid.
12. NA Kew, CAB 1/29/18, Hankey to Lloyd George, 22 July 1920.
13. Wyszczelski, *Polska Myśl Wojskowa 1914–1939*, Warsaw, MON, 1988, pp.58, 190–1.

Chapter 3

1. McCauley, *The Soviet Union 1917–1991*, London, Longman, 1994, p.30.
2. Plokhy, *The Gates of Europe. A History of Ukraine*, London, Allen Lane, 2015, pp.239–41.
3. Korbonski, 'Civil-Military Relations in Interwar Poland' in *Poland Between the Wars: 1918–1939. A Collection of Papers and Discussions from the Conference 'Poland between the Wars 1918–1939' held in Bloomington, Indiana, February 21–23 1985*, (ed.) Timothy Wiles, Bloomington, Indiana University Polish Studies Center, 1989, pp.39–54.
4. Garlicki, *Piłsudski 1867–1935*, edited and translated by John Coutouvidis, Aldershot, Scolar Press, 1995, p.74.
5. Wiatr, *The Soldier and the Nation. The Role of the Military in Polish Politics, 1918–1985*, Boulder, Westview, 1988, p.26.
6. Biskupski, 'The Military Elite of the Polish Second Republic, 1918–1945: A Historiographical Review', *War & Society*, 14 (1996) 49–86.
7. Ibid.
8. Korbonski, 'Civil-Military Relations in Interwar Poland' in Wiles (ed.) pp.39–54.
9. Michta, *Red Eagle, The Army in Polish Politics, 1944–1988*, Stanford, Hoover Press, 1990, p.27.
10. Polonsky, *Politics in Independent Poland, 1921–1939*, Oxford, Clarendon Press, 1972, p.130.
11. Korbonski, p.43.
12. Michta, p.27.
13. Korbonski, p.43.
14. Jędrzejewicz, *Piłsudski: A Life for Poland*, New York, Hippocrene, 1982, p.235.
15. Garlicki, 'Relations between Sikorski and Piłsudski, 1907–28' in Sword (ed.) pp.24–42.
16. Ibid. p.39.
17. de Wiart, *Happy Odyssey: The Memoirs of Lt-Gen. Sir Adrian Carton de Wiart*, London, Jonathan Cape, 1950, p.96.
18. Wiatr, p.26.
19. Michta, p.26.
20. Michta, *Red Eagle: The Army in Polish Politics, 1944–1988*, Stanford, Hoover Press, 1990, p.29.
21. Poliakov, 'Piłsudski' *The Slavic Review*, 14 (1935–1936) pp.44–52.
22. Michta, *The Soldier-Citizen*, p.27.
23. Wiatr, p.63.
24. Rothschild, *Piłsudski's Coup d'état*, New York, Columbia University Press, 1966, p.28.
25. Rothschild, *East-Central Europe Between the Two World Wars*, Seattle, University of Washington, 1990, 6th edition, p.58.
26. de Gaulle, *War Memoirs. Volume One. The Call to Honour, 1940–1942*, Translated by Jonathan Griffin, London, St James Place, 1955, p.57.
27. Romeyko, *Przed i po maju*, Warsaw, MON, 1967, p.99.
28. Jędrzejewicz, p.96.
29. French 'The Mechanization of the British Cavalry between the World Wars' *War in History*, 2003, pp.296–320.

30. Sikorski, *Modern Warfare*, New York, Roy Publishers, 1943, With a note by General George C. Marshall, Chief of Staff of the US Army, p.177.
31. Antony Polonsky, 'Sikorski as opposition politician 1928–39' in Sword (ed.) pp.43–74.
32. Ibid. p.47.
33. Ibid. pp.49–50.
34. Ascherson, *The Struggles for Poland*, London, Michael Joseph, 1987, p.75. Romeyko, pp.334–5.
35. Polonsky, p.58.
36. Wynot, *Polish Politics in Transition: The Camp for National Unity and the Struggle for Power, 1936–39*, Athens, Georgia, University of Georgia Press, 1974, p.40.
37. Ascherson, p.83.
38. Wynot, pp.140–1, 162.
39. Ascherson, p.83.
40. Hugh Dalton, *The Fateful Years: Memoirs 1931–1945*, London, Frederick Muller, 1957, p.271.
41. Suchcitz, *A Brief Survey of Military Planning and Preparations for the Defence of Poland, October 1938-August 1939*, MA dissertation, University of London, 1981, p.2.
42. Ibid. pp.3–4.
43. Sikorski, 'Poland's Defences', *The Slavic Review* (17) 1938–1939, pp.343–355.
44. Karski, *The Great Powers & Poland, 1919–1945. From Versailles to Yalta*, Lanham, University of America Press, 1985, p.234.
45. Kośminder, *Planowanie Wojenne w Polsce w Latach 1921–1926*, Toruń, Adam Marszałek, 2001, pp.112–14. See also Tomasz Kośminder, 'Dorobek Sztabu Generałnego w Zakresie planowanie operacyjmego mobilizacji w latach 1921–1928' in Tadeusz Panecki, Franciszek Puchała, Jan Szostak (eds) *Sztab Generałny (Głowny) Wojska Polskiego, 1918–2003*, Warsaw, Bellona, pp.81–93.
46. Polonsky, p.492.
47. Ascherson, pp.75–6.
48. Deszczyński, *Ostantnio Egzamin. Wojsko Polskie Wobec Czechosłowachiego, 1938–1939*, Warsaw, Neriton, 2003, p.424.
49. Polonsky, p.66.
50. Ibid. p.67.
51. Bethell, *Gomułka. His Poland and his Communism*. London, Penguin, 1972, p.32.

Chapter 4

1. NA Kew, Prime Ministers' Office, PREM 1/331A, Roseway to Rucker, August 1939.
2. Karski, *Story of a Secret State: My Report to the World*, London, Penguin, 2011, pp.98–9. Originally published in USA by Houghton Mifflin, 1944.
3. Ibid. pp.132–3.
4. Winstone, *The Dark Heart of Hitler's Europe. Nazi Rule in Poland under the General Government*, London, I.B. Tauris, 2015, pp.27–8.
5. PISM, PRM 12/17, 'The Whitehall Letter', 1 March 1940.
6. Article 24 of the Constitution of 23 April 1935 provided that during wartime the President had to designate his successor by a special act that was to be published in *Monitor Polski*, the official journal of the Polish government, should the presidency become vacant before the conclusion of peace. The successor was to remain in office for three months before any such peace treaty. The decree nominating the new president was promulgated in *Monitor Polski* on 29 September 1939 and published in Paris.

F.E. Oppenheimer, 'Governments and Authorities in Exile' *The American Journal of International Law*, 36 (1942) pp.568–95,

7. NA Kew, FO 371/22949/C15019/62, 'Setting up of Polish and Czech Governments', 25 September 1939.
8. Dubicki & Stanisław Jan Rostworowski, *Sanatorzy Kontra Sikorszczycz Czyli Walka o Władze na Uchódzstwie w Rumanii 1939–1940*, Warsaw, Adiutor, 1995, p.5.
9. Duraczynski, *Rząd Polski na Uchódzstwie 1939–1945*, Warsaw, Książka i Wiedza, 1993, pp.15–21.
10. NA Kew, CAB 85 Allied Forces (Official) Committee, CAB 85/1 MR (39) Meeting (Mtg) Anglo-French Liaison, 16 September 1939.
11. Terlecki, p.84. See FN 85.
12. NA Kew, CAB 65, War Cabinet Meetings, CAB 65/29 (39) Minute 10, 26 September 1939.
13. Ibid.
14. NA Kew, FO 371/23152C/15147, Phipps to Halifax, 26 September 1939.
15. NA Kew, CAB 65/29 (39) Minute 10, 27 September 1939.
16. Raczyński, *In Allied London*, London, Weidenfeld & Nicolson, 1962, pp.42–4.
17. Beauvois, *Les Relations Franco-Polonaises Pendant Le 'Drole de Guerre'*, Paris, L'Harmattan, 1989, p.73.
18. Duraczynski, p.35.
19. Suchcitz, *A Brief History of the Military Planning*, pp.3–4.
20. Beauvois, pp.66–7.
21. Meiklejohn Terry, p.175.
22. Ibid.
23. Prażmowska, *Britain and Poland, 1939–1943: The Betrayed Ally*, Cambridge, Cambridge University Press, 1995, p.11.
24. Terlecki, *Generał Ostatniej Legendy. Rzecz O Gen. Władysławie Sikorskim*, Chicago, Bookstore & Publishers Co., 1976, p.87.
25. Ibid, p.84.
26. Ibid.
27. Prażmowska, p. 11. Beauvois, p.73.
28. *The Manchester Guardian*, 21 February 1939.
29. PISM (Polish Institute and Sikorski Museum, Kensington, London) PRM, Prime Ministers' Office (Polish), PRM 14B/40, '*Notatka Słuzbowa ppłk. J. Kornaus, Bucharest*', March 1940.
30. NA Kew, FO 371/23151C/14615/456, Kennard to Halifax, 22 September 1939.
31. NA Kew, FO 371/23152C/15148/8526/55, Norton to Sargent, 27 September 1939.
32. Iwańska, *Exiled Governments, Spanish and Polish. As Essay in Political Sociology*, Cambridge, Mass, Schenkman Inc, 1981, pp.30–1.
33. *Papers and Memoirs of Juliusz Łukasiewicz, Ambassador of Poland. Diplomat in Paris, 1936–1939* (ed.) Jędrzjewicz, New York, Columbia University, 1970, p.358.
34. Ibid. pp.357–9.
35. Terlecki, p.86.
36. Ibid, p.87.
37. Ibid. pp.87–8.
38. Ibid. p.88.
39. Ibid.
40. Raczyński, p.39.

41. Tendyra, *General Sikorski and the Polish Government-in-Exile, 1939–1943: A Study of Polish Internal Émigré Politics in Wartime*, Ph. D thesis, The London School of Economics and Political Science, 2000, pp.35–6.
42. Terlecki, p.89.
43. Ibid. p.37.
44. Joanna K.M. Hanson, *The Civilian Population and the Warsaw Uprising of 1944*, Cambridge, CUP, 1982, p.47.
45. Meiklejohn Terry, p.183.
46. PISM, PRM 3/8a, Record of Conversation Between General Sikorski and Lord Halifax, 14 November 1939.
47. Ibid.
48. PISM, PRM 3/10, Prime Minister's Conversation with General Sikorski, 16 November 1939.
49. NA Kew, FO 371/23152/C15314/8525/35, telegram from Sir R. Hoare (Bucharest) to FO, 29 September 1939.
50. NA Kew, FO 371/23152/C15358/8526/55, telegram from Sir Eric Phipps (Paris) to FO, 1 October 1939.
51. NA Kew, FO 371/23152/C15796/8526/55, 'Polish Government in Paris', 28 September 1939.
52. Stachura, 'Władysław Sikorski, Soldier, Politician, Statesman, 1881–1943', *Scottish Slavonic Review*, 21 (1993) pp.71–94.
53. Polonsky (Sword) pp.43–74.
54. Korpolska, *Władysław Eugeniusz Sikorski: Biografia Polityczna*, Wrocław, Zakład Narodowy im. Ossolińskich Wydawnictwo, 1981, p.155.
55. NA Kew, FO 371/23152/C16383/8526/55 'Reaction of Poles in Romania to the new Polish Government', 3 October 1939.
56. PISM, PRM 24/1, 23 December 1939.
57. Karski, p.410.
58. NA Kew, FO 371/24474/C1667/252/55, Sir Howard Kennard (Angers) to Strang, 26 January 1940.
59. PISM, PRM 13/2, 20 January 1940; PRM 13/7, 24 April 1940.
60. *Polski Siły Zbrojne w Drugiej Wojnie Światowej* (Henceforth *PSZ*) Vol. 2, part 1, London, Instytut Historyczny im. gen. Sikorskiego, 1959, pp.153–6; 177–91; 203–8, Adam Zamoyski, *The Forgotten Few: The Polish Airforce in the Second World War*, London, J. Murray, 1995, pp.44–77.
61. Joseph Rothschild, *East Central Europe Between the Two World Wars*, Seattle, University of Washington Press, 1974, pp.190–192.
62. PISM, KOL 1. Journal of the Activities of the Supreme Commander (Polish) KOL 1/2, 28 September 1939.
63. PISM, A.48 Civil Chancellery of the President of the Polish Republic, A.48 1/N/24-30, 23 October 1939; A.48 1/N/33-36, 7 November 1939, A.48 1/N/44, 7 November 1939.
64. Karasiewicz-Tokarzewski, 'Jak powstała Armia Krajowa' *Zeszyty Historyczne* 6, 1964, pp.17–44.
65. Karski, *Polish Fortnightly Review*, 15 December 1943.
66. PISM, PRM 24/7, 30 September 1939.
67. PISM, PRM 12/1, Situation in Poland. Sent from Warsaw, December 1939.
68. Ibid.

69. Andreski, *Military Organisations and Society*, London, Routledge & Kegan Paul, 2nd Edition, 1968, p.106.
70. McGilvray, *Red Trojan Horse. The Berling Army and the Soviet Annexation of Poland, 1943–45*, Warwick, Helion, 2019, pp.54–74.
71. Andrzej Friszke, 'Rząd na Obczyznie Wobec Panstwa Podziemnego w Kraju' in Z. Blazynski, *Materiały Polskiego Niepodległośćiowego* Vol. 1. London, Polskie Towarzystwo Naukowe na Obczyznie, 1994, pp.562–623.
72. Buczek, 'Tragedia Ryszarda Świętochiego', *Zeszyty Historczne* 26 (1973) pp.150–69.
73. Gross, *Polish Society Under German Occupation. The Generalgouvernment, 1939–1944*, Princeton, Princeton University, 1979, pp.273–4.
74. Tendyra, p.60.
75. Winstone, pp.211–25.
76. Szudek, pp.75–97.
77. Martin S. Alexander, *The Republic in Danger. General Maurice Gamelin and the Politics of French Defence, 1933–1940*, Cambridge, Cambridge University Press, 1992, p.315.
78. Jeffery A. Gunsburg, *Divided and Conquered. The French High Command and the Defeat of the West, 1940*, London, Greenswood, 1979, pp.92–3.
79. Alexander, pp.344–8.
80. Thomas, *The Spanish Civil War*, Middlesex, Penguin, 1979 third edition, originally published 1961, pp.944–5.
81. Szudek, p.93.
82. Terlicki, *Generał Sikorski*, Vol. 1, Kraków, Wydawnictwo Literackie, 1981, pp.234–5.
83. Mikołajczyk, p.9.
84. Szudek, p.95.
85. Coutouvidis, 'Sikorski's thirty-day crisis, 19 June–19 July 1940' in Sword (ed.) *Sikorski*, pp.114–37.
86. Lunkiewicz, 'Naczelne Władze Polskich Zbrojnych na Obczynie w latach 1939–1945' *Bellona*, II, 1957, pp.42–55.
87. Kukiel, *Generał Sikorski, Żołnierz i Mąż Wałczącej*, London, Polska Fundacja Kulturalna, 1995, 3rd Reprint, pp.112–14.
88. PISM, KOL 1/3, Part 1, 11 October 1939; KOL 1/6, Part 1, 'Rozkaz Oficerski Tajny' Nr. 6, 22 January 1940; KOL 1/3, Part 1, 'Dodowodej Wojsk Wobozie' 9 October 1939; PRM 6, Unnumbered Section III, Sikorski to Sławoj-Składkowski & Kasprzycki.
89. PISM, KOL 1/11/3, Letter from Air Ministry to Air Force Attaché, 17 June 1940.
90. PISM, A.5., Minutes of the Meetings of the Polish National Defence Council, A.5 1/21a, 30 August 1940.
91. PISM, KOL 1/11, Part 2, Z. Bohusz-Szyszko, 16 June 1940.
92. Tendyra, p.89.
93. Raczyński, p.54.
94. Terlecki, *Generał Ostatniej Legendy. Rzecz O Gen. Władysławie Sikorskim*, Chicago, Polonia, 1976, p.107.
95. Ibid. p.108.
96. Ibid.
97. Ibid, p.109.
98. Ibid, pp.109–10.
99. Ibid. p.111.
100. Ibid.
101. Ibid, p.112.

102. Ibid. p.113.
103. Ibid. p.114.
104. Pomian, *Józef Retinger. Życie i pamiętniki "szarej eminencju"*, Warsaw, Pelikan, 1990, p.113.
105. Ibid, pp.1110–14.
106. *King's Counsellor. Abdication and War. The Diaries of Sir Allen Lascelles*, edited by Duff Hart-Davis, London, Phoenix, 2007, diary entry 20 August 1942, p.48. Hereafter referred to as *Lascelles*.
107. Ibid. p.114.
108. Pomian, pp.114–15.
109. Ibid, p.115.
110. PISM, PRM 24/24, *Nastroje Ogólne Społeczeństwo*, 1940.
111. PISM, PRM 25/34, 18 September 1940.
112. PISM, PRM 26/5, Dąb-Biernacki to Sikorski, 13 July 1940.

Chapter 5

1. PISM, KOL 1/11/15, 'Aide Memoir in relation to the formation of a Polish Army in the USSR', 19 June 1940. TNA, PREM 3/395/1, Sikorski to Cripps, June 1940.
2. Macksey, *The Partisans of Europe in World War II*, London, Hart-Davies, MacGibbon, 1975, p.38.
3. PISM, KOL 1/11, Part 1, Sikorski to Klimkowski, 30 June 1940; KOL 1/12, Part 1, Sikorski to Lange, 25 July 1940.
4. PISM, A.5 1/16, 18 July 1940.
5. Tendyra, pp.88–90, 103.
6. PISM, PRM 26/2, Paszkiewicz to Sikorski, 3 July 1940; PRM 37a/1, Kukiel to Sikorski, 19 July 1940.
7. PISM, PRM 26/7, 16 July 1940.
8. PISM, PRM KOL 1/11, Part One, 22 June 1940.
9. PISM, A.48. 1/0/2, 24 June 1940.
10. PISM, PRM-K. 102, Minutes of the Meetings of the Council of Ministers, PRM-K. 102/27e, 11 July 1940; PRM 37b/14, 12 July 1940; A.48.2.114A/9, 12 July 1940; PRM 37b/11, 11 July 1940.
11. PISM, PRM 26, 'Open Letter from Dąb-Biernacki to Sikorski, 13 July 1940.
12. PISM, PRM-K.102/16, 1 February 1940; KOL 1/10, Part One, 10 May 1940.
13. PISM, PRM-K. 102/27f, 12 July 1940; PRM 37b/11, 13 July 1940; PRM 37b/15, 14 July 1940.
14. Tendyra, p.102.
15. Kazimierz Sosnkowski, *Materiały Historyczne*, London, Gryf, 1966, pp.5–8.
16. PISM, PRM 37c/10, 18 July 1940.
17. PISM, PRM 25/22, Budapest, 25 July 1940.
18. PISM, PRM 25/22, Budapest, 25 July 1940.
19. PISM, PRM 12/17, 1 March 1940.
20. PISM, PRM 55/1, Activities of General Sikorski and the Polish Government from the Fall of France, 1941. This document was published by the Polish Foreign Ministry, dated 17 June 1940.
21. PISM, PRM 55/1, 19 June 1940.
22. NA Kew, FO 371/24474/C8090/252/55, 30 July 1940.
23. NA Kew, FO 371/24474/C7639/252/55, 20 July 1940.
24. NA Kew, FO 371/24474/C7639252/55, Kennard to Savery, 31 July 1940.

25. *Great Britain. Foreign Office Weekly Intelligence Summaries* (Hereafter, *Weekly Intelligence*) Introduction, Clifton Child, New York, Kraus, 1983, *Weekly Intelligence*, Vol. 2, July-December 1940, nos.39–64, no.42, 23 July 1940, pp.4–5.
26. NA Kew, CAB 66, War Cabinet Memoranda, CAB 66/36 WP (43) 175, 26 April 1943.
27. NA Kew, FO 800, Halifax Papers, FO 800/321, Eden to Halifax, 9 October 1940.
28. NA Kew, FO 371/24474/C7639/1252/55, Report by F.K. Robert, 30 July 1940.
29. NA Kew, FO 371/24474/C101115/252/55, Savery, British Embassy to Poland, 15 September 1940.
30. Ibid.
31. NA Kew, FO 371/24474/C8736/252/55, Savery to Roberts, 1 October 1940, minute by F.K. Roberts, 25 October 1940.
32. PISM, PRM 39a/2, Sikorski to Eden, 16 January 1941.
33. PISM, PRM 39a/7, Sir Alexander Cadogan to Sikorski, 17 February 1941.
34. *The Maisky Diaries. Red Ambassador to the Court of St James's, 1932–1943*, edited by Gabriel Gorodetsky, translated by Tatiana Sorokina & Oliver Ready, New Haven and London, Yale University Press, 2015, (hereafter referred to as *Maisky*) p.289, diary entry, 28 June 1940.
35. Ibid.
36. Catherine Epstein, *Model Nazi: Arthur Greiser And The Occupation Of Western Poland*, Oxford, Oxford University Press, 2010, pp.190–1.
37. Kacewicz, *Great Britain, the Soviet Union and the Polish Government-in-Exile (1939–1945)*, The Hague, Nijhoff, 1979, p.85. *Documents on Polish-Soviet Relations, 1939–1945, Volume 1, 1939–1943*, (Hereafter referred to as *DPSR1*), London, Heinemann, 1961, p.95.
38. Meiklejohn Terry, p.6.
39. Ibid.

Chapter 6

1. Peszke, 'The Polish Armed Forces in Exile, Part 1, September 1939-July 1941', *The Polish Review*, 26 (1987) pp.67–113.
2. PISM, PRM 26/5, Open Letter to Sikorski from Dąb-Biernacki, 13 July 1940.
3. PISM, PRM 37c/18, 7 December 1940; PRM 37c/5, undated, *Rozkaz do Wojska Nr. Sąd Połowy nr. 3* (Orders for Military Field Court no. 3), Tendyra, p.108.
4. PISM, KOL 1/11, Sikorski to Klimecki, 30 June 1940; KOL 1/12, Part 1, Sikorski to Langer, 25 July 1940.
5. PISM, A.5, Minutes of the Meetings of the Polish National Council, A.5. A 1/15a, Minutes by Jóźwiak, Żeligowski and Jaworski, 7 July 1940.
6. PISM, PRM 26/7, Stefczyk to Sikorski, 16 July 1940.
7. PISM, KOL 1/12, Part 1, Sikorski to Burhardt-Bukacki, 31 July 1940; PRM 37a/3, 2 August 1940; PRM 37a/5, 5 August 1940.
8. NA Kew, FO 371/26733/C6528, Savery to Roberts, 7 July 1940.
9. NA Kew, FO 371/2448/C5143, Butler to Pritt, 27 July 1940.
10. PISM, KOL 1/13, Part One, *Odprawa*, 30 August 1940; PRM 48/4, 26 October 1940.
11. PISM, PRM 26/35, 11 December 1940.
12. Ibid.
13. Mitkiewicz, *Z Generałem Sikorski na Obczynie*, Paris, Kultury, 1968, pp.98–9.
14. NA Kew, FO 371/24474/C7639, Enclosure C, Savery, 20 July 1940.

15. NA Kew, FO 800/321, Halifax to Eden, 11 October 1940; FO 800/321, Cazalet to Halifax, 24 October 1940.
16. Peszke, pp.26, 71, 74–75.
17. NA Kew, CAB 85, Allied Forces (Official) Committee, CAB 85/19 AFO (40) 1st Meeting (mtg) Allied Forces (Official) Sub-committee, Minute 2, 29 July 1940.
18. Peszke, p.109.
19. Terlecki, p.127.
20. NA Kew, CAB 83 Military Co-ordination Committee, CAB 83/2 WM (39) 84th Conclusion, Minute 6, 14 November 1939.
21. NA Kew, CAB 65/2 (39) Minute 5, 16 November 1940.
22. NA Kew, CAB 85/3 MR (40) 59 mtg, Allied Military Committee, 7 March 1940; CAB 85/4 MR (40) 73 mtg, Allied Military Committee, 29 March 1940.
23. NA Kew, CAB 85/4, MR (40) 106 mtg, Allied Military Committee, 6 May 1940.
24. NA Kew, CAB 85/11, FBC (J) (40) 45, 13 May 1940; CAB 85/11, FBC (J) 46, 14 May 1940.
25. NA Kew, PREM 3, Prime Ministers' Office, PREM 3/351/3, 14 November 1940.
26. Tendyra, p.114.
27. PISM, PRM 20/8, 7 August 1940.
28. PISM, PRM 20/7, 7 August 1940.
29. Kacewicz, pp.65–6. PISM, PRM 20/35, Raczyński to Sikorski, November 1940.
30. PISM, PRM 20/17, Eden to Sikorski, 17 September 1940.
31. PISM, PRM 20/23, Sikorski to Churchill, 15 October 1940.
32. PISM, PRM 25/19, Sosnkowski to Kot, 12 June 1940.
33. PISM, PRM 25/13, '*Nota dla Premierem i Naczełego Wodza*' 24 May 1940.
34. Archiwum AKT Nowych (Warsaw) AAN, Sygnal 135, *Ministerstwa Informacji i Dokumentacji Rząd/Emigracyjnego/RP w Londynie*, AAN 135/27, Stefan Werner, Istanbul to Professor Stanisław Kot, 11 November 1943.
35. NA Kew, PREM 3/296/1, 16 August 1940.
36. PISM, PRM 39a/5, Churchill to Sikorski, 24 January 1941.
37. NA Kew, FO 371/26735/C1868, Minutes by Makins & Strang, 9 & 21 January 1941; Eden to Churchill, 13 January 1941; Halifax to Eden, 25 February 1941.
38. Churchill Papers, Churchill College, University of Cambridge, CHAR 20/21B/124, Churchill to Sikorski, 6 March 1941.
39. PISM, PRM 49, April 1941.
40. *Documents on Canadian External Relations 1939–1941, Vol. 7, Part One* (hereafter referred to as *DCER*) Ottawa, Queen's Printer, 1974, pp.974–5.
41. Ibid. pp.176–7.
42. John Coutouvidis, *The Formation of the Polish Government-in-Exile and its Relationship with Great Britain, 1939–1941*, Ph. D thesis, Keele University, pp.158, 228.
43. NA Kew, CAB 66/30 WP (42) 499, 31 October 1942.
44. NA Kew, FO 371/26734/C12847/395/55, Dormer to Eden, 18 November 1941.
45. PISM, PRM 20/42, PAT, Helsinki, December 1940.

Chapter 7

1. Terlecki, pp.141–2.
2. PISM, PRM 22/3, T. Szumowski, *c.*1939.
3. PISM, PREM 22, Letter to Sikorski, Lisbon, 11 November 1940.
4. PISM, PRM 54/4/5, Eastern Europe's Future, 21 February 1941.

5. Ibid.
6. Ibid.
7. PISM, PRM 63 tII/38, Władysław Sikorski, *Bellona* 'The Higher Military School and its Aims', (Translation) February 1941.
8. Radek Sikorski, interview with author, June 1999.
9. PISM, PREM 42/1/1, 23 June 1941.
10. *Maisky*, pp.365–369, diary entry, 22 June 1941.
11. Ibid.
12. Ibid, p.377, diary entry, 30 July 1941.
13. Ibid.
14. De Gaulle, pp.250–1.
15. NA Kew, FO 371/24474/C7639/252/55, Roberts, 19 July 1940.
16. Siebel-Achenbach, *Lower Silesia from Nazi Germany to Communist Poland, 1942–49*, London, Macmillan, 1994, p.33.
17. PISM, PREM 63, Sikorski, Speech, 15 January 1941.
18. Tendyra, p.145. 'Federacja Zachodnio-Słowiańska' in *Biuletyn-Zachodno-Słowiański*, 2 1940, pp.3–11, No author identified.
19. PISM, PRM 35c/15, 24 August 1940; PRM-K. 102/28c, 24 August 1940.
20. *Armia Krajowa w Dokumentach, 1939–1945, Volume 1* (hereafter referred to as *AK1*), London, Studium Polski Podziemnej, 1970, pp.88–9, 267, 272, 297–9.
21. PISM, PRM-K. 102/21a, 2 December 1940.
22. Hinsley, *British Intelligence in the Second World War. Its Influence on Strategy and Operations.* Volume 1, London, HMSO, 1979, pp.457–8.
23. NA Kew, PREM 3/403/7, T. 18, Telegram from Churchill to Cripps, 3 April 1941.
24. NA Kew, PREM 3/351/17, 8 June 1941; PREM 3/395/16, Churchill to Sikorski, 4 June 1941; PREM 3/395/46, Sikorski to Churchill, 25 May 1941; PREM 3/395/16, Churchill to General Ismay, 3 June 1941.
25. PISM, PRM 60a/4, 19 June 1941; PRM 39b/71, Note by General Sikorski in conversation with Sir Stafford Cripps, 18 June 1941.
26. PISM, PRM 60A/4, Sikorski to Raczkiewicz, 19 June 1941.
27. Ibid.
28. PISM, PRM 63/67, An address delivered by General Sikorski at a luncheon organised by the National Defence Public Interests Committee, 2 July 1941.
29. Ibid.
30. PISM, PRM 60A/4, Sikorski to Raczkiewicz, 19 June 1941.
31. PISM, PRM 61/13, Adam Romer, 1 March 1941.
32. Ibid.
33. Tendyra, p.146.
34. *Cadogan*, p.390, diary entry, 23 June 1940.
35. Tendyra, p.147.
36. *Documents on Polish Soviet Relations 1939–1943 Vol. 1*, London, Heinemann, 1961 (hereafter referred to as *DPSR1*) p. 109.
37. NA Kew, FO 371/26756/C8306, Dormer to Eden, 22 July 1941.
38. NA Kew, FO 371/26755/C7016, Minute by Makins, 1 July 1941.
39. NA Kew, FO 371/26755/C7016, 24 June 1941.
40. Maisky, *Memoirs of a Soviet Ambassador. The War, 1939–43*, translated by Andrew Rothstein, London, Hutchinson, 1967, pp.170–5.
41. Bethell, p.39.

42. *DSPR1*, p.116.
43. NA Kew, FO 371/26758/C8803, Dormer to Sikorski, 5 August 1941.
44. NA Kew, FO 371/26755/C7422, C7423, 4 July 1941, *DSPR1*, pp.114–16.
45. Kacewicz, pp.94–5.
46. PISM, PRM-K.102/37a, 5 July 1941.
47. Bethell, p.41.
48. *DPSR1*, pp.128–32.
49. Tendyra, p.157.
50. PISM, PRM 41/3/2, 4 July 1941.
51. PISM, PRM 41/2/11, Kot to Wyszyński, 10 October 1941.
52. Tendyra, pp.138–9.
53. PISM, PRM-K.102/37c, 21 July 1941.
54. PISM, KOL 1/24, I, Sikorski to Sosnkowski; Sosnkowski to Sikorski, 20 July 1941.
55. NA Kew, KV Intelligence Reports, KV2/516, (General Wladyslaw Sikorski – General Kazimierz Sosnkowski) Captain Derbyshire to Major Alley, 22 April 1941.
56. Harvey (ed.) *The War Diaries of Oliver Hardy*, London, Collins, 1978, p.23.
57. NA Kew, CAB 65/33 74 (41) 2, 24 July 1941.
58. PISM, PREM 43/11/3, *Daily Sketch*, 23 July 1941.
59. Kot, *Listy z Rosji do Gen. Sikorskiego*, London, Jutro Polski, 1955, pp.10–14.
60. PISM, PRM 47h/5, 2 October 1941.
61. PISM, PRM-K. 102/37d, 25 July 1941.
62. Tendyra, p.164.
63. Ibid. pp.164–5.
64. *Great Britain. Weekly Political Intelligence Summaries*, Vol. 4, July–December 1941, nos.92–117, New York, Kraus, no. 101, p.5, 11 September 1941.
65. Bethell, p.41.
66. PISM, PRM 44/5/3, 20 December 1941.
67. PISM, PRM 45A/9, 22 August 1941.
68. PISM, PRM 46A/4, 1941.

Chapter 8

1. PISM, PRM 48/13, 8 June 1941.
2. Żochowski, *British Policy in Relations to Poland in the Second World War*, New York, Vantage Press, 1988, p.123.
3. Sword, *Deportation and Exile. Poles in the Soviet Union, 1939–48*, Basingstoke, Macmillan, 1996, p.31. Applebaum, *Gulag. A History of Soviet Camps*, London, BCA, 2003, pp.403–4, 407. Alexopoulos, 'Amnesty 1945: The Revolving Door of Stalin's Gulag' *Slavic Review*, 64, 2005, pp.274–306.
4. Kot, *Listy*, p.21.
5. PISM, PRM 42/4/2, 14 August 1941.
6. PISM, KOL 1/27, I, Sikorski to Anders, 1 October 1941.
7. PISM, KOL 1/26, I, 1 September 1941.
8. Quoted in Meiklejohn Terry, p.39.
9. Mitkiewicz, *Dokumenty. Z Gen. Sikorskim na Obczyźnie (Fragmenty Wspomnień)*, Paris, Kultury, 1968, p.193.
10. PISM, PRM 39a/12, Sikorski to Lt Gen. Archibald P. Wavell, 17 March 1941.
11. PISM, KOL 1/27, I, Sikorski to Anders, 1 October 1941.

12. Kot, *Listy*, p.82. PISM, 22/1/19, 18 September 1941. Władysław Anders, *Bez Ostatniego Rozdziału*, Newtown, Montgomeryshire Printing Co., 1949, pp.82–3.
13. NA Kew, FO 371/31088/C11653, Hankey to Makins, undated, 1942.
14. NA Kew, FO 371/3108/C130909, Memorandum by Hills, 29 October 1942; Kot, *Listy*, pp.334–7; Sword, pp.107–12.
15. PISM, KOL 1/26, Kot to Sikorski, 22 September 1941.
16. Anders, *An Army in Exile. The Story of Second Polish Corps*, London, Macmillan, 1949, pp.61–2, 76.
17. Klimkowski, *Byłem Adiutantem Generała Andersa*, Warsaw, MON, 1959, pp.134–5; Zygmunt Berling, *Wspomnienia. Z Łagrów do Andersa*, Warsaw, Polski Dom Wydawniczy, 1990, pp.111–12; *DPSR1*, p.159; NA Kew, FO 371/26760/C1090, Foreign Office to Moscow, 17 September 1941.
18. PISM, PRM 41/3/26, Sikorski to Churchill, 17 December 1941; PRM 41/5/5, note of conversation between General Mason-MacFarlane and General Szyszko-Bohusz, 21 November 1941; PRM 41/6/13, Ciechanowski (Washington DC) to Council of Ministers (Polish Government-in-Exile Cabinet), 25 November 1941.
19. *DPSR1*, pp.149–51, 187, 207.
20. Prażmowska, 'Poland's Eastern and Western Frontiers in General Sikorski's Foreign Policy' in *General Władysław Sikorski's Wartime Leader Conference Papers*, (4 November 2003), Ciechanowski & Suchcitz (eds) London, Polish Institute & Sikorski Museum, 2007, pp.106–22.
21. Churchill Papers, Churchill College, University of Cambridge, CHAR 20/22A/77-79, Churchill to Sikorski, 28 August 1941.
22. CHAR 20/21B/197-198, 15 April 1941.
23. Foster, 'The Beaverbrook Press & Appeasement: The Second Phase' *European History Quarterly*, 21, 1991, pp.5–38.
24. PISM, PRM 42/4/4, 11 September 1941; PRM 42/5/10, 12 September 1941; PRM 42/4/9, Anders to Sikorski, 5 October 1941; PRM 41/3/20, Polish Ambassador to the USA to President Franklin D. Roosevelt, 31 October 1941. NA Kew, PREM 3/351/81, Sikorski to Churchill, 11 September 1941, FO 371/26760/C10394, 15 September 1941; CAB 66/19 WP (41) 238, 8 October 1941; CAB 66/19 WP (41) 256, 4 November 1941.
25. PISM, KOL 1/27, I, Sikorski to Churchill, 8 October 1941. TNA, FO 371/26760/C11104, Sikorski to Churchill, 8 November 1941, Minute by Strang, 13 November 1941.
26. Gorodetsky, *Stafford Cripps in Moscow, 1940–1942. Diaries and Papers*, London, Vallentine Mitchell, 2007, pp.218–19, diary entry, 7 December 1941.
27. NA Kew, FO 371/26766/C12318/3226/55, Polish Postulate Present to the Government of the USSR, 27 November 1941.
28. PISM, PRM 39a, Sikorski to Churchill, 17 September 1941.
29. NA Kew, FO 371/267/C11104, C10331, Minute by Strang, 13 October 1941 from War Office (Communicated) received 16 October 1941.
30. NA Kew, PREM 3/353/18, Sikorski to Churchill, 11 September 1941.
31. NA Kew, CAB 65/19 WM (41) 102nd Conclusion, Minute 9, 13 October 1941.
32. PISM, A.XII, Papers of the Ministry of Defence (Poland), A.XII 1/36, Sikorski to General Szyszko-Bohusz, Polish Embassy, Moscow, to be forwarded to General Hastings Ismay, 26 September 1941; A.XII 1/57, Churchill to Sikorski, 29 March 1942.
33. PISM, PRM-K.102/39, 1a, 3 October 1941; PRM-K 102/39 1d, 27 October 1941.
34. PISM, PRM 43/812, 27 September 1941; PRM 43/8/13, 29 October 1941; PRM 43/8/15, undated.

35. PISM, KOL 1/27, 1, Januszajtis to Sikorski; 24 October 1941; Sikorski to Januszajtis to Sikorski, 26 October 1941.
36. NA Kew, FO 371/26760/C11514, Eden to Cripps, 13 November 1941; FO 371/26758/C9066, 12 August 1941.
37. PISM, KOL 1/27, I, 24 October 1941. TNA, FO 371/26760/C11837, 24 October 1941; FO 371/26761/C12041, Minute by Millard, 28 October 1941.
38. PISM, PRM 20/26, Conversation between General Sikorski and Ernest Bevin, Minister for Labour, November 1940; PRM 37B/37, Polish Consulate, Istanbul to London, 14 September 1940, re: moving Polish troops to Egypt.
39. PISM, A.XII 1/48c, Sikorski to Kopański, 6 September 1941.
40. Kopański, *Wspomnienia Wojenne, 1939–1946*, London, Veritsas, 1961. pp.147–148, PISM, PRM-K. 102/42a, *Sprawodnie z Podroży Generała Sikorskiego na Średni Wschód i do Rosji*, 12 January 1942.
41. PISM, KOL 1/28, I, Sikorski to Mikołajczyk, 15 November 1941; PRM 42/2/10, 9 November 1941.
42. PISM, PRM 44/1/11, 21 November 1941; PRM 44/4/19, 7 November 1941; KOL.1/28, Kuśnierz to Sikorski, 11 November 1941.
43. Anders, *Bez Ostatniego Rozdziału*, p.103 Klimkowski, pp.188–9, 191–2.
44. *DPSR1*, pp.227–8.
45. Coutouvidis & Reynolds, *Poland 1939–1947*, Leicester, Leicester University Press, 1987, pp.113–23.
46. Stefania Stanisława (ed.) *Sprawa Polska w Czasie Drugiej Wojny Światowej na Arenie Międzynarodowej. Zbiór Dokumentów*, Warsaw, Pańsтowy Instytut Naukowe, 1965, pp.241–9.
47. PISM, KOL 1/29, I, 3 December 1941. *DPSR1*, pp.231–43.
48. PISM, KOL 1/29, I, 4 December 1941. *DPSR1*, pp.244–6, 365.
49. Gorodetsky, pp.218–19.
50. Kot, *Listy z Rosji*, pp.65–66.
51. *Foreign Relations of the United States*, 1942, III, Washington DC, Government Printing Office, 1961, p.102.
52. *DPSR1*, pp.227–8.
53. Anders, *Bez Ostatniego Rozdziału*, p.129.

Chapter 9

1. Ibid. PISM, KOL 1/29, I, 10 December 1941.
2. Anders, *An Army in Exile*, p.81.
3. PISM, PRM 44/5/3, 20 December 1941.
4. Anders, *An Army in Exile*, Introduction by Harold Macmillan, p.xiii.
5. Black, *Franklin Delano Roosevelt. Champion of Freedom*, London, Weidenfeld & Nicolson, 2004, p.1125.
6. PISM, KOL 1/37, I, Anders to Sikorski; Sikorski to Anders, 6 August 1942.
7. *DPSR1*, pp.421–3.
8. NA Kew, FO 371/31686/C7661, Minute by Roberts, 6 August 1942, Sikorski to Churchill, 3 August 1942, Brown to Lawford, 4 August 1942.
9. NA Kew, PREM 3/354/6, Redman to Lawford, 17 August 1942. PISM, KOL 1/37, I, *Komunikat Naczelnego Wodza* Nr. 4, 8 August 1942, Sikorski to Anders, 18 August 1942.
10. PISM, KOL 1/37, Part 2, *Dziennik Podroży Szefa Sztabu N. W. Gen-Brig. T. Klimeckiego na Śr. Wschód*, 20 August 1942–30 September 1942, (hereafter *Klimecki 1942 Report*) pp.287–9.

11. PISM, PRM 73/1/38, 24 August 1942, *Klimecki 1942 Report*, p. 299. NA Kew, FO 371/31086/C7661, Sikorski to Churchill, 3 August 1942.
12. PISM, *Klimecki 1942 Report*, p. 284; KOL 1/38, I, Kot to Sikorski, 1 September 1942.
13. PISM, *Klimecki 1942 Report*, pp.289–290, KOL 1/38, I, Kot to Sikorski, 31 August 1942. NA Kew, PREM 3/254/6, Rowan to Churchill, 26 August 1942.
14. PISM, KOL 1/40, I, *Ocena Sytacji i Możliwości Działaina*, 17 November 1942, Sikorski to Anders, 25 & 26 November 1942, TNA, PREM 3/351/11, 17 November 1942.
15. Tendyra, p.259. PISM, *Klimecki 1942 Report*, pp.293–9, 306, 308.
16. Ibid. p.299.
17. NA Kew, FO 371/31089/C13090, Report to Major C. Bryson on the British Army in the East, 108, 25 November 1942. Piotr Zaroń, *Armia Andersa*, Toruń, Adam Marszałek, 1996, pp.174–7.
18. NA Kew, FO 371/31089/C8428/74/55, Polish Political Situation, Minister of State, Cairo, 30 August 1942; C8428/74/55, Draft telegram (FO) to Mexico City, 14 December 1942.
19. NA Kew, FO 371/31089/C13090/74/55, Report by Major C. Bryson on the Polish Army in the Middle East, 108, 25 November 1942.
20. NA Kew, FO 371/31089/C13090/74/55, Report by Major C. Bryson on the Polish Army in the Middle East, no. 2, 10 November 1942.
21. PISM, *Klimecki 1942 Report*, p.69.
22. Ibid., p.320.
23. NA Kew, FO 371/31088/C11652, Hankey to Makins, 10 November 1942. PISM, KOL 1/39, I, Kot to Sikorski, 27 November 1942.
24. Kot, pp.389–90, PISM, PRM 80/17, 24 September 1942; KOL 1/38, I, Sikorski to Anders, 26 September 1942; KOL 1/39, I, Anders to Sikorski, 4 October 1942; Sikorski to Anders, 7 October 1942.
25. Kopański, pp.270–271.
26. Sarner, *General Anders and the Soldiers of the Second Polish Corps*, Cathedral City, Brunswick, 1997, pp.29, 73, 155, 282.
27. NA Kew, FO 371/31082/C3950/G, Sikorski to General Boruta, 7 April 1942.
28. NA Kew, FO 371/26760/C7402/G, 30 Military Mission, Moscow, to WO, 27 July 1942.
29. NA Kew, PREM 3/354/2, Minister of State, Cairo to Foreign Office, 6 February 1943; FO 371/34563/C1723/G, Minute by Allen, 12 February 1943. For essays on inter-war Polish youth see: Micewski, 'Polish Youth in the Thirties' *Journal of Contemporary History*, 4 (1969) pp.155–67; Wynot Jr. 'The "Service of Youth"; A Polish Experiment in Social Modernization, 1937–1939' *Canadian Slavic Studies*, 5 (1971) pp.213–25.
30. NA Kew, PREM 3/354/2, Minute by Secretary of State, Cairo, to Foreign Office, 6 February 1943.
31. PISM, KOL 1/14, I, Lieutenant-Colonel De Chair, No.4 Military Mission, to Sikorski, 23 September 1940.
32. *Generał Broni Władysław Sikorski – Generał Dywizji Władysław Anders. Korespondencja 1941–1943. Wybór Dokumentów*, Bogusław Polak (ed.), Koszalin, Politechnika Koszalinka, 2000, pp.74–77, General Anders – report to General Sikorski, Moscow, 25 September 1941.
33. PISM, KGA, General Anders' Collection, KGA/11, Klimkowski to Anders, 19 January 1943.
34. NA Kew, FO 371/34593/C4597/940/G, Baghdad to Minister of State, Cairo, 22 April 1943.

35. Sarner, p.56.
36. PISM, KGA/11, 30 June 1943; KOL. 1/47,I, Klimecki to Kukiel, Deputy Chief of Staff, 8 June 1943 & 13 June 1943; Sikorski to Kukiel, 10 June 1943; KOL. 1/48, I, Sikorski to Mitkiewicz, 1 July 1943, Sikorski to Anders, 3 July 1943. Anders, *Bez Ostatniego Rodziału*, pp.179, 193, 200.
37. Sarner, pp.73, 282–83.

Chapter 10

1. *Polski Siły Zbrojne w Drogiej Światowej*, Vol. II, part 2, London, Instytut Historyczny im. gen. Sikorskiego, 1959, pp.320–1.
2. PISM, KOL. 1/38,I, Anders to Sikorski, 22 & 26 September 1942; Sikorski to Anders, 24 September 1942; PRM 80/12; PRM 80/18, Kot to Sikorski, 14 September 1942; *Klimecki 1942 Report*, p.322. NA Kew, FO 371/31088/C11309, C-in-C Persia to War Office, 9 November 1942.
3. NA Kew, FO 371/31088/C11632, 10 November 1942.
4. NA Kew, FO 371/31089/C13090, Bryson Report, 25 November 1942; FO 371/31088/C11652, 25 November 1942.
5. PISM, KOL. 1/40, I, 17 November 1942, Sikorski to Anders, 25 & 26 November 1942. NA Kew, PREM 3/351/11, 17 November 1942. Black, p.852.
6. *DPSR1*, pp.473–5.
7. NA Kew, PREM 3/351/11, 17 November 1942.
8. See Meiklejohn Terry, p.37.
9. PISM, PRM 104/4/2, Colonel Cazalet, *The Polish Eastern Frontier*, 13 March 1943.
10. Ibid.
11. Ibid.
12. Ibid.
13. Ibid.
14. PISM, PRM 69/138, undated. Jan Ciechanowski, *Defeat in Victory*, New York, Doubleday, 1947, pp.122–3.
15. NA Kew, FO 371/34563/C910/910/G, FO to Washington, 7 February 1943.
16. NA Kew, KV, British Security Service Files, KV 2/516, Sikorski's Visit to the USA, 17 February 1943.
17. NA Kw, FO 371/34563/C910/910/G, FO to Washington, 7 February 1943.
18. Kot, *Listy z Rosji*, pp.418–423. PISM, PRM 107/12, received 9 February 1943.
19. NA Kew, FO 371/34593/C3742, Eden to Churchill, 11 April 1943.
20. PISM, PRM 107/12, received 9 February 1943.
21. PISM, PRM-K. 102. 102/55a, 11 February 1943.
22. Kopański, pp.270–1.
23. PISM, PRM 107/28; PRM 107/31, both undated.
24. PISM, KOL. 1/43, I, Anders to Sikorski, 18 February 1943.
25. NA Kew, FO 371/34593/C3375, Hopkins to Strang, 17 March 1943. Previously Hulls, as a lieutenant colonel had been the Imperial General Staff's Liaison Officer for the Polish commander in the USSR liaising with Soviet officials. Zaroń, p.39.
26. NA Kew, FO 371/34593/C3375, Minute by Lambert, 8 April 1943.
27. NA Kew, FO 371/34593/C3602, Minute by Roberts, undated.
28. NA Kew, FO 371/31088/C10946/G, WO to C-in-C, Persia-Iraq, 3 November 1942; C11048/G, Minister of State, Cairo to the Undersecretary of State, FO, 12 November 1942; C9293/74/G, Minister of State, Cairo to FO, 20 November 1942.

29. NA Kew, FO 371/34593/C3623, Minister of State, Cairo, to FO, 1 April 1943.
30. Tendyra, p.285. NA Kew, FO 371/34593/C1938, Eden to Cadogan, 20 February 1943; PREM 3/354/2, 20 February 1943.
31. PISM, KOL. 1/44, I, 15 & 17 March 1943.
32. NA Kew, FO 371/345593/C3742/G, Prime Minister's Personal Telegram, M.2224/3, 3 April 1943.
33. NA Kew, FO 371/34593/C3742/G, Eden to Churchill, 11 April 1943.
34. NA Kew, FO 371/34593/C3623/335/G55, Minister of State, Cairo, to FO, 2 April 1943.

Chapter 11

1. Meiklejohn Terry, p.334.
2. Conquest, *The Great Terror: Stalin's Purge Of The Thirties*, Harmondsworth, Penguin, 1971, p.180.
3. Sebag Montefiore, *Stalin: The Court of the Red Tsar*, London, Phoenix, 2004, p.34.
4. PISM, PRM 98/2/34, Onacewicz to Sikorski, 14 April 1943.
5. Kryska-Karski; Stanisław Żurakowski, *Generałowie Polski Niepodległej*, Warsaw, Spotkania, 1991, p.167.
6. Conquest, *Stalin: Breaker of Nations*, London, Weidenfeld, 1993, p.229.
7. *DPSR1*, pp.504–19.
8. PISM, PRM 102/4, *Dziennik Polski*, 17 April 1943.
9. McGilvray, *Red Trojan Horse. The Berling Army and the Soviet Annexation of Poland 1943–45*, Warwick, Helion, 2019, pp.50–5.
10. Ibid, p.177.
11. PISM, PRM 102/4/13, Anders to Sikorski, 26 April 1943.
12. Ibid.
13. PISM, PRM 102/4/16, Anders to Sikorski, 27 April 1943.
14. PISM, PRM 102/4, 19 April 1943.
15. PISM, PRM 102/4, 19 April 1943.
16. PISM, PRM 102/4, *Kozielsk: Oficerski obóz jeńców polskich koło Smoleńska*. Minister Professor W. Komarnicki, 20 April 1943.
17. PISM, PRM 102/4, Anders (Baghdad) to Sikorski, 21 April 1943.
18. PISM, PRM 102/4/3, 17 April 1943.
19. PISM, PRM 102/4/11, Anders to Sikorski, 23 April 1943.
20. PISM, PRM 98/2/37, Washington DC to Sikorski, 19 April 1943.
21. PISM, PRM 102/4, Statement by Katarzyna Gaszciecka, 26 January 1943.
22. For examples of this form of Soviet propaganda see *Soviet War News*, 22 February 1943; 3 March 1943; 10 March 1943; 30 March 1943; 2 April 1943. Wasilewska's article 'The Real Poland' was published on 30 April 1943.
23. Raack, *Stalin's Drive to the West, 1938–1945, The Origins of the Cold War*, Stanford, Standford University Press, 1995, p.80.
24. Puacz, *Problems of the Exile Governments*, London, Free Poland Library, Pamphlet no.11, 1943.
25. Iwańska, *Exiled Governments: Spanish and Polish. An Essay in Political Sociology*, Cambridge, Mass, Schenkman, 1981, p.93.
26. Foreign and Commonwealth Office, Departmental Series of Eastern Europe and Soviet Departments, The Memorandum, DS 2/73, 10 April 1973, www.fco.gov.uk (hereafter referred to as '*Butler*') p. 8. fn.12.
27. *Butler*, p.8. fn.12.

28. Rees, p.270.
29. Beria, *Beria. My Father: Inside Stalin's Kremlin*, London, Duckworth, 2001, pp.90, 319, fn. 43.
30. Jacek Ślusarczyk, *Polityka Rządu Generała W. Sikorskiego Wobec ZSRR*, Warsaw, PAN, 1985, p.88. Davies, *Rising '44 'The Battle for Warsaw'*, London, Macmillan, 2003, p.91.
31. Bór-Komorowski, *Armia Podziemna*, 3rd Edition, London, Veritas, 1967, p.48.
32. *Butler*, p.8.
33. *Dziennik Polski*, 21 April 1943.
34. NA Kew, FO 371//34571/C4828, C4778, Pownall to Anders, 29 April 1943.
35. NA Kew, FO 371/ 34569/C4396, Minute by Roberts, 22 April 1943. Raczyński, *W Sojusziczym Londynie: Dziennik Ambasadora Edwarda Raczyńskiego 1939–1945*, London, Orbis, 1960, p.172. *DPSR1*, pp.525–7. PISM, PRM-K. 102/57c, 28 April 1943.
36. NA Kew, FO 371/34570/C4664, Minute by Roberts, 21 April 1943.
37. Black, pp.742, 830.
38. Conquest, *Stalin: Breaker of Nations*, p.261.
39. NA Kew, PREM 3/354/10, General Smuts to Churchill, 28 April 1943.
40. PISM, PRM 96/10, Discussion between General Sikorski, Raczyński, Prime Minister Churchill and Sir Alexander Cadogan, 15 April 1943.
41. Kimball, *Churchill & Roosevelt. The Complete Correspondence, Volume 2*, Princeton, Princeton University Press, 1984, p.393.
42. *Cadogan*, p.537, diary entry, 18 June 1943.
43. NA Kew, PREM 3/354/8, Churchill to Eden, 28 April 1943.
44. Rees, p.273.
45. Churchill Papers, CHAR 20/111/8-9, Telegram, Churchill to Stalin, 'Private and Most Secret' T 606/3, 28 April 1943.
46. PISM, PRM 103/4/4, *The Origin of the Curzon Line*, Dr. T. Piszczowski, May 1943.
47. Stanford, *Poland, the Conquest of History*. Amsterdam, Harwood, 1999, p.97.
48. Stalin to Roosevelt, 21 April 1943. *Correspondence Between the Chairman of Ministers of the USSR and the Presidents of the USA and the Prime Minister of Great Britain during the Great Patriotic War of 1941 and 1945, Volume 2*, Moscow, Progress, 1957, pp.54–5 (Hereafter referred to as *Correspondence II*).
49. Churchill Papers, CHAR 20/111/12, telegram private and most secret, T 608/3, Churchill to Roosevelt, 28 April 1943.
50. Churchill Papers, CHAR 20/111/13-14, telegram private and most secret, Churchill to Roosevelt, T 609/3, 28 April 1943.
51. Winstone, pp.142–6.
52. McCrum, *Wodehouse: A Life*, London, Penguin/Viking, 2004, p.337.
53. NA Kew, PREM 3/354/8, FO to the Minister of State, Cairo, 26 April 1943.
54. Sanford, p.97.
55. NA Kew, PREM 3/354/8, FO to Moscow, 30 April 1943.
56. Beria, p.55.
57. Stalin to Churchill, 4 May 1943, *Correspondence Between the Chairman of the Council of Ministers of the USSR and the Presidents of the USA and the Prime Ministers of Great Britain During the Great Patriotic War of 1941–1945, Volume 1*, Moscow, Progress 1957, pp.131–132, (Hereafter *Correspondence I*) See also Stalin to Roosevelt, 29 April 1943, *Correspondence II*, pp.56–7.
58. NA Kew, PREM 3/354/8, Churchill to Stalin, 26 April 1943. Churchill to Stalin, 26 April and 30 April 1943, *Correspondence I*, pp.126–7; 129–30. Roosevelt to Stalin,

26 April 1943, *Correspondence II*, p.56. Kimball, *Churchill & Roosevelt, The Complete Correspondence Volume 2*, Princeton, Princeton University Press, 1984, pp.203–5.

59. NA Kew, FO 371/34574/C5138, Churchill to Eden; Eden to Churchill, 10 May 1943.
60. NA Kew, PREM 3/354/8, Churchill to Roosevelt, 28 April 1943.
61. Churchill Papers, CHAR 20/111/66-67, Telegram, Stalin to Churchill, T 656/3, 6 May 1943.
62. Churchill Papers, CHAR 20/111/105, Telegram, Churchill to Stalin, personal and most secret, T 689/3, 12 May 1943.
63. NA Kew, FO 371/345675/C5295, Eden to Clark-Kerr, 11 May 1943.
64. NA Kew, FO 371/34574/C5189, Clark-Kerr, 8 May 1943.
65. PISM, KOL. 1/45, II, *Dziennik Podróży Szefa Naczelnego Wodza Gen. Bryg. Tadeusza Klimeckiego na Śred. Wschód. Kwiecień, Maj, Czerwiec, Lipiec, 1943 rok.* (Henceforth, *Klimecki 1943 Report*) Notatka Nr. 270, 27 April 1943.
66. PISM, *Klimecki 1943 Report*, pp.171–3.
67. Ibid. p.192.
68. NA Kew, FO 371/34593/C3742, FO to the Minister of State, Cairo, 13 April 1943.
69. NA Kew, PREM 3/354/8, Churchill to Sir Alexander Cadogan, 3 April 1943.
70. PISM, *Klimecki 1943 Report*, p.202.
71. Jerzy Klimkowski, *Katastrofa w Gibraltarze. Kulisy Śmierci Generała Sikorskiego*, Bielsko-Biała, Wydawnictwo Śląsk, 1965, p.62.
72. NA Kew, KV 2/516, 'General Władysław Sikorski – General Kazimierz Sosnkowski' Robinson-Scott to Captain Derbyshire, 19 April 1943.
73. NA Kew, FO 371/34577/C5843/910/G, Roberts to Moscow, 25 May 1943.
74. NA Kew, FO 850, Foreign Office Communications. FO 850/84 Y2391/G, F.K. Roberts, 19 April 1943.
75. PISM, PRM 98/2/55, Washington DC to Sikorski, 18 May 1943.

Chapter 12

1. Meiklejohn Terry, p.339.
2. Tendyra, p.304. PISM, KOL 1/47, I, 10 June 1943. NA Kew, FO 371/34594/C6892/G, Minister of State, Cairo, to FO, 16 June 1943.
3. NA Kew, FO 371/34593/C3375/G, Hopkins, Cairo, to Strang, 17 March 1943; Minister of State, Cairo to FO, 31 March 1943.
4. NA Kew, FO 371/34593/C3623/335/G55, Minutes by Roberts and Allen, 2 April 1943.
5. Ibid.
6. PISM, A.5. Minutes of Meetings of the Polish National Council, A.5.3/74, 74th Sitting, 19 April 1943.
7. PISM, KOL. 1/47, I, 10 June 1943.
8. NA Kew, FO 371/34593/C3375, Hopkins to Baghdad, to Minister of State, Cairo, 27 May 1943.
9. NA Kew, FO 371/34614 A/C5992, Minister of State, Cairo to FO 27 May 1943. PISM, KOL. 1/48, I, Report by T. Żażuliński, 8 July 1943.
10. Tendyra, p.305.
11. NA Kew, FO 371/34594/C6892, Minister of State, Cairo to FO, 16 June 1943. *Polskie Siły Zbrojne w Drugiej Wojnie Światowej*, (PSZ, Part 2) pp.328–9.
12. PISM, PRM 66/31, Duff Cooper to Sikorski, 21 July 1942.
13. PISM, PRM 6/32, Sikorski to Duff Cooper, 23 July 1942.
14. Irving, *Accident. The Death of General Sikorski*, London, William Kimber, 1967, pp.155–6.

15. PISM, A.XII, Papers of the Polish Ministry of National Defence, A.XII 3/81, 26 April 1943.
16. NA Kew, PREM 3/354/1, 26 April 1943.
17. Irving, p.157.
18. PISM, PRM 69/138, undated. Ciechanowski, *Defeat in Victory*, London, Gollancz, 1948, p.134.
19. Rhodes James, *Victor Cazalet. A Portrait*, London, Hamilton, 1976, p.282.
20. Irving, pp.152–63.
21. PISM, KOL 1/47, I, Sikorski to Raczkiewicz, 4 June 1943; KOL. 1/48, I, 3 July 1943. NA Kew, FO 371/34594/C7463, Minister of State, Cairo to FO, 3 July 1943.
22. Terlicki, Vol. 2, pp.226–7. Wojtkiewicz, *Sikorski i Jego Żołnierz*, Łódź, Księgarni Ludowej, 1946, p.66. Kopański, p.282. PISM, PRM.K. 102/59f, 25 June 1943. Michał Sokolnicki, the Polish Ambassador to Turkey, recorded in his diary, 12 May 1943, the eighth anniversary of Piłsudski's death, the choir in Ankara sang '*Pierszwą Brygadę*' before Mass. Michał Sokolnicki, *Dziennik Ankarski, 1939–1943*, London, Gryf, 1965, p.514. Sikorski was not present at this incident, yet it illustrated the influence of Piłsudski and the First Brigade to many Poles even eight years after Piłsudski's death. Sokolnicki was a veteran of the Legions.
23. Tendyra, p.307. Sokolnicki, pp.541–3.
24. NA Kew, CAB 122 British Joint Staff Missions, CAB 122/141, Eden to Halifax, 1 June 1943.
25. NA Kew, FO 371/34594/C6892/G, Minister of State, Cairo, to FO, 16 June 1943.
26. NA Kew, FO 371/34594/C763/335/55Pol/43/47, Minister of State, Cairo, to FO, 3 July 1943.
27. PISM, KGA 1b, *Dziennik Czynności Gen. Andersa od 30/X/42 do 14/III/44.* General Maitland Wilson in a letter made a reference to Anders' illness, KGA. 3a, Wilson to Anders, 17 July 1943.

Chapter 13

1. Burleigh, *Small Wars, Far Away Places. The Genesis of the Modern World*, London, Macmillan, 2013 p.173.
2. Ibid. p.406.
3. Djilas, *Conversations with Stalin*, London, Penguin, 1969, p.61.
4. Ibid, p.144.
5. Łubieński, 'The Last Days of General Sikorski: An Eyewitness Account' in Sword *Sikorski*, pp.146–53.

Chapter 14

1. Ibid. p.155.
2. Ibid, pp.154–5.
3. Ibid. p.155.
4. Ibid. p.156.
5. Ibid.
6. Courtauld, *Footprints in Spain. British Lives in a Foreign Land*, London, Quarter Books, 2017, p.179.
7. Rees, *Hitler and Stalin. The Tyrants and the Second World War*, London, Penguin, 2021, p.209.
8. Irving, p.145.

9. Ibid. p.146.
10. McGilvray, *Man of Steel and Honour: General Stanisław Maczek. Soldier of Poland, Commander of the 1st Polish Armoured Division in North-West Europe 1944–45*, Solihull, Helion, 2015, pp.177–81.
11. Irving. pp.146–7.
12. Ibid. p.148.
13. Ibid. p.149.
14. Ibid. p.161.
15. Zurowski, 'British Policy Towards The Polish Second Corps' *East European Quarterly*, XXVII, No.3, 1993, pp.271–300.
16. McGilvray, *Anders' Army. General Władysław Anders & The Polish Second Corps 1941–46*, Barnsley, Pen & Sword, 2018, pp.236–9.
17. Ibid., pp.189–93.

Bibliography

Unpublished Archival Sources

Archiwum AKT Nowych AAN, Warsaw,
Sygnał 135, *Ministerstwa Informacji i Dokumentacji*
Churchill Collection, Churchill College, University of Cambridge,
CHAR 20
Polish Institute & Sikorski Museum (PISM), Kensington, London
A.XII, Papers of the Ministry of Defence (Poland)
A.5, Minutes of Meetings of the Polish National Defence Council
A.48, Civil Chancellery of the President of the Polish Republic
KGA, General Anders Collection
Kol.1, Journal of the Activities of the Supreme Commander
PRM, Prime Ministers' Office (Poland)
PRM -K.102, Minutes of the Meetings of the Council of Ministers
The National Archives (TNA), Kew, London, UK
CAB/1 Mission to Poland
CAB 65, War Cabinet Meetings
CAB 66, War Cabinet Memoranda
CAB 83, Military Co-ordination Committee
DS 2/73, (Foreign and Commonwealth Office) 'Butler Report' [Katyń]
FO 371, Foreign Office Correspondence
FO 800, Halifax Papers
KV, Intelligence Reports
PREM/1, Prime Minister's Office
PREM/3, Prime Minister's Office
WO, War Office

Published Primary Sources

Armia Krajowa w Dokumentach, 1939–1945, (4 Vols.), London, Studium Polski Podziemniej, 1970

Churchill & Roosevelt. The Complete Correspondence (3 Vols.). (ed.) Warren F. Kimball, Princeton, Princeton University Press, 1984

Correspondence Between the Chairman of the Council of Ministers of the USSR and the Presidents of the USA and the Prime Ministers of Great Britain During the Great Patriotic War of 1941–1945, (2 Vols,) Moscow, Progress, 1957

Documents on Canadian External Relations, 1939–1941, Vol. 7, Part One, Ottawa, Queen's Printer, 1974

Documents on Polish-Soviet Relations, 1939–1945, (2 Vols.) London, Heinemann, 1961 & 1967

Foreign Relations of the United States, 1942, III, Washington DC, Government Printing Office, 1981

Generał Broni Władysław Sikorski – Generał Dywizji Władysław Anders, Korespondencja 1941–1943. Wybór Dokumentów, (ed.) Bogusław Polak, Koszalin, Politechniku Koszalinka, 2000

Great Britain, Foreign Office Weekly Intelligence Summary, (ed.) Clifton Child, New York, Kraus, 1983

King's Counsellor. Abdication and War. The Diaries of Sir Allen Lascelles, (ed.) Duff Hart-Davis, London, Phoenix, 2007

Papers and Memoirs of Juliusz Łukasiewicz, Ambassador of Poland. Diplomat in Paris, 1936–1939, (ed.) Wacław Jędrzejewicz, New York, Columbia University, 1970

Sprawa Polska w Czasie Drugiej Wojny Światowej na Arenie Międzynarodowej. Zbiór Dokumentów, (ed.) Stefania Stanisława, Warsaw, Państowy Instytut Naukowe, 1965

Stafford Cripps in Moscow, 1940–1942. Diaries and Papers, (ed.) Gabriel Gorodetsky, London, Vallentine Mitchell, 2007

The Diaries of Sir Alexander Cadogan, 1938–1945, (ed.) David Dilks, London, Cassell, 1971

The Maisky Diaries. Red Ambassador to the Court of St James's, 1932–1943, (ed.) Gabriel Gorodetsky, translated by Tatiana Sorokina and Oliver Ready, New Haven and London, Yale University Press, 2015

The War Diaries of Oliver Hardy, Oliver Hardy, London, Collins, 1978

W Sojusziczym Londynie: Dziennik Ambasadora Edwarda Raczyńskiego 1939–1945, London, Orbis, 196

General Władysław Sikorski

Works by:

Sikorski, Władysław, *Modern Warfare*, New York, Roy Publishing, 1943. With a note by General George C. Marshall, Chief of Staff, US Army

Sikorski, Władysław, 'Poland's Defences' *The Slavic Review*, (17) 1938–1939, 343–55

Sikorski, Władysław, 'The Higher Military School and its Aims' (Translation) *Bellona*, February 1941, PISM, PRM 63 t11/38

Works on:

Ciechanowski, Jan, Suchcitz, Andrzej, (eds) *General Władysław Sikorski. Wartime Leader Conference Papers*, London, PISM, 2007. Conference held 4 November 2003

Irving, David, *Accident: The Death of General Sikorski*, London, William Kimber, 1967

Klimkowski, Jerzy, *Katastrofa w Gibraltarze. Kulisy Śmierci Generała Sikorskiego*, Bielsko-Biała, Wydawnictwo Śląsk, 1965

Korpalska, Walentyna, *Władysław Eugeniusz Sikorski: Biografia Polityczna*, Wrocław, Zakład Narodowy im. Ossolińskich Wydawnictwo, 1981

Kot, Stanisław, *Listy z Rosji do Gen. Sikorskiego*, London, Jutro Polski, 1955

Kukiel, Marian, *Generał Sikorski, Żołnierz i Mąz Walczącej*, London, Polska Fundacja Kulturalna, 1995, 3rd reprint

Meiklejohn Terry, Sarah, *Poland's Place in Europe: General Sikorski and the Origin of the Oder-Neisse Line, 1939–1943*, Princeton, Princeton University Press, 1983

Mitkiewicz, Leon, *Z Generałem Sikorskim na Obczyźnie*, Paris, Kultury, 1968

Stachura, Peter D., 'Władysław Sikorski, Soldier, Politician, Statesman, 1881–1943' *Scottish Slavonic Review* (21) 1993, 71–94

Strumph Wojtkiewicz, Stanisław, *Gwiazda Władysława Sikorskiego*, Warsaw, Czytelnik, 1946

Strumph Wojtkiewicz, Stanisław, *Sikorski i Jego Żołnierz*, Łódź, Księgarni Ludowej, 1946

Sword, Keith (ed.), *Sikorski: Soldier and Statesman. A Collection of Essays*, London, Orbis, 1990.

Ślusarczyk, Jacek, *Polityku Rządu Generała W Sikorskiego Wobec ZSRR*, Warsaw, PAN, 1985
Terlecki, Olgierd, *Generał Sikorski* (2 vols) Kraków, Wydawnictwo Kraków, 1981 and 1983
Terlecki, Olgierd, *Generał Ostatniej Legendy. Rzecz O Gen. Władysławie Sikorskim*, Chicago, Polonia, 1976

Published Secondary Sources

Alexander, Martin S., *The Republic in Danger: General Maurice Gamelin and the Politics of French Defence, 1933–1940*, Cambridge, Cambridge University Press, 1992
Anders, Władysław, *Bez Ostatniego Rozdziału*, Newtown, Montgomeryshire Printing Co., 1949
Anders, Władysław, *An Army in Exile: The Story of Second Polish Corps*, London, Macmillan, 1949
Andreski, Stanislav, *Military Organisation and Society*, London, Routledge & Keegan Paul, 1968
Applebaum, Anne, *Gulag: A History of the Soviet Camps*, London, BCA, 2003
Ascherson, Neal, *The Struggles for Poland*, London, Michael Joseph, 1987
Beauvois, Yves, *Les Relations Franco-Polonaises Pendant Le 'Drole de Guerre'*, Paris, L'Harmattan, 1989
Beevor, Antony, *Russia, Revolution and Civil War, 1917–1921*, London, Wiedenfeld & Nicolson, 2022
Beria, Sergo, *My Father: Inside Stalin's Kremlin*, London, Duckworth, 2001
Berling, Zygmunt, *Wspomnienia. Z Łagrów do Anders*, Warsaw, Polski Dom Wydawniczy, 1990
Bethell, Nicholas, *Gomułka: His Poland and his Communism*, London, Penguin, 1972
Black, Conrad, *Franklin Delano Roosevelt: Champion of Freedom*, London, Weidenfeld & Nicolson, 2004
Blazynski, Z., *Materiały Polskiego Niepodległośćiowego*, Vol 1, London, Polskie Towarzystwo Naukowe na Obczyznie, 1994
Bór-Komorowski, Tadeusz, *Armia Podziemna*, London, Verita, 1967, 3rd edition
Burleigh, Michael, *Small Wars, Far Away Places: The Genesis of the Modern World, 1945–65*, London, Macmillan, 2013
Carton de Wiart, Adrian, *Happy Odyssey: The Memoirs of Lt Gen. Sir Adrian Carton de Wiart*, London, Jonathan Cape, 1950
Ciechanowski, Jan, *Defeat in Victory*, New York, Doubleday, 1947
Conquest, Robert, *Stalin: Breaker of Nations*, London, Weidenfeld, 1993
Conquest, Robert, *The Great Terror: Stalin's Purge of the Thirties*, Harmondsworth, Penguin, 1971
Courtauld, Simon. *Footprints in Spain: British Lives in a Foreign Land*, London, Quarter Books, 2017
Coutouvidis, John, Reynolds, Jaime, *Poland 1939–1947*, Leicester, Leicester University Press, 1987
Dalton, Hugh, *The Fateful Years: Memoirs 1931–1945*, London, Frederick Muller, 1957
Davies, Norman, *Rising '44: 'The Battle for Warsaw'*, London, Macmillan, 2003
De Gaulle, Charles, *War Memoirs: Volume One – The Call to Honour, 1940–1942*, Translated by Jonathan Griffin, London, St James Place, 1955
Deszczyński, Marek Piotr, *Ostantnio Egzamin. Wojska Polskie Wóbec Kryzysu Czechosłowachiego, 1938–1939*, Warsaw, Neriton, 2003
Djilas, Milovan, *Conversations with Stalin*, London, Penguin, 1969
Dubicki, Tadeusz, Rostworowski, Stanisław, Jan, *Sanatorzy Kontra Sikorszczycz Czyli Walka o Władze na Uchództwie w Rumanii 1939–1940*, Warsaw, Adiutor, 1995

Duraczynski, Eugeniusz, *Rząd Polski na Uchódzstwie 1939–1945*, Warsaw, Książla i Wiedza, 1993

Epstein, Catherine, *Model Nazi: Arthur Greiser and the Occupation of Western Poland*, Oxford, Oxford University Press, 2010

Garlicki, Andrzej, *Piłsudski 1867–1935*, edited and translated, John Coutouvidis, Aldershot, Scolar Press, 1995

Gross, Jan Tomasz, *Polish Society Under German Occupation: The Generalgouvernment, 1939–1944*, Princeton, Princeton University Press, 1979

Gunsburg, Jefferey A., *Divided and Conquered: The French High Command and the Defeat of the West, 1940*, London, Greenswood, 1979

Hanson, Joanna, *The Civilian Population and the Warsaw Uprising of 1944*, Cambridge, CUP, 1982

Iwańska, Alicja, *Exiled Governments, Spanish and Polish: An Essay in Political Sociology*, Cambridge, Mass, Schenkman Inc., 1981

Jędrzejewicz, Wacław, *Piłsudski: A Life for Poland*, New York, Hippocrene, 1982

Kacewicz, G.V., *Great Britain, the Soviet Union and the Polish Government-in-Exile (1939–1943)* The Hague, Nijhoff. 1979

Karski, Jan, *Story of a Secret State: My Report to the World*, London, Penguin, 2011, originally published in the USA, 1944

Karski, Jan, *The Great Powers & Poland, 1919–1945: From Versailles to Yalta*, Lanham, University of America Press, 1985

Klimkowski, Jerzy, *Byłem Adiutantem Generała Andersa*, Warsaw, MON, 1959

Kopański, Stanisław, *Wspomnienia Wojenne, 1939–1946*, London, Veritas, 1961

Kośmider, Tomasz, *Planowanie Wojenne w Polsce w Latach 1921–1926*, Toruń, Adam Marszałek, 2001

Kryska-Karski, Tadeusz, Żurakowski, Stanisław, *Generałowie Polski Niepodległej*, Warsaw, Spotkania, 1991

Macksey, Kenneth, *The Partisans of Europe in World War II*, London, Hart-Davies, 1975

Maczek, Stanisław, *Od Powody do Czołga: Wspomnienia Wojenne, 1918–1945*, Edinburgh, Tomar, 1961

McCauley, Martin, *The Soviet Union, 1917–1991*, London, Longman, 1994

McCrum, Robert, *Wodehouse: A Life*, London, Penguin/Viking, 2004

McGilvray, Evan, *Man of Steel and Honour: General Stanisław Maczek. Soldier of Poland, Commander of the 1st Polish Armoured Division in North-West Europe, 1944–45*, Solihull, Helion, 2015

McGilvray, Evan, *Anders' Army: General Władysław Anders and the Polish Second Corps, 1941–46*, Barnsley, Pen & Sword, 2018

McGilvray, Evan, *Red Trojan Horse: The Berling Army and the Soviet Annexation of Poland, 1943–45*, Warwick, Helion, 2019

Michta, Andrew A., *Red Eagle. The Army in Polish Politics, 1944–1988*, Stanford, Hoover Press, 1990

Panecki, Tadeusz, Puchała, Franciszek, Szostak, Jan, (eds) *Sztab Generały (Głowny) Wojska Polskiego, 1918–2003*, Warsaw, Bellona, 2003

Peploński, Andrzej, *Wywiad w Wojne Polsko-Bolszewickiej, 1919–1920*, Warsaw, Bellona, 1999

Plokhy, Serhii, *The Gates of Europe. A History of Ukraine*, London, Allen Lane, 2015

Polonsky, Antony, *Politics in Independent Poland, 1921–1939*, Oxford, Clarendon Press, 1972

Pomian, John, *Józef Retinger. Życie i pamiętniki 'szarej eminencju'* Warsaw, Pelikan, 1990

Prażmowska, Anita, *Britain and Poland, 1939–1943: The Betrayed Ally*, Cambridge, Cambridge University Press, 1995

Puacz, Edward, *Problems of Exile Governments*, London, Free Poland Library, Pamphlet No. 11, 1943

Raack, Richard C., *Stalin's Drive to the West, 1938–1945: The Origins of the Cold War*, Stanford, Stanford University Press, 1995

Raczyński, Edward, *In Allied London*, London, Weidenfeld & Nicholson, 1962

Rees, Laurence, *Hitler and Stalin. The Tyrants and the Second World War*, London, Penguin, 2021

Rhodes James, Robert, *Victor Cazalet. A Portrait*, London, Hamilton, 1976

Romeyko, Marian, *Przed i po maju* (2 vols) Warsaw, MON, 1967

Rothschild, Joseph, *East-Central Europe Between the Two World Wars*, Seattle, University of Washington, 1990, 6th edition

Rothschild, Joseph, *Piłsudski's Coup d'état*, New York, Columbia University Press, 1966

Sanford, George, *Poland, the Conquest of History*, Amsterdam, Harwood, 1999

Sarner, Harvey, *General Anders and the Soldiers of the Second Polish Corps*, Cathedral City, Brunswick, 1997

Sebag Montefiore, Simon, *Stalin: The Court of the Red Tsar*, London, Phoenix, 2004

Siebel-Achenbach, Sebastian, *Lower Silesia from Nazi Germany to Communist Poland, 1942–49*, London, Macmillan, 1994

Sokolnicki, Michał, *Dzienik Ankarski, 1939–1943*, London, Gryf, 1965

Sosnkowski, Kazimierz, *Materiały Historyczne*, London, Gryf, 1966

Sword, Keith, *Deportation and Exile. Poles in the Soviet Union, 1939–48*, Basingstoke, Macmillan, 1996

Thomas, Hugh, *The Spanish Civil War*, Middlesex, Penguin, 1979 (3rd edition)

Wiatr, Jerzy J., *The Soldier and the Nation. The Role of the Military in Polish Politics, 1918–1985*, Boulder, Westview, 1988

Winstone, Martin, *The Dark Heart of Hitler's Europe. Nazi Rule in Poland under the General Government*, London, I.B. Tauris, 2015

Wynot, Edward D., *Polish Politics in Transition: The Camp for National Unity and the Struggle for Power, 1936–39*, Athens, Georgia, University of Georgia Press, 1974

Wyszczelski, Lech, *Polska. Myśl Wojskowa, 1914–1939*, Warsaw, MON, 1988

Zamoyski, Adam, *The Forgotten Few. The Polish Airforce in the Second World War*, London, John Murray, 1995

Zaroń, Piotr, *Armia Andersa*, Toruń, Adam Marszałek, 1996

Żochowski, Stanisław, *British Policy in Relation to Poland in the Second World War*, New York, Vantage Press, 1988

Polski Siły Zbrojne w Drugiej Światowej (PSZ) Vol. 2, part 1, London, Instytut Historyczny im gen. Sikorskiego, 1959, no author identified

Journals

Alexopoulos, Golfo, 'Amnesty 1945: The Revolving Door of Stalin's Gulag' *Slavic Review* (64) 2005, 274–306

Buczek, Roman, 'Tragedia Ryszarda Świętochiego' *Zeszyty Historczne* (26) 1973, pp.150–69

Biskupski, M.B., 'The Military Elite of the Polish Second Republic, 1918–1945: A Historical Review' *War & Society* (14) 1996, pp.49–86

Foster, Alan, 'The Beaverbrook Press & Appeasement: The Second Phase' *European History Quarterly* (21) 1991, pp.5–38

French, David, 'The Mechanization of the British Cavalry between the World Wars' *War in History*, 2003, pp.296–320

Micewski, Andrzej, 'Polish Youth in the Thirties' *Journal of Contemporary History* (4) 1969, pp.155–67

Oppenheimer. F.E., 'Governments and Authorities in Exile' *The American Journal of International Law*, (36) 1942, pp.568–95

Peszke, Michael Alfred, 'The Polish Armed Forces in Exile, Part 1, September 1939-July 1941' *The Polish Review* (26) 1987, pp.67–113

Wynot Jr, Edward, 'The "Service of Youth". A Polish Experiment in Social Modernization, 1937–1939' *Canadian Slavic Studies* (5) 1971, pp.213–25

Zurowski, Michael, 'British Policy Towards the Polish Second Corps' *East European* Quarterly, (3) 1993, pp.271–300

'Federacja Zachodnio-Słowiańska' *Biuletyn-Zachodno-Słowiański* (2) 1940, pp.3–11, no author identified

Theses

Coutouvidis, John, *The Formation of the Polish Government-in-Exile and its Relationship with Great Britain, 1939–1941*, Ph. D. thesis, Keele University

Suchcitz, Andrzej, *A Brief Survey of Military Planning and Preparations for the Defence of Poland, October 1939-August 1939*, MA Dissertation, University of London, 1981

Tendyra, Bernadeta I., *General Sikorski and the Polish Government-in-Exile, 1939–43. A Study of Polish Internal Émigré Politics in Wartime*, Ph. D thesis, The London School of Economics and Political Science, 2000

Press

Dziennik Polski
Manchester Guardian
Polish Fortnightly Review
Soviet War News

Interview

Radek Sikorski, Warsaw, June 1999

Index

AK (*Armia Krajowa* – Home Army [Polish Military Underground]), 35, 69, 114, 193
Algeria, 71
Anders, General Władysław (1892–1970), vii, 5, 15, 25, 45, 52, 67, 69, 87, 111–20, 123–36, 139–43, 147–53, 157–8, 161, 165–7, 169–72, 1745, 177, 183, 190–4
Angers, France, 58–69
Anglo-Polish Military Agreement, 5 August 1940, 88
Ankara, Turkey, 90
Anti-Semitism, 20, 25, 84
Antonescu, General Ion, Conducător of Romania (1882–1946), 101–103
Arethusa, 62–3
Argentina, 90
APW (*Armia Polska na Wschódzie* – Polish Army in the East – commonly known as 'Anders' Army'), 129–30, 133–6, 141–2, 157, 166–72, 174–5, 191–2
Atler, Wiktor (1890–1943), 168
Auchinleck, General Sir Claude, C-in-C, Middle East (1884–1981), 121
Axis Powers, 116, 185

Baku, 102
Barbarossa, Operation, German Invasion of the Soviet Union, 102
Baudouin, Paul, French Foreign Minister (1894–1964), 62
BBWR (*Bezpartyjny Blok Wspołpracy z Rządu* – Non-Party Bloc), 29
Beaverbrook, Lord, First Baron Aitken, William Maxwell (1879–1964), 119–20
Beck, Colonel Józef, Polish Foreign Minister (1894–1944), 27–9, 31–2, 34–36, 40, 42, 44, 49, 58, 76, 80
BEF (British Expeditionary Force), 56
Beirut, 178
Belgium, 66, 87–8
Belgrade, 80
Benedykt, Captain, 14
Beria, Lavrenti (1899–1953), 104
Beria, Sergo (1924–2000), son of Lavernti, 156–7, 160, 164
Berlin, 145
Berling, General Zygmunt (1896–1980), 54, 146–9, 153–4
Beseler, General Hans Hartwig von (1850–1921), 8–9
Bessarabia, 46, 101
Bevin, Ernest (1881–1951), 14
Biddle, Anthony Joseph Drexel Jr (1897–1961), 39, 43, 65–6, 155
Blackbushe Airport, Yateley, Hampshire, 65
Blitzkrieg, 55–6
Bohin, Major, 132
Bohusz-Szyszko, General Zygmunt (1893–1982), 58, 115, 119, 135
Bolshevik, 6, 9, 11–14, 16, 19, 24–5, 28, 46, 60, 96, 110–11, 130, 144–5, 152, 156, 158, 162–3, 172
Bordeaux, France, 58, 61–6
'Borecki', 34–5
Bór-Komorowski, General Tadeusz (1895–1966), 157
Brazil, 90
Britain, 68, 88, 102, 161, 167, 192
British Military Mission to Poland, 1920, 15, 19
Brooke, General Sir Alan (CIGS) (1883–1963), 118, 128
Bryson, Major, British Intelligence, 129–30, 136
Brześć, Treaty of, 3 March 1918, 9
Bucharest, 36–7, 39, 42–3, 76

Budapest, 5, 36, 76
Budyonny, Semyon, Soviet Commander (1883–1973), 14–15
Burhardt Bukacki, Major General Stanisław, General Inspector Polish Army (1890–1942), 84
Butler Report, Katyń, Rohan Butler, Advisor to Foreign Secretary (UK) (1917–1996), report published 1973, 157

Cadogan, Sir Alexander, Permanent Undersecretary, FO (1884–1968), 103, 158, 160, 167
Cairo, Egypt, 112, 127–8, 132, 141, 143, 179, 182
Canada, 89, 91–2, 139, 174
Carpathian Brigade, 86–7, 90, 92, 116, 121–2, 124
Casey, Richard (1890–1976), 141–2, 171
Caucasus Mountains, 98, 121
Cazalet, Colonel Victor MP MC, British Liaison Officer to Sikorski (1896–1943), 67, 85, 137–9, 174, 179, 186
Central Powers, 4, 7–11
Chamberlain, Neville (1869–1940), 47, 162
Churchill, Winston (1874–1965), vii, 11, 13, 60, 64, 66–71, 76–9, 81–3, 85, 87–91, 94, 98–9, 101–104, 111, 118–21, 127, 135–6, 142, 151, 159–67, 176–8, 183, 185, 191–2, 194
Ciołkosz, Adam (1901–1978), 171
Coëtquidan, 42
Constitution, 1921, Polish, 6, 21, 36
Constitution, 1935, Polish, 36
Cripps, Sir Stafford (1889–1952), 72, 101, 103–104, 110, 120, 124
Curzon Line, 136, 161–2
Cyprus, 80

Danzig (Gdańsk), 17, 28
Dąb-Biernacki, General Stefan (1890–1959), 71, 74–5, 83
Declaration of Friendship and Mutual Assistance, Treaty signed between Sikorski and Stalin, December 1941, 124
Dill, General Sir John (CIGS), 121
Djilas, Milovan (1911–1995), 176–7
Dmowski, Roman (1864–1939), 17
Dowbór-Musnicki, General Józef (1867–1937), 16
Dudzinski, Major, Sikorski Inquiry, 186
Dulfalva Internment Camp, 9

Eden, Anthony, Foreign Secretary (1897–1977), 76, 79–80, 89, 91, 104–106, 108–10, 120, 124, 140–2, 156, 158, 160–2, 166, 174
Edinburgh, Scotland, 52, 172, 190
Egypt, 92, 122, 127, 178
Einsatzgruppen, 151
Election, 1928, Poland, 26
Erlich, Henryk (1882–1942), 168
Estonia, 33, 46, 97

Falange (Polish interwar youth movement), 29
Ferek-Błeszyński, Brigadier General Jerzy (1888–1945), 41–2
First Brigade, 4, 19–20, 23–4, 174
First World War, 3, 11, 18, 25, 87
Franco, General Franciso (1892–1975), 26, 95, 102
Franco-Polish Military Alliance, 41
Franco-Polish Military Accord, 9 September 1939, 50
France, 14, 17, 26–7, 31–2, 34–9, 415, 48, 50–52, 54, 56–78, 80, 84, 86–8, 90, 95, 115, 120, 159, 162, 177
Free French, 69, 87, 99
Front Morges, 54

Gafencu, Gregor (Grigore), Romanian Foreign Minister (1892–1957), 37
Galicia, 2, 5, 9–10, 19
Gamelin, General Maurice (1872–1958), 55–7
Gaszciecka, Katarzyna, 154–5
Gaulle, General Charles de (1890–1970), 24, 50, 69, 87, 99, 119, 193
Generalgouvernment (GG), 54
Gent, Sir Edward (1895–1948), 176
George VI, 58

Germany, vi–vii, 4, 6–7, 11–13, 18–19, 24–5, 27–36, 45–50, 60, 63, 65, 67, 71–3, 75–7, 81–3, 85–8, 92–103, 105–106, 108, 110, 115, 120, 123, 126–7, 130, 133, 136–7, 139–40, 142, 148, 151–2, 156–60, 162–5, 167, 177–8, 191–4
Gestapo, 54, 104, 145, 157
Gibraltar, vii, 67, 77, 144, 176–82, 184–9, 191, 194
Głowna Rada Polityczna (GRP) – Main Political Council, 54
Goebbels, Joseph (1897–1945), 156
Göring, Hermann (1893–1946), 103
Greiser, Arthur (1897–1946), 81
Griazov, Soviet Union, 146, 149
Grobicki, Colonel Jerzy (1891–1972), 133
Gulag, 95, 107, 190

Halifax, Lord (1881–1959), 38, 40, 46–7, 85, 140
Haller, General Józef (1873–1960), 16–17
Haller, General Stanisław (1872–1940), 115
Hammarskjöld, Dag, United Nations Secretary General (1905–1961), 176
Hankey, Sir Maurice (1877–1963), 17–18, 135
Harriman, W. Averell (1891–1986), 120, 170
Helsinki, Finland, 93
Henrys, General Paul (1862–1943), 18
Himmler, Heinrich (1900–1945), 81, 104
Hitchcock, Alfred (1899–1980), 26
Hitler, Adolf (1889–1945), 23, 25, 29, 31–2, 34–5, 46–7, 81, 95, 98, 102–103, 108, 127, 156, 161, 165
Hlond, Cardinal August (1881–1948), 44
Hulls, Colonel L.R., 141
Hungary, 9, 36, 46, 51, 74, 76, 147

International Red Cross (IRC), 158, 162
Iran (Persia), 111, 121, 125, 128, 132, 160, 166, 175
Iraq, 111, 118–19, 128, 141, 157, 170, 175
Iron Guard, 103
Ironside, Field Marshal Edmund (1880–1959), 34
Italy, 37–8, 60, 87, 111, 119, 122, 192
Iżycki, Colonel Mateusz (1898–1952), 64–5

Japan, 13, 73, 126–7
Jarewicz, Second Lieutenant Eugeniusz, 173
Jędrychowski, Stefan (1910–1996), 123
Jersey, Channel Island, UK, 65, 67
Jews, 5, 31, 35, 53, 81, 168
Jolly George, 14
Juchnov (Yukhnov) Soviet Union, 149, 153
July 1940 Coup, Portland Place, London, 85

Kaczyńska, Maria, First Lady, Republic of Poland (1942–2010), 149
Kaczyński, Lech, President of Poland (1949–2010), 149
Karasiewicz-Tokarzewski, Major General Michał (1893–1964), 52, 129–30
Karski, Jan né Kozielewski (1914–2000), 34–5, 49
Katyń, 115, 139, 144–6, 148–50, 152–4, 156–67, 169–70, 183, 190
Kawałkowski, General Aleksander (1899–1965), 41
Kennard, Sir Howard (1878–1955), 40, 50, 62, 77
Kharkov, Soviet Union (Kharkiv, Ukraine), 146, 149
Kiev/Kyiv, Ukraine, 13, 27, 102
Kirkpatrick, Sir Ivone (1897–1964), 48
Kleczynski, Wing Commander Eugeniusz (PAF), 172–3, 181
Klimecki, Brigadier General Tadeusz, Chief of Polish General Staff (1895–1943), 75, 127–8, 166–8, 179, 182, 184
Klimkowski, Captain Jerzy (1909–1991), 117, 130–4, 140, 168
Klimkowszczyna, 130–2, 140
Koc, Adam (1891–1969), 43, 48, 133
Kopański, General Stefan (1895–1976), 90, 119, 122, 140
Kormanicki, Wacław (1891–1954), 152
Kornaus, Colonel Jan, 40
Korneichuk, Alexander (Oleksandr) (1905–1972), 154–5

Kot, Stanisław (1885–1975), 60, 64, 66, 74–6, 90, 107, 116–17, 120, 123–4, 135
Kowalewski, Colonel Jan, 42
Kozielsk (Soviet Union), 145–6, 148–9, 152–4
Kraków, 54, 157
Kresy, 19, 83
Krogulski, Colonel, 133
Kukiel, General Marian (1885–1972), 1–2, 57, 60, 62, 73, 80, 84
Kułakowski, Adam, Personal Secretary to General Sikorski (1916–1943), 179
Kwienciński, Colonel Bogdan, Air Attache (1895–1981), 64

Lascelles, Sir Alan (1887–1981), 67
Latvia, 33, 46, 97, 149
Leclerc, General Phillippe François Marie de Hauteclocque (1902–1947), 193
Leipzig, Germany, 93
Lenin, Vladimir Ilyich né Ulyanov (1870–1924), 11, 14, 24, 69, 114, 144
Leśniowska, Zofia née Sikorska (1912–1943), 179
Liberator AL523, 178, 184
Libya, 122
Lieberman, Herman (1870–1941), 43–4
Lithuania, 33, 46, 97, 149
Lloyd George, David (1863–1945), 14, 17–18
Lock, Walter Heathcote (1900/1–1943), 179
London, 6, 34, 36, 44, 48, 52, 58, 61–2, 64, 66–7, 69–70, 74–6, 79–82, 88, 104, 109, 114, 116, 118, 122, 135, 140, 154, 156–8, 165, 168–70, 174, 176, 181–3, 188, 192
Łubieński, Lieutenant Ludwik, Chief of the Polish Military Mission, Gibraltar, 1943 (1912–1996), 178, 184
Łukasiewicz, Juliusz, (1892–1951), 41, 43, 45
Lwów (L'viv), 1–2, 12, 24, 130, 138

Mackiewicz, Stanisław 'Cat', (1896–1966), 59
Macmillan, Harold (1894–1986), 126
Maczek, General Stanisław (1892–1994), 25, 51–2, 187, 193
Madrid, Spain, 178
Magdeburg, Germany, 11
Maginot Line, 57, 60
Maisky, Ivan, Soviet Diplomat (1884–1975), 81, 99, 104–107, 115, 157, 166, 179–81, 191
Maisky-Sikorski Treaty, July 1941, 191
Majdanek, 153
Marecki, Colonel Andrzej, Chief of (Polish) Operations Staff (1898–1943), 179, 182
Marshal-Cornwall, Lieutenant General Sir James (1887–1985), 87
Marx, Karl (1818–1883), 12–13, 69, 114
Mason-MacFarlane, Lieutenant General Sir Noel, Governor Gibraltar (1889–1953), 178–82
May 1926 Coup, Warsaw, 18, 24
McCarthy, Joseph (1908–1957), 189
Mediterranean, 69, 119, 167, 175, 177, 191
Middle East, 67, 86, 90, 94, 98, 111, 116, 118–19, 121–2, 124, 127–8, 130, 132–3, 135, 140–3, 167–72, 174–5, 177–8, 180, 191, 194
Miechowo, village in Poland, 3
MI6, 183, 189
Mikołajczyk, Stanisław (1901–1966), 189
Military Department, 3–8
Military Mission 30, British, 132
Miranda del Ebro, Spanish Internment Camp, 177, 181
Mitkiewicz, Colonel Leon (1896–1972), 61, 85, 87
Mohl, Aleksander, Polish diplomat (1899–1956), 65
Molotov, Vyacheslav Mikhaylovich né Skryabin (1890–1986), 32, 95, 104, 107, 114, 120, 146, 149, 185, 191, 193
Molotov-Ribbentrop agreement (Nazi-Soviet Pact) August 1939, 32
Momentowicz, Włodzimierz, 2
Montreal, Canada, 139, 174, 189–90
Mościcki, Ignacy, Polish President (1867–1946), 37, 43–4
Moscow, 82, 95, 99, 102, 104–105, 109–10, 115–16, 118–21, 123–4, 127, 177, 179, 181
Motorised Brigade, 10th, 51
Mussolini, Benito (1883–1945), 95, 102, 127

Naczelny Komitet Narodowy (Supreme National Council), 3
Narutowicz, Gabriel, President of Poland (1865–1922), 22
Nasmith-Dunbar, Admiral Martin VC (1883–1965), 68
National Question, 8
NATO (North Atlantic Treaty Organisation), 14, 96–7, 100
Nazi, 25, 27–9, 32–3, 35, 46, 52–4, 72, 81, 95–6, 98, 103–106, 126, 151, 159–60, 164, 194
Nicholas II, Tsar (1868–1918), 8
NKVD, People's Commissariat for Internal Affairs (Soviet Security Police), 54, 82, 104, 115, 131–2, 134, 145, 147–8, 151, 156–7, 168
Noël, Léon (1888–1987), 39–40, 42
North Africa, 25, 62, 87, 90, 94, 119, 122, 137, 159, 167, 178, 185
Norway, 62, 64, 88, 147
Norwegian Campaign, 1940, 88
Nowogródska Cavalry Brigade, 15

Oath Crisis, July 1917, 8–9
Oder, river, 100
Oder-Neisse Line, 82
Okulicki, Colonel Leopold (1898–1946), 132
O'Malley, Owen (1887–1974), 159–60
Onacewicz, Colonel Włodzimierz, Polish Military Attache, Washington DC (1892–1986), 145
Operation AB (AB-Aktion) 1940, 157
Operation Unthinkable, 194
Oran, Algeria, 68
Orkan, Polish Destroyer, 184
Ostashkov, 146
OUN (Organisation of Ukrainian Nationalists), 19
OZON, Camp of National Unity (Poland), 29–30

Paderewski, Ignacy (1860–1941), 15–16, 18, 22, 38, 42, 44–5
PAIC (Persia and Iraq Command), 128
Palestine (British Mandate), 31, 90, 98, 119
Paris, vii, 15, 37–40, 43–5, 50–1, 59–60, 63, 65, 193
Paszkiewicz, General Gustaw (1892–1955), 73
Peake, Sir Charles (1897–1958), 67
Pearl Harbor, 102, 126–7
Pétain, Marshal Philippe (1856–1951), 60–4, 95
Philby, Harold Adrian Russell 'Kim' (1912–1988), 189
Phipps, Sir Eric (1875–1945), 38, 48
Piłsudski, Józef (1867–1935), vi, 1–11, 13, 15–30, 32, 34, 36, 44–5, 52, 54–5, 57, 70, 74–5, 78–9, 90, 100, 111, 117, 129, 136, 174
Plan 'W' (*Wschód*) Polish eastern defensive plan, 1939, 30
Plan 'Z' (*Zachód*) Polish western defensive plans, 1939, 30
Podhalian Brigade, 63
Poland, *passim*
Polish Air Force (PAF), 51, 86, 92, 124, 128, 172
Polish Communist Party (KPP – *Komunistyczna Partia Polski*), 95, 123
Polish Government-in-Exile, 1939–1990, vii, 6, 34, 36, 39, 43, 45, 48, 50–1, 55, 57–9, 61–2, 65, 67–8, 70–2, 78–81, 85–6, 88–91, 98–101, 103–10, 117, 120, 122–4, 127–8, 130–1, 136, 138–43, 145–6, 150–2, 154–60, 162, 164–9, 171, 177–9, 183–4, 190, 192
Polish Presidential Protocol, 63
Polish Question, 3, 5, 7, 104, 138
Polish Riflemen, 3
Polish Second Republic (1918–1939), vi, 6
Polish-Soviet War, 1919–1920, vi, 14, 23–4, 144
Polish Workers' Party (PPR – *Polska Partia Robotnicza*), 123
Polska Organizacja Wojskowa (POW) [Polish Military Organisation], 8
Polski Stronnictwo Postępowe (Polish Progressive Party), 2
Polish II Corps, 170, 172
Ponikiewski, Lieutenant Józef, Naval ADC to General Sikorski (1916–1943), 179
Portugal, 94–5, 178

Pownall, General Henry, C-in-C Persia and Iraq Command (1887–1961), 157
Pragier, Adam (1886–1976), 43
Prchal, Flight Lieutenant Eduard (Czech Air Force) (1911–1984), 178–82, 184–8
Pruszyński, Ksawery (1907–1950), 126
Puacz, Edward (1905–1985), 156
Putin, Vladimir (born 1952), 97, 149, 189

Qizil Ribat, Iraq, 174
Quayle, Major Anthony, later Sir Anthony, actor (1913–1989), 179

Raczkiewicz, Władysław, President of Poland (1885–1947), 37–8, 44–5, 48, 58, 62–3, 70–1, 74–6, 78, 83, 100–101, 111, 141, 164
Raczyński, Edward (1891–1993), 28, 38, 44–5, 61–2, 68, 158, 184, 193
Raczyński, Roger (1889–1945), 42–3
Radcliffe, Major General Sir Percy (1874–1934), 15–16
Rataj, Maciej (1884– murdered by German forces in 1939 or 1940), 53
Red Army, 12–15, 17, 19, 24–5, 47, 60, 94, 104–105, 114, 118, 120, 130, 137–9, 144–6, 148, 150–1, 159, 161, 164, 168, 172, 183, 193–4
Rennes, France, 63, 67
Retinger, Józef (1888–1960), 64–71, 115
Reynard, Paul, French Prime Minister (1878–1966), 57, 60–2
Riga (Treaty of 1921), 19, 104, 106
Roberts, F.K. Frank (1907–1998), 77, 79, 127, 141, 158, 171
Romania, vii, 34, 36–40, 42–3, 46, 49, 52, 57, 80, 87, 101–102, 147, 187
Romer, Tadeusz (1894–1978), 146
Roosevelt, Franklin D., President USA (1882–1945), 56, 60, 68–9, 87, 91, 102, 111, 117, 126, 136, 139–40, 159, 162–5, 181, 183
Rosmarin, Henryk (1882–1955), 122
Rothesay, Isle of Bute, 42
Rowecki, Colonel Stefan (1895–1944), 52
Royal Air Force (RAF), 49, 176, 180–1
Royal Air Force Volunteer Reserve (RAFVR), 51
Royal Navy, 32, 51, 68–9
Rozwadowski, General Tadeusz (1866–1928), 17
Rumbold, Sir Horace (1869–1941), 18
Russia, vi–vii, 2–5, 7–9, 11–15, 18, 20–1, 27–8, 30, 46, 59, 69, 72, 81, 87, 95–100, 102, 105, 108, 111, 114–17, 121, 124–5, 127, 130, 137, 143–4, 149, 158–9, 161, 164, 172, 189
Rzeszów, Poland, 2

Sanacja, interwar Polish military junta, vii, 23, 113, 190
Scotland, 42, 73–4, 79–80, 84–5, 124, 175, 187
Second Front, 159
Seyda, Marian (1879–1967), 76, 110
Sicily, 159, 167, 185
Sikorska, Emilia née Habrowska, 1
Sikorski, Radek (born 1963), 96, 191
Sikorski, Tomasz, 1
'Sikorski's Tourists', 52
Sikorski, General Władysław (1881–1943), *passim*
Simpson, Air Commodore Sturley, Air Commander, Gibraltar (1896–1966), 180
Sławek, Walery (1879–1939), 27
Służba Zwyciestwo Polski (SZP) Victory for Poland Service, 52, 54
Smolensk, 144–6, 150, 153, 160
Smuts, Field Marshal Jan, Prime Minister South Africa (1870–1950), 159
Sokolnicki, Michał (1880–1967), 3
Sosnkowski, General Kazimierz (1885–1969), 1–2, 38, 55, 58, 62, 74–6, 79–80, 84, 89, 100–101, 108–10, 115, 142
Soviet-Czechoslovak Treaty of Friendship, 18 July 1941, 107
Soviet-Polish Agreement, July 1941, 99
Soviet Union, vi–viii, 6, 18, 20, 28–30, 32–4, 36, 47–8, 53–4, 69, 71–3, 77, 79–83, 87, 90, 92–111, 113–21, 123–32, 134–40, 143–8, 150–60, 162–3, 165–6, 168, 170–1, 173–5, 177–9, 181, 184–5, 191–4
Spanish Civil War (1936–1939), 26, 56
Stalin, Joseph Vissarionovich né Jugashvili (1878–1953), vii, 5–6, 13–14, 19, 23, 28, 34, 36, 43, 45–6, 69, 72, 78, 82, 87, 94–8,

104, 106, 108, 111–12, 114, 117–18, 121, 123–5, 127, 137–9, 144–9, 151–3, 156, 159–62, 164–7, 170, 172, 174, 176–7, 183, 185, 191, 193–4
Stalingrad, 137
Starobielsk, 146, 148–9, 153, 155
Stefczyk, Lieutenant Colonel Kazimierz, Head of General Staff, First Bureau (Intelligence) (1891–1941), 74, 84
Strasburger, Henryk (1887–1951), 74–5
Stroński, Stanisław (1882–1955), 42
Supreme War Cabinet, 87
Sweden, 97, 147
Switzerland, 27, 63, 158
Świętochowski, Ryszard (1882–1941), 54
Syria, 86, 90, 122, 149

Tel Aviv, 122
Teschen, annexation by Poland, 1938, 30, 45, 108–109
The 39 Steps (1935 Film), 26
Thoma, General Wilhelm Josef Ritter von (1891–1948), 56
Tilea, Viorel (1896–1972), 103
Tito, Josip né Broz (1892–1980), 176
Tobruk, 90, 121–2
Treblinka, 153
Trotsky, Leon né Bronstein, Lev Davidovich (1879–1940), 14, 46, 144
Turkey, 90, 122, 147

Ukraine, vi, 9, 12–13, 19, 97, 102, 149, 155, 193
Ullmann, Tadeusz, 186
United Kingdom (UK), 6, 14, 32, 35–8, 42–5, 48, 50–2, 57–9, 62–3, 65–70, 73, 75–7, 79–81, 83–9, 92–5, 98, 102, 106, 109, 111, 113, 116, 118, 120, 122, 126–8, 132, 135, 139, 161–3, 167–8, 172–3, 175–6, 178, 180, 184, 187, 194
United States (USA), 48, 69, 87, 90–1, 102, 110–11, 115, 118–20, 126–7, 133, 139–40, 154, 172–4, 176, 189, 194
USSR, 81, 115, 161–2
Uzbekistan, 120

Vichy, 61–3, 67, 72, 90
Vijnita (Wyźnica), Romania, 39
Villa Reale, 178
Volga, 120, 124, 144
Volhynia, 20
Volksdeutsch, 53

Wałęsa, Lech, President of Poland (born 1943), 193
Warsaw, Poland, 8–9, 17, 22, 24, 29, 44, 53–5, 59–60, 69, 82, 97, 114, 131, 144, 157, 182, 193
Washington, DC, 23, 139–40, 145, 154, 159, 168, 174
Wasilewska, Wanda (1905–1964), 123, 155–6, 164
Wavell, General Sir Archibald (1883–1950), 116, 119
Way, Brigadier, 26th Military Mission, 141
Welles, Sumner (1892–1961), 189
Wenda 'Madam', 36, 76
Werner, Stefan, 90
Western Ukraine, 9, 12
Weygand, General Maxime (1867–1965), 16–17, 24, 57, 59–62
Whiteley, Brigadier John Percival MP (1898–1943), 180, 184
Wiart de, General Sir Adrian Carton (1880–1963), 18, 22
Wieniawa-Długoszowski, Bolesław (1881–1942), 37–8, 44, 49
Wilno (Vilnius), Lithuania, 93, 130, 138
Wilson, General Sir Henry Maitland (1881–1964), 128
Wilson, Woodrow, President USA (1856–1924), 12
Witos, Wincenty (1874–1945), 48
Wodehouse, P.G. (1881–1975), 163–4

Yalta, 68
Yugoslavia, 80, 101

Zając, General Józef (1891–1963), 129
Zakopane, Poland, 145, 157
Zakrzewski, Lieutenant Colonel Tadeusz (1897–1964), 42
Zaleski, August (1883–1972), 43–5, 61–3, 75–6, 78, 100, 104, 108–10
Związek Strzlecki (Riflemen's' Union), 2
Związek Walki Czynnej (Union for Active Struggle), 2
Związek Walki Zbrojnej (ZWZ) (Union of Armed Struggle), 55